Striking In

The
Early
Notebooks
of James Dickey

Edited with Introductions by Gordon Van Ness

UNIVERSITY OF MISSOURI PRESS
COLUMBIA & LONDON

Notebooks copyright © 1996 by James Dickey

Notes and introductions copyright © 1996 by
The Curators of the University of Missouri
University of Missouri Press, Columbia, Missouri 65201

Printed and bound in the United States of America

ALL RIGHTS RESERVED

5 4 3 2 1   00 99 98 97 96

Library of Congress Cataloging-in-Publication Data

Dickey, James.
    Striking in : the early notebooks of James Dickey / edited with an
introduction by Gordon Van Ness.
          p.   cm.
    ISBN 0-8262-1056-2 (alk. paper)
    1. Dickey, James—Notebooks, sketchbooks, etc. I. Van Ness,
Gordon, 1950–   . II. Title.
PS3554.I32S85   1996
818'.5403—dc20   96-2553
                                                               CIP

♾™ This paper meets the requirements of
the American National Standard for Permanence of Paper
for Printed Library Materials, Z39.48, 1984.

Text design and typesetting: Stacia Schaefer
Jacket Design: Kristie Lee
Printer and binder: Thomson-Shore, Inc.
Typeface: Bembo

Striking In

This book is dedicated to my father and mother, Gordon and Rosaline Van Ness, who got through it all by doing what needed to be done, holding in themselves all things on all sides, exactly right, in the one world widening for me.

Contents

Acknowledgments

Clichés of acknowledgment are sometimes accurate. I am grateful to my colleagues at Longwood College, who have enabled me to do my research. Ellery Sedgwick, chair of the English department, graciously provided all within his means. Vera Williams, dean of the Graduate School when the final drafts of this manuscript were being prepared, awarded me a Faculty Research Grant, which hastened the completion of this project. Bill Frank, dean of the School of Liberal Arts and Sciences, offered encouragement. He believed.

Herb Hartsook of the South Caroliniana Library of the University of South Carolina facilitated my access to the notebooks and assisted me in their duplication. Rebecca Laine and Norma Taylor, respectively, of the Longwood College Library allowed me unrestricted access to stored materials and worked relentlessly to secure my requests for interlibrary loans. Their prompt efforts greatly assisted the editing and annotation of these notebooks.

I am indebted to the following for their expertise and advice: Mc Amoss, Matthew J. Bruccoli, Craig Challender, Liz Flynn-Chapman, Martha Cook, Donald Greiner, Charles Kinzer, Mike Lund, Susan May, Bruce Montgomery, Frank Moore, Geoff Orth, John Reynolds, Massie Stinson, Herb Taylor, Vince Taylor, Graves Thompson, and Cam Tinnell.

Angelin Brewer, Cathy Gaughran, Debbie Spears, and Liz Watkins provided research assistance when they could least afford the time. Their willingness to help continues to astonish me. I am especially grateful to Jennifer Steib. Wherever her eyes turn, light slants and becomes something more.

Chris Langner selflessly gave of her time to answer all my questions regarding WordPerfect. Her computer knowledge commands my respect. Ken Autrey and Joyce Pair read and critiqued portions of the manuscript, providing indispensable counsel that only bettered this project. I value their friendship. Beverly Jarrett, Clair Willcox, and Jane Lago from the University of Missouri Press provided sound editorial advice. Their acumen continually guided my efforts.

Pat Pilkinton, Ned Crawley, John Boggs, and Welford Taylor were there when I sang young and easy under the apple boughs. They were guardians of my green world, and I am better for what they did and do.

My wife, Janet, has graciously accepted her subordination to James Dickey for twelve years. She read the manuscript and corrected my awkward sentences, never urging me to pursue another line of endeavor. I have neglected my children, who retaliated by growing up. They continually remind me of the pastness of the present.

My greatest debt is to Jim Dickey, who patiently and thoroughly answered my many questions about his life. I am thankful for his coming and his continuing. *Il donne un sens plus pur aux mots de la tribu.*

Striking In

Before I made a move, though, I sat for maybe twenty seconds, failing to feel my heart beat, though at that moment I wanted to. The feeling of the inconsequence of whatever I would do, of anything I would pick up or think about or turn to see was at that moment being set in the very bone marrow. How does one get through this? I asked myself. By doing something that is at hand to be done was the best answer I could give; that and not saying anything about the feeling to anyone.

—James Dickey, from *Deliverance*

                                                         O claspable
Symbol   the unforeseen on home ground   The thing that
    sustains us forever
In other places!

—James Dickey, from "Coming Back to America"

Introduction

James Dickey entered Vanderbilt University in the summer of 1946 after serving in World War II as a member of the 418th Night Fighter Squadron. Three years later he graduated Phi Beta Kappa with a major in English and a minor in philosophy. His 2.67 grade-point average (on a 3.0 scale) earned him honors and the rank of 14th in a class of 446. Following graduation, he entered the graduate school at Vanderbilt. He received his master's degree on June 4, 1950, and then accepted a teaching position as instructor of English at Rice Institute (now Rice University). The Korean conflict, however, caused the Air Force to recall him to duty after only a semester. He was sent first to Maxwell Field in Montgomery, Alabama, and then to training command centers at Keesler Air Force Base in Gulfport, Mississippi, and Connally Air Force Base in Waco, Texas. Not until the fall of 1952 did he return to his classroom activities at Rice.

While teaching in 1950, Dickey purchased four bound ledgers, each approximately seven and a half by twelve inches, having heard that Thomas Wolfe wrote in such notebooks and hoping the method would facilitate his own creative efforts. He additionally used two ringed, loose-leaf notebooks, one blue and the other red. Both measure four and a half by seven inches. He intended in these separate notebooks or journals (he used the words interchangeably) to discuss his novels and short stories, to comment on books and essays that he read, and to record observations or specific events he felt significant. He also planned to keep notes for and drafts of his own poems and to analyze formally other poetic works. In practice, however, individual notebooks never achieved such specialized purposes and were never explicitly labeled according to purpose. While loosely centered on a particular concern, each became a literary catchall in which Dickey continually briefed himself to determine his artistic mission. He often worked simultaneously in all notebooks, the entries in one journal sometimes reflecting or developing concerns raised in another. The six notebooks, in other words, are not sequential. Dickey did not finish one notebook before beginning another, although generally they reveal a chronological progression during the fifties. Moreover, he rarely dated any entries (the latest dated entry is August 1956), and he did not number the notebooks; they have been numbered insofar as possible to reflect the chronology and the overall development of his major interests or principal concerns.

Dickey's early notebooks, a kind of reconnaissance, were undertaken to confront the possibilities of language and to address immediate literary interests. They assume critical importance in allowing us to understand his artistic apprenticeship. Vanderbilt's literary magazine, *Gadfly,* had published four of Dickey's poems while he was a student: "Christmas Shopping, 1947" (winter 1947), "Sea Island" and "King Crab and Rattler" (spring 1948), and "Whittern and the Kite" (summer 1949). Although he was not certain he possessed literary talent, these acceptances encouraged him. In addition, *Sewanee Review* accepted his poem "The Shark at the Window" while Dickey was a student at Vanderbilt. The poem was not published, however, until the April–June 1951 issue, after the Air Force had recalled him to duty and as he struggled in his notebooks to chart his artistic course. Its publication was, as he notes in *Self-Interviews,* "one of the things that sustained me during the trauma of being recalled into the service."[1]

During the fifties Dickey published more than three dozen poems in literary reviews such as *Poetry, Kenyon Review, Quarterly Review of Literature, Sewanee Review,* and others, all publications he studied as part of his apprenticeship.[2] Another twenty-one poems were published in 1960. That year Scribner's published Dickey's first volume of poetry, *Into the Stone,* as part of its Poets of Today series. The notebooks manifest the genesis of many of his fictional and poetic ideas and images and reveal not only how acutely he understood his literary mission but also how luminous his imagination was during those early years. They display, too, Dickey's determined effort to acquire the skills, techniques, and readings necessary to become an artist. Notebook entries mention some of the previously unpublished or uncollected poems contained later in this book; together these apprentice efforts show how Dickey discovered the subjects, forms, and rhythms of what he calls his early motion.

American poetry during the fifties still confronted the formidable presence of T. S. Eliot. Although *Time* magazine had viewed *The Waste Land* as a hoax in its March 3, 1923, issue, labeling it a "new kind of literature . . . whose only obvious fault is that no one can understand it," it enthroned Eliot on its March 6, 1950, cover, acknowledging his "Olympian judgments" and declaring, "Mr. Eliot is secure and honored in his high place as one of the foremost men of English letters." Although Delmore Schwartz had argued in his 1949 essay "The Literary Dictatorship of T. S. Eliot" that "it might be desirable to have no literary dictators," and Edmund Wilson in a January 1954 journal entry had

1. *Self-Interviews* (Garden City, N.Y.: Doubleday, 1970), 41.
2. See the Appendix for a list of the poems Dickey published during the fifties.

called Eliot "an obsolete kind of American,"[3] poetry continued to be judged by its adherence to New Critical principles even as artists attempted to discover a new voice or direction. Pound and Williams, whose *Pisan Cantos* and *Paterson,* respectively, had proved them capable of advancing modernism, also remained firmly entrenched in the literary firmament. Poets who were just starting their literary careers, therefore, such as Robert Lowell, Randall Jarrell, and John Berryman, stressed (at least initially) artistic impersonality and a poetics grounded in irony and linguistic construction. Indeed, beginning in 1955, Dickey himself wrote Pound, praising the older poet and emphasizing their shared sensibilities. Their correspondence continued for three years.

The ambivalence that poets felt toward modernism as they struggled to achieve their own distinctive voices paralleled the uncertainties and tensions Americans generally felt during the fifties, a decade that glittered on the surface with prosperity and leisure but that also confronted McCarthyism, the Cold War, and the development of the hydrogen bomb. Far from being a time, as the October 16, 1972, issue of *Newsweek* nostalgically regaled in its cover story, "when hip was hep, good was boss and everything nice was copacetic," the Eisenhower years are more accurately described as conservative, tired, and anxious. While poets were no longer viewed, as Schwartz admitted in his 1958 lecture "The Present State of Poetry," as "strange and exotic being[s],"[4] art did not flourish. The number of poetry prizes, awards, grants, and honors had increased, but poets needed to teach to secure a living and often to supplement their incomes with occasional public readings. The change in the public's perception of poets from self-serving bohemians to respected educators elevated artists in one sense and bewildered them in another because society now asked them to teach, become editors, or write book reviews or critical essays. What they were not asked to do, or not do with the frequency to which they had been accustomed, was to write poetry. To attempt a poetic career, therefore, resembled volunteering for a hazardous mission.

That Dickey believed himself on such a mission is suggested by the military image in *Sorties,* the volume in which he published his later notebooks in 1971.[5] *Sorties* consists of undated prosaic ramblings in which Dickey himself—his ideas, interests, and beliefs—becomes the focus not of a search for artistic understanding, but of a declaration of attitudes on particular writers and works as well as political, cultural, and

3. Schwartz's essay appeared in *Partisan Review* (February 1949): 119–37; Wilson's comment is included in *The Fifties: From Notebooks and Diaries of the Period,* ed. Leon Edel (New York: Farrar, Straus and Giroux, 1986), 127.

4. Schwartz's lecture was published in *American Poetry at Mid-Century* (Washington, D.C.: Library of Congress, 1958), 15–31.

5. *Sorties* (Garden City, N.Y.: Doubleday, 1971).

even personal concerns. His voice is at once broader and more egocentric in *Sorties* than in these early notebooks, motivated partly by the belief that he is under attack by Robert Bly and other liberals and partly by his principle that the self must be syntactically related to the larger world to achieve meaning. The early notebooks, by contrast, are an extended briefing on literary topics in which he discusses the nature of fiction and poetry and experiments with subject matter and style. Dickey knew his intended destination. He hoped to become an artist; publication, if it came at all, would come later. He determined to use these notebooks to chart the course, a conscious "striking in" to pursue his objective.

Editorial Note

To edit is to alter. The principle of selection for this volume was to retain most of the entries dealing with the practice of literature and to omit most of the entries in which Dickey comments either on personal or family matters or on concerns related to daily teaching duties. The notebooks, overwhelmingly literary, detail Dickey's efforts to discover and pursue an artistic career. Few entries are completely private; I have included here those private entries that reinforce or complement the literary intent. In addition, I have generally included words or phrases Dickey found interesting, lines or passages he felt would be of possible literary use, drafts or outlines of poems and stories, and critical analyses of specific writers or works. They anticipate his later poetry and fiction, reveal the development of his style and subject matter, or contribute to understanding his method of composition. I have also for the most part kept those entries identifying or listing books he intended to purchase or had recently read, particularly since many of those books had just been published. They assist in determining the time frame of each notebook because Dickey quickly acted on such directives. Other references that date a notebook, such as the date of an exam while he was teaching at Rice Institute or the University of Florida, have also been included.

Dickey closely read certain works, often quoting passages verbatim and occasionally commenting on the efficacy of the ideas. I have incorporated some of these entries to reveal their extension into his later thoughts or works. Moreover, references to other entries have been allowed to remain so as to reveal Dickey's simultaneous use of the notebooks and the development of his thought processes. On the other hand, names of individuals he wanted to write and lists of test questions he intended to ask his classes add little to understanding the origins and development of his literary ideas. Therefore, I have excluded these. Except where stipulated, all entries are complete.

Dickey occasionally revised an entry as he wrote it, making a modification or an addition above or below the original line in order, on reflection, to better convey his intent. Often he parenthetically inserted the change, but in some instances he overlooked the parentheses. To represent the notebooks as exactly as possible, the revisions have been included as they appear in the notebooks, with or without their parentheses; all revisions are marked with an up arrow before and a down arrow after each individual insertion: ↑She capable of↓. Text that Dickey crossed through or deleted has been rendered by the use of angle brackets: <limit>. Material that I have inserted to date the notebooks more effectively has been placed within squiggle brackets: { }. When Dickey placed parentheses around text containing another parenthesis, I have changed the outer marks to square brackets. Dickey frequently used a dash instead of a period or a comma, and a colon or semicolon instead of a dash. Sometimes he capitalized the first word of a new sentence or phrase; sometimes he did not. To avoid confusion and to enhance comprehension, I have standardized spelling, punctuation, and capitalization.

Autobiographical names, places, or events in Dickey's life have been annotated wherever possible, as have references to essays or books that significantly affected his proposed creative or critical efforts and with which the reader might not be familiar. Publication information on essays or books that he listed has also been given when it can date the entries. Otherwise, such information is not included. Wherever appropriate, entries that anticipate Dickey's later work have been noted, and historical or mythological allusions have been explained. Finally, where entries refer to material in other notebooks or suggest their simultaneous use, I have cross-referenced the annotations.

Notebook I

The first notebook is the longest in length (152 written pages in a bound ledger), and its content is the most varied. The entries range from Dickey's ideas for his fiction and poetry to explorations of the literary techniques he wanted to employ. They cover a period of approximately two years. None of the entries is dated. Internal evidence suggests that Dickey began writing in the notebook during late 1950. On page 2 he quotes from and comments on an essay by Kenneth Burke that appeared in the winter issue of *Sewanee Review* for that year, and an entry on page 9 identifies a colleague with whom Dickey was teaching at Rice during the fall of 1950 as someone to whom he needed to talk. Page 43 lists an anthology he wanted to obtain, *Modern Poetry, American and British,* edited by John Malcolm Brinnin and Kimon Friar and published in 1951. On the following page, Dickey listed ten questions for a Shakespeare test; because the Air Force had recalled him to active duty during 1951, that entry likely dates from the fall of 1952 when he had returned to teaching at Rice. Most of the entries in the first journal therefore seem to have been written during 1952 after Dickey returned to teaching following his recall to military service.

Dickey had undertaken a large novel tentatively titled *The Casting.* The title, derived from Sir Walter Baldwin Spencer and Francis James Gillen's anthropological study *The Native Tribes of Central Australia,* published in 1938, suggests that the unfinished novel centered on the initiation into manhood. Although the conception of the plot remains unclear, important characters and scenes anticipate his novel *Alnilam,* published in 1987 but begun during the fifties. The protagonist of *The Casting,* an enigmatic figure named Julian Glass, resembles Joel Cahill of *Alnilam;* both are estranged from their fathers and both seek to control others. A notation concerning an old man suffering "cancer in the center of his forehead 'like a diadem'" anticipates Frank Cahill, Joel's diabetic father, and the shuttling gold sparks he sees in his blindness. Dickey also plans a crucial scene involving a sudden nosebleed, which foreshadows the one involving Frank Cahill and Hannah Pelham. Another entry projects a short story that seems to allude directly to the central character in *Alnilam*—a young airman who believes his entire career has been a preparation to confront himself "in the center ↑crater↓

of the flame of a burning aircraft." Although he had not yet conceived the narrative for *Alnilam,* Dickey had discovered aspects of it.

Evidence in the first notebook suggests that Dickey wants his fiction to treat a large subject in a large way. Entries show that his thematic concerns include kingship and king-killing; faith, decadence, and resurrection; war and conspiracy; and exile and repatriation. Although his primary interest lies in characterization, he shuns the subtle, analytical approach of Henry James, asserting in one entry that "the bigness (melodrama and all) must be there in big (great) writing." He adds, "The purveyors of super and refined subtleties are not Shakespeare and Melville but Henry James and the 'explicators' of James, Melville, and Shakespeare." Dickey deliberately seeks not so much to present an archetype in his fiction as to create one. However, he realizes that his overall conception has to be enriched by minor details and incidental insights because "the spray defines the fountain." Notes on *The Casting* indicate that Julian attempts through force of will and intensity of imagination to determine or discover an independent self. Dickey describes him as "an acute non-literary sensibility," wearing a dragon on his shirt and, alienated from his father, often acting instinctively, even primitively. Insecure but imaginative, he reveals a kind of "masterful instability," evoking admiration and disgust.

Occasionally in this first notebook Dickey contemplates combining ideas set aside for later works. He proposes wedding them into a single, big novel to depict a sense of men—or a man—moving in history in a narrative supported by philosophical speculation. At one point, for example, he considers a second novel uniting his concern for fraternal repatriation with his interests in kingship and war. Its focus is also large: "the preoccupied inanity of modern life . . . and the paradoxical apocalyptic *vision* which proceeds from it." Whatever the subject, however, aspects of ritual and myth pervade his notes for the fiction. For example, Jack Corbett, the athletics coach in *The Casting,* possesses a "shaman-like power," and Julian is described as "one of *Penelope's suitors,* who cannot bend Ulysses' bow." Dr. Arrington, another character in the planned novel, calls himself a "medicine man."

Dickey seems to believe poets are born, not made, and to have decided that while he may reasonably become a good critic, he has arrived at poetry too late to consider it as a career. He formulates an extensive article on the similarities between jazz and the poetry of Hart Crane, listing works he should consult to develop his ideas. Another intended essay would detail the methods by which the poetry-making mind operates. To determine his standards as well as to practice poetic analysis, he reads and critiques the works of writers such as John Donne, Andrew Marvell, Cyril Tourneur, Thomas Hardy, Emily Dickinson, and

Randall Jarrell. Particular poems, stanzas, lines, and even words catch his attention and receive his scrutiny. Despite this critical inclination, however, Dickey devotes much of this first notebook to the discovery of his own poetic subjects and techniques. Believing that a good poet must thoroughly explore the possibilities of language, he discusses or experiments with diction, imagery, stanzaic form, and meter. The quality of ghostliness in Coleridge's "Ancient Mariner" intrigues him, as do Robert Lowell's violent, physical imagery and George Barker's projection of self into history.

The nature of poetry itself also constitutes a large concern. Entries reveal his constant attempt to define or characterize it, as if briefing himself in this manner will narrow and therefore better chart his artistic destination. On the one hand, Dickey believes that good poetry shows "the *exploratory* sense of language," so that words, derived from the unconscious, manifest previously unseen or undiscovered meanings. Such poetry involves a willingness to explore what Dickey terms "the implications of association." Hopkins, Mallarmé, Rilke, and Hart Crane exhibited this "word-led" or "word-choked" poetry. On the other hand, he understands that he may logically construct or "rig" a poem. Just as the critic analyzes a poem by line and stanza to determine how it succeeds, so too may the poet assemble a poem by planning elements such as sound and imagery in advance and fitting them together to accomplish an intended effect. If the structure of such a poem is good, the reader will likely anticipate what happens next. Yet Dickey does not want simply an accumulation of detail or a listing of common objects such as he detects in the poetry of Jarrell and Elizabeth Bishop. To deny to any poem aspects either of the unconscious or of the rational, he asserts, would be "to impoverish it altogether needlessly, to thin it." Dickey therefore separately pursues both approaches, hoping each will develop independently. Any coalescence must reveal a linguistic vitality and not simply a mechanical synthesis. The distinction, however, remains difficult for him to maintain, for he believes his own poetry combines aspects of both kinds, or what he terms a "*cultivated* spontaneity."

The first notebook reveals that while he recognizes that a poet always begins as an imitator, he also understands that he needs to discover his own material and assume a relationship to it. He declares, "Poetry is yourself, your personality, whatever things peculiar to you as a human being, smashed, forced, and bled through whatever poetical techniques you have mastered." What matters most is correlating one's insight with a particular point of view. Attitude not only determines the meaning of an object or experience but also becomes "the necessary prologue" to all technical devices. Dickey explores a broad range of poetic subjects, including the historical, religious, hypothetical, allegorical, and abstract, or what he calls "a poetry of ideas." Particular ideas often derive from his readings, but these are either filtered through or expanded by his own interests and personal experiences. Regardless of perspective, however, his poetic philosophy is explicit: "'Don't tell 'em, show 'em'; or at any rate, show 'em more than you tell 'em."

As with the notes on his fiction, the poetic material is largely historical and mythological. Dickey works extensively on a poem titled "Sennacherib at Babylon" as well as on poems involving alchemists, the sacrifice of children at Carthage, and the Carthaginian general Hamilcar Barca. He also considers a poem presenting man's awakening knowledge of discoveries such as fire, the wheel, and the arch. Other entries examine how George Barker, Hart Crane, Saint-John Perse, and others used history in their poetry. Mythological subjects mentioned in the entries include Christ, Mulciber, Philomel, a Bacchic celebration, and Creation, and mythic images of the falconer, knight, king, and sorcerer pervade the apprentice poems. In addition, Dickey projects several poems involving angels, which may have led to "The Angel of the Maze," published in the June 1955 issue of *Poetry*. Drafts of "The Kingly Lover," which concerns the sexual union of a lion and a woman, and "The Lady in the Statue" depict his interest in exchanging states of being. An entry about a man crucified on the side of a moving freight car anticipates "A Folk Singer of the Thirties," published in the August 1963 issue of *Poetry,* and his interest in writing a deeply religious poem, tentatively titled "Prayer Becoming," likely led to "Approaching Prayer," which Dickey included in *Helmets,* published in 1964. Other poems involve a criminal, a poor woman, or a hobo, all figures that appear in later published work such as "At Darien Bridge," "Chenille," and "Bums, on Waking," respectively. As with his fiction, autobiographical elements also appear in the poems. One involves his father, and another concerns the "voyage" of a son, likely a reference to his combat in the Pacific during World War II.

To support his critical and creative examinations, Dickey regularly studies scholarly journals. The first notebook reveals dozens of essays and books he is reading or that he wishes to read. He carefully examines articles from *Partisan Review, Kenyon Review, Sewanee Review, Hudson Review, Quarterly Review of Literature, New York Times Book Review,* and *Accent.* Moreover, books in the fields of philosophy, mythology, music, psychology, and history, as well as works of literature and criticism, continually provide Dickey with new perspectives. In these readings he identifies ideas, technical concepts, and "type figures" (generalized or archetypal images). As if their publication has rendered them free literary material, he notes all that intrigue him and adapts them to his own interests by placing them in new or unusual poetic contexts. His preoccupation with images supports Dickey's later statement in *Self-Interviews* on the influence of modernism: "the poetry I wrote before *Into the Stone* was influenced stylistically not so much by individual writers as by an amalgam of writers: something called in capital letters, MODERN POETRY."[1]

These entries clearly reveal the intensity with which Dickey studies literature. From widely differing poetic traditions, he scrutinizes particular ideas and images to provide a bank of fictional and poetic material. He feels his participation in World War II had impeded his academic and intellectual efforts, describing himself in *Veteran Birth* as "desperately behind the position he should have been in: behind because of the war and the convulsions of history."[2] He is determined to overcome the loss of time.

In the first journal Dickey admits to his flawed literary efforts. He notices that his poetic criticism is better than his poems, and he is already involved in rewriting sections of the novel when he finishes the first ledger. Not discouraged, he believes his primary mission is the exploration of diction.

1. *Self-Interviews*, 46.
2. *Veteran Birth* (Charlotte, N.C.: Palaemon Press, 1978). The quotation appears in the untitled, unpaginated preface.

{Dickey was teaching at Rice Institute in the fall of 1950 when he began writing in Notebook I. At the end of that semester, the Air Force recalled him.}

Novel: work for a pervading *strangeness,* something like *The Cannibal* or *The Plenipotentiaries.*[3] (Visit to draft board: *Mohan*) *not too obviously Kafkian.* "Jigging on railing." (Thinks) Marrowbone Lake. Clothed fall: laughing under water: hand trails algae.

Novel's end: *essential* that the force (love, attraction, etc.) is working on the pro. and that he is *unaware* of it. "Perhaps she is dead"—"but no, she was standing there," etc. Place for some mood description—"...," I said. "..." This has to be worked on *terrifically.*

71 *Sewanee Review:* K. Burke:[4] "begins with such a natural scene as would require a *genius loci* to make it complete." Idea of a "completing" or "fulfilling" presence. "As would require" here the suggestive phrase. Scene which you set up during which the audience waits for an unknown inevitability to be fulfilled, to complete the scene which requires it. Sense of presence. Might be fruitful. Can be terribly hammed up.

Counterparts of movement, sound, etc., shape: swaying tree, swaying fish, or any *combination* of these: *sound* (similar) suggests sight (similar). Structural device—"structure by counterpart." Then different *things* move, sound, etc., *linked* by the counterparts, etc.

Burke on snail (72): "A series of repetitive attempts to arrive at the same end from different images as starting point." This may be useful not as a hag-riding device but more or less fragmentarily, tentatively, withholdingly, suggestively.

Burke's phrase: "a world of masks." In Roethke these are flowers, etc.

Mary McCarthy — *Cast a Cold Eye* and *The Company She Keeps.*
Aiken — *Short Stories.*
Stevens — *Auroras of Autumn.*
Aymé — *The Barkeep of Blémont.*
Leroy Leatherman — *The Caged Birds.*
Ford Madox Ford — *Parade's End.*
R.V. Cassill — *Eagle on the Coin.*

3. John Hawkes, *The Cannibal* (New York: New Directions, 1949), and Harold J. Kaplan, *The Plenipotentiaries* (New York: Harper, 1950).
4. Kenneth Burke, "The Vegetal Radicalism of Theodore Roethke," *Sewanee Review* 58 (winter 1950): 68–108.

Make more complex, complicated. See T. Weiss "4 Lay-Saints + a Satyr."[5]

Roethke: verb *not* required by noun: "spiders cry," "cracked pod cells." Insects figure in dreams as surrogates for children.

Burke (103–104) on metaphor: tremendously stimulating. Two apparently opposed figures are *caught up* and resolved by a third figure through kinesis, meaning, form, etc., that is peculiar to them both: fish sways + girl sways = tree sways over water.

Great thing is sense of *history*—all right in Lowell (though could be immeasurably bettered), not so good in Jarrell (mere reference to *events* in history is not the same thing, nor is economic causation).

Novel: it is part of my job to show that physical sex-fulfillment is only the prelude to a greater hunger which is unappeasable, but which is related to the idealized *image* of sex. Consummation does not destroy but enhances it. The image seems to me inextricably bound up in what are naively called "perversions," the <limit> effort to push the "poor flesh" *in any way* beyond what has already been discovered to be inadequate to its vision.

The great effort to treat a big thing "bigly" involves elements of melodrama precisely because the effort is incapable of being employed by all who wish to do so. The lesser efforts tend to make the grander ones ridiculous.[1] Who can read the scene in *Moby-Dick* where Ahab anneals the harpoon in blood without smiling? And yet the bigness (melodrama and all) must be there in big (great) writing. The purveyors of super and refined subtleties are not Shakespeare and Melville but Henry James and the "explicators" of James, Melville, and Shakespeare.

[1]They fall from "grandness" to "bombast." In Longinus' terms, those who attempt the "elevated" or "sublime" style and fail in reaching it achieve only "bombast."

George: "where the most characteristic gesture is arrested at the peak of motion." Tapestry (probably used by James Merrill): knighthood: *Sagen and Sänge.*[6]

Jarrellism: "as though he were trying to swim with a hundred-years' load of *Partisan Reviews* on his back."

5. Weiss's "Four Lay-Saints and a Satyr" appeared in the winter 1949 issue of *Sewanee Review.* Dickey alludes to an untitled poem about his brother on which he was working.

6. Literally, "legends and songs." George is a character in the novel on which Dickey was working.

Novel: at crucial moment, absurd nosebleed—"a (a certain) freshening of the skull immediately behind the face" (secret). Emphasize, but do not use this word.

Order *Janus* — Barker.
   "Bete Noire" — Keith Douglas.
   Summer *Kenyon.*
   Fall *Kenyon.*
   Fall *Sewanee.*
   September–October *Poetry.*
   Fall *Hudson.*
      —Gotham Book Mart
Read *Loving.*[7]

"Poem of Splintered References": (in *Partisan*).

   ———   ———   ———

    ——   ——   ————

   ————   ——

   ———   ———   ———

(Eliz. Bishop) except much, much bigger and more "experimental" in the best sense.[8]

Apollinaire — *Selected Writings.*
Henry Green — *Back* (Viking).
Osbert Sitwell — *Noble Essences.*
Fry
   Venus Observed
   A Phoenix Too Frequent.
D. S. Savage
   The Personal Principle
   The Withered Branch.
Frost — *Collected Poems.*

↑She capable of↓ "a sustained wildness of (intemperance)"—an intemperate and sustained wildness of pain. (An) aesthetic of pain: use cautiously.

A continuous use of "if" or "if it had" metaphor, signifying a wish to remake things "to the heart's desire."

7. Henry Green, *Loving, a Novel* (London: Hogarth Press, 1945; New York: Viking Press, 1949).

8. Bishop's "Over 2,000 Illustrations and a Complete Concordance" appears in *Partisan Review* 15:6 (1948), "O Breath" in 16:9 (1949), and "Poems" in 18:1 (1951). The last of these consists of three sections, the first of which is titled "Rain Towards Morning." In "O Breath," unlike the other poems, each line is gapped or split into two uneven parts.

They are right. The novel is artifact. *Within this* the human thing may move.

"O Loud, hear the wee beseech of thees
<of these> of each of these thy unlitten ones!"
    —*Finnegans Wake*

Winters: "Preliminary Problems."[9]

Yeats: masks and antimasks—self and otherself.

Look up Freud's dream symbolism of flying.

For Thurs. 1. Correct rest of G. themes.
    2. Correct 200 G. papers. *Record them*. Make test questions and prepare literature. Get former grades.
    3. Correct 100 H. papers.
    4. Go by office and get questions.
    5. Ask Jim Young.[10]

Covertly associational factors: Perse's "green peacocks of fame":[11] (pride, vanity, etc.)(in which this is fulfilled). Also make the adjectives *tell* in subtle ways.

Isherwood of *Goodbye to Berlin*.[12]

Excitement: "I bled through my veins." Natural running of blood conceived as bleeding. Needs working on. Perhaps a quick reflection under

9. The essay appears in Yvor Winters, *The Anatomy of Nonsense* (New York: New Directions, 1943). It logically examines twelve "problems" through a series of deductions, beginning with the idea that one may determine the better of two poems and concluding with the nature of the critical process.

10. James Dean Young, who had received his Master's degree from Stanford University in 1950, joined Rice Institute along with Dickey as an instructor in English in the fall semester of that year. English 100, required of all freshmen, was titled "English Composition; Study of Fundamental Literary Forms." While its primary purpose was to give students a command of written English, a second purpose was to examine the principal types of prose and poetry. English 200 was titled "Outlines of the History of English Literature." The *General Announcements* for Rice that year describes the course as "collateral reading of major authors representative of the various periods." The letters designate time periods during which courses were taught.

11. From "Rains," *Exile and Other Poems* (New York: Bollingen Foundation, 1949). The notebook entry has an arrow connecting "green" with "vanity" and another linking "this" and "adjectives."

12. Christopher Isherwood's fictional sketches, *Goodbye to Berlin*, were published in 1939 and involve a character bearing the author's name. The protagonist resembles Julian Glass, the central figure in the novel Dickey was writing. Like Julian, Christopher is an outsider, uncertain of his identity.

pressure—the realization that the natural running of the blood is a kind of bleeding-away.

Another *kind* of figure: example: "*his isopod curiosity.*" *Noun as adjective.*

Jack Corbett: "his lucid, uncomprehending eyes."

Sara's hands have "greenish veins."

Metaphor: when you strain against something overpowering, etc., with no chance and you exert your best efforts (almost) as a joke.

This of Sara's home—word: "evening," "evening-colored": "a (sad) *artificial* ↑stress↓ world, like that of ballet." ↑and yet: qualify↓

"Where all (passion) is perfectly presented, and therefore not really passion."

Tentative title: *The Casting.*
    Use tomorrow: maneuvered our situations toward requisite "pure moment." Use "pain" here—image of the ballet dancer (injured)(pain and beauty). Image of "watching her from audience." She "carried out my will," etc.[13] Also, Laverne had a "dancer-like" quality in drum-majorette uniform (absurd, etc., but somehow serious). Stress Sara's Orientalism by "dancer's slanted eyes," etc.

Show that Julian's aspirations (ballet theme) about her are fictions, are forestalled by their extreme familiarity "which I could never get behind."

It is late August ↑or first week in September↓: thus *swimming* and *watermelons* (perhaps a sentence on the transition from summer to fall: manifestations): the game they have come in from, or perhaps it was a practice of some kind (an all-star game, school bands, etc.): the distribution of Hallowe'en costumes, saved from year to year and redistributed (or something else), taken up and stored and swapped among the <several> ↑two (one Catholic and one county)↓ orphanages, etc., by the kind ladies, unseasonably early.
    When he first sees Laverne, he is a little startled by her outfit, but then remembers the game Jack is coaching. Then (the game) <that> is where she has gone before beating scene.

13. Compare Dickey's "The Lyric Beasts" in *Puella* (Garden City, N.Y.: Doubleday, 1982). Unless otherwise noted, all poems alluded to in the notes are available in *The Whole Motion: Collected Poems, 1945–1992* (Hanover and London: Wesleyan University Press and University Press of New England, 1992).

Metaphor: "[All] (noun) which does [does not] (verb) is (soon ___),
where. . . ." (Variations on this).

Also, *metaphor* instead of simile: instead of is *like, is* such and such: "an
exile, the young prince strolls through his marmoreal shows," etc. Your
heart *is* a such and such.

Epigram from Auden:
  "Dear heart, do not
  Think lightly to contrive his overthrow."

Type figure: "warming his hands at the fires of her anxiety" ↑at her anxious fires,↓ etc. Personification, pathetic fallacy.

In ritual scene: the shaman-like power of the coach, "as though he alone
were in touch" with so and so.

Poem on Eskimo: Sedna: from Radin.[14]

Next novel: inweaving of war and old man. Perhaps deal somehow in
magic. See Dr. Faustus (Mann), *Ritual Magic* (Butler).

Kingship (Hocart).[15]

In the ritual scene, make sure that you say that Julian "knew perfectly
what he was supposed to do, had been instructed," etc., but simply
failed. And after it is over they treat him as if "for them, I did not exist."
This failure is basis for his rejection.

Type figure: *enrich* my resignation. Something (from another category)
done to an attitude or state of mind.

"Smiling" pain: ↑characteristic or suggestive↓ noun as adjective.

Metaphor: animal frozen in ice: "requires only the ice's ___ release" for
corruption to set in, etc.

On Jack Corbett: make plain: he enjoyed a solid reputation in the community "as coaches usually do," etc.

  14. Paul Radin discusses the Eskimo and Sedna, the Eskimo deity of the sea, in his
anthropological study *Primitive Religion* (New York: Viking, 1937).
  15. Arthur Maurice Hocart, *Kingship* (London: Oxford University Press, 1927). The
study suggests that the ceremony crowning a king or installing a chief, regardless of the
society, involves approximately twenty-six features. Initiation and marriage ceremonies,
moreover, are modified versions of the royal ritual, regardless of where they occur.

Description of someone: "*masterful instability*"—as the gull each instant attempts to improve his position with respect to the wind: "minute shiftings."

Fantasy like the sleeping priest in "Lions, Harts, Leaping Does."[16]

Perhaps combine:
    2nd novel: old man on Fla. and war.
    3rd: *Two Brothers*—repatriation.

Poetry: Aivaz article: symbols.[17]

Poem on lycanthropy: end line: "(the half-room furnished by my ↑new-come blood↓ furred eyes)."

As ready to bloom as the sand.

Armor image in first of *Casting.*

(I) "smoke through the stone"—Hafiz.[18]

Taz Lighthorn—Hugh Newton.[19]

Orgasm linked with riding waves: "and in that small chaos you lie still."

In the first chapter, change the whole business about the statue. Make it *much* more farcical, much more consciously ironic; let the seriousness intrude only a little. "Inventing a novel around myself as a girl who falls in love with a statue," etc.

First chapter must be *much amplified* but not padded. Add details in light of later developments.

Perhaps quoted: "faith involves a kind of stagnation, perhaps the worst kind."

16. J. F. Powers's short story was published in the autumn 1943 issue of *Accent.*
17. David Aivez, "The Poetry of Dylan Thomas," *Hudson Review* 3 (fall 1950): 382–404. The essay argues that Thomas's poems are structured by an accumulation of images that extend the descriptive or symbolic context, that this context stresses the affirmation of process, and that within these images almost always lies an empathetic identification of objects, ideas, and emotions.
18. Persian poet who died in 1389(?) and whose lyrics always display vehemence, especially his amatory verses, his drinking songs, and his invective. His poetry, written in rhyming couplets, appears as *Divan,* an anthology published in hundreds of variations.
19. A classmate who, along with Dickey, played football at North Fulton High School.

Fantasy transference a sacrifice: perhaps 2 persons: "persisted in doing this" as through a prism. Theme of sacrifice—"sacrifice of reconciliation": Radin 179–180—beast and suppliant.[20]

Poem: "Prayer Becoming." Radin 186—a *deeply* religious poetry.[21]

Chapter 1: Sara (on visit to child psychiatrist which *she* may or may not have taken): "I was always afraid he would ferret out of me the things I did to my dolls."

Julian is *also* one of *Penelope's suitors,* who cannot bend Ulysses' bow.

Also in Chapter 1, mention his looking at Sara in conjunction with a very subtilized *mirror* image. *Subtilized,* I said, "as though she appeared in disturbing water."

"Simplification by exclusion" as by telescope.

Projected: a possible article on the analogies between jazz and the poetry of Hart Crane: a little like Valéry on da Vinci.[22]
    1. Jazz and Crane essentially Dionysiac.
    2. Both improvisatory: endlessly inventive.
    3. Crane's stanzas in "Faustus and Helen" in praise of the "new music" (Frank's review of Weber's book)[23] are not nearly so near (?) the spirit (?) or method of jazz as are the mere verbalizations, intonations, selections of words, entire poetic strategy. Concept of composition.
    4. Possible analogy between Crane and Beiderbecke[24] (sense of form, devotion to art, life).
    5. Crane's concept of jazz is ultimately false, like Van Vechten's,[25] but the methods, probably inadvertently on his part, are much the same.
    6. Jazz and Crane's poetry essentially American. Then analyze poems

---

20. See "The Conciliation of the Supernatural," *Primitive Religion,* 169–91. The "sacrifice of reconciliation" is a purification rite in which the killing of an animal and the drinking of its blood cleanse the sinner.

21. Radin argues that, in the order of evolution, wish-fulfillment precedes the performance of a magical spell and that a wish "is practically always on the verge of becoming a prayer." Compare Dickey's poem "Approaching Prayer" and see his comments regarding prayer in *Self-Interviews,* 134–35.

22. "Introduction to the Method of Leonardo da Vinci," *Oeuvres I: Les divers essais sur Léonard de Vinci* (Paris: N.R.F., 1938); reprinted separately with Valéry's marginal notes in *Tout l'oeuvre peint de Léonard de Vinci* (Paris: N.R.F. [Galérie de la Pléide], 1950).

23. Brom Weber's *Hart Crane: A Biographical and Critical Study* (New York: Bodley Press, 1948) was reviewed by Joseph Frank in the winter 1949 issue of *Sewanee Review.*

24. Leon Bismarck ("Bix") Beiderbecke (1903–1931) was an American jazz composer and cornetist, noted for his brilliant phrasing and clarity of tone.

25. Carl Van Vechten was an assistant music critic for the *New York Times* and drama critic for the *New York Press.*

for rhythms, etc. The *verbal* quality, intoxication with words, sounds, for *their own sakes* is the essential point of correspondence.

References: (1) Susanne Langer on music (*Hudson Review*).[26]
  (2) Frank article.[27]
  (3) French critics on jazz. Perhaps use the play-off of improvised rhythms, etc., against a basic chord structure and beat and give an analogy between this and Crane's verbal and metrical practices (perhaps use *tradition* here, also).
  (4) *American Jazz Music:* Wilder Hobson.[28]
  (5) Music in *The Nation:* Haggin.[29]

Aesthetic of pain: Laverne in pain and sunlight: "red and gold," "veins like twisted strands of violets."

"The *circumstances* of (light, air, fire, water)."

The thing is taking a good deal from philosophical speculation. I believe this to be good.

Parable of artist: the twin personality and its control. These two are *really* one and inevitably color and influence each other, but for each's development (and for that of the composite whole) they are separable, it being the business of the unseen and necessary to give direction to the seen and unnecessary in order to feed the unseen and necessary. Only in moments of great agitation, and not infrequently then also, do the two become inseparable and indistinguishable one from the other.

The unconscious kind of writing of Crane, Graham, and Thomas must be resolved into the consciousness, the logicalness past logic, of Valéry. May this not be made the poet's task, mine?
  Both the shaping and the singular *athleticism* of the unconscious bubbling-up of words and images may be acquired, at least to a degree. The latter is simply a willingness to explore, somehow passively, the implications of association, a tremendous territory, and the former is training oneself to discard and put into and out of conjunction what must be treated so.

26. Susanne K. Langer's "The Principles of Creation in Art" was published in the winter 1949 issue of *Hudson Review.* A second, related essay, "The Primary Illusions and the Great Orders of Art," appeared in the summer 1950 issue.
  27. Joseph Frank's "A Metaphysic of Modern Art," *Partisan Review* 17:2 (1950): 174–88.
  28. New York: Norton, 1939.
  29. B. H. Haggin regularly reviewed music and records for the *Nation* in the forties and fifties.

"The associative constructions of water": then this must be frozen into ice and shaped like statuary or architecture.

"The conflagration of consciousness"—"burned away (out of existence) by meditation": perhaps image in, of this.

Being: "sensibility is its home; knowledge, its profession": Mathews on Valéry.[30]

"The controlled ↑ordered↓ wildness, like an actor's, of a tree in the wind."

Control of the *widest* opposites: "the wheeling fern of the ferris wheel." If you stretch this far enough, you may arrive at Graham, but in better shape. Perhaps this is the best way—through rationality and its widest extension to the kind of piling-up of effect and richness that I want.

The *wheeled* fern—the ferned steel.

The Casting proper: Australian aboriginal societies: Spencer and Gillen: p. 259.[31]

Word: brass, brassy—light on (pain and beauty) scene of Laverne at lake.

Poems: <The> "Two Wild Songs ↑Poems↓ and One Sober."
       (Controlled Associative)   Traditional

"The Thorn Tree Shade": "scaling prince": "(birds) gang his soft weeping eaves and shriek (shrill)."[32]

Image of Christ as lawyer: "pleads man's case." Title: "Poem in Broken Metaphor for the Possibility of All Easters" or (of Easter).

His mind engages like a *cam,* not a cog (look up).

Book: *Make Light of It* — Wm. Carlos Williams.
Ritual Magic — E. M. Butler (Brown's) $5.00.
A Poet's Notebook — Edith Sitwell.

30. Jackson Mathews's review of Valéry's *Reflections on the World Today* appeared in *Partisan Review* 15:7 (1948).

31. Sir Walter Baldwin Spencer and Francis James Gillen, *The Native Tribes of Central Australia* (London: Macmillan, 1938). Chap. 7, "Initiation Ceremonies," details the rite of passage from boyhood into manhood. The initiate casts his boomerang in the direction in which his mother, who is the reincarnation of the tribe's mythical ancestors, supposedly lived prior to her birth. The ritual "may in all likelihood be regarded as intending to symbolize the idea that the young man is entering upon manhood and thus is passing out of the control of women and into the ranks of men."

32. See Notebook IV, n. 27, concerning Graham Sutherland's series of paintings titled *Thorns.*

Type figure: "*drink* the *passage.*" Disparity: perhaps with explanation.

Visual: drying blood in palm (skin) of hand "like a vast and unbelievably (orderly) systematic (system) of irrigation."

Easter poem: "over '*jurying*' ↑godded↓ raiment."

Type figure: "and *conceives* by *idleness.*"

Type figure: "rotting rest."

Type figure: "Good not let up for midnight's cheered centurions / Come home again"—(Graham).[33]

Type figure: "that *feed* your *inquiries* like aerial wine." Abstractions in "distraught" but compelling relationship.

Poetry: "the fine trained animal spring(ing) of the imagination."

Type figure: "we hauled in the net of our routes."

Book: *News of the World* ⎫ George Barker.
    The Dead Seagull ⎭

Look up books in library on prosody, versification, metrics.

Type figure: "trees *threw* a *moment* of shade."
                physical   time
Intermixed, and all variants of these.

Book: *Ceremony and Other Poems* — Richard Wilbur — Harcourt Brace ($2.50).
    The Poems and Plays of Thomas Lovell Beddoes — ed. H. W. Donner ($2.50) — Harvard University Press.

Title: "Angel Embattled."

In fantasy transference have [dimly (masked) adumbrated] executioner make her rise from floor where she is staked between two bolts on a polished surface—white reflecting surface: frozen milk: smooth-cast: billowed smooth and cast. "Her shaven sex": the *cool* reflection.

---

33. From W. S. Graham's "The White Threshold," *The White Threshold* (London: Faber and Faber, 1949; New York: Grove Press, 1952).

Orozco print: masked ritualist:[34] "taped-off sex."

Mulciber is Angel Embattled.[35]

The architect of heaven: concept of form. It is the *seeking* for the form that is the creative power of the architect (artist). The achieved form (buildings in Heaven) does not satisfy this. Perhaps have him addressed as Mulciber: *dive* is *form*—he *wills* it.

Research on Vulcan.

Type figure: "*honor is flashed off exploit.*"

Tate on Greenberg: "the shift of the seeing eye of the poet into the thing seen."[36]

Union of opposites, of opposite *scenes* and themes to make the poem, with images drawn from these and selected and cut and slanted to fit. See Thomas #11, "Then was my neophyte."[37]

Photography: death: evolution: the child: the sea.

In fantasy transference, the orgasm comes when the dancer rears, with her back to him (use word "audience" here), and in "accumulated strickenness," stands rigid in the statuesque(,)(+) pure immobility of pain and beauty, and he feels an unabeyant rising and a *pure direction*. But this time the dancer will not stop dancing. Show here that this is a portrayal of his impotence.

Poems 1935–1948 — Clifford Dyment (Dent).
Collected Poems — Roy Campbell (The Bodley Head).

The poet and Dead poem: "baring his only eye."

"Mirrored page."

Type figure: "Adam's brine" (Thomas).[38]

---

34. José Clemente Orozco (1883–1949), Mexican painter and muralist. His work dealt compassionately with social themes, particularly that of man versus machine. Dickey likely is referring to *Ancient Human Sacrifice,* part of a vast scheme of frescoes divided into two parts, *The Coming* and *The Return of Quetzalcoatl.*

35. Mulciber in Milton's *Paradise Lost* was the architect of Heaven before being thrown "by angry Jove / Sheer o'er the Crystal Battlements" (1.741–42), where he fell for an entire day. See Dickey's entry on p. 26 and Notebook III, n. 40. Mulciber was also known as Vulcan.

36. See "Preface," *Poems by Samuel Greenberg* (New York: Holt and Co., 1947).

37. Dylan Thomas, *Selected Writings* (New York: New Directions, 1946).

38. From "I dreamed my genesis."

"A darkness in the weather of the eye
Is half its light."[39]

Lowell's violent, physical, kinetic imagery concerning mythological figures: "so and so snaps / Across Poseidon's shins," etc. This seems useful.
His telescoping of mythology and the present as though they were in-
teractive.

Image of falconer: "gyve," "tethered" or "tether" as noun.

Hourglass (reversal) technique of Kent's criminal-sailor poem and
Thomas' "Conversation of Prayers."

Type figure: Hopkins' "mined with a motion":[40] "comb(ed)."

Book: Leavis' two or three books from George Stewart I don't have—
Great Tradition.[41]

Image: identification of heart and sun: Harvey: "the heart is the beginning of life, the sun of the microcosm."[42]

Type figure: "shaded," "shadowed" (these are participles) *in* the fennel
stalk, etc.

Poem on Carthage: sacrifice of children (perhaps soliloquy by child: a
happiness in the prospect of the fire: a kind of sacrificial *game*).

Type figure: "the sharp song with sun under its radiance" (Pound).[43]

Carthage poem: "Hamilcar (waiting)."[44]

Experimentation with logically unrelated images: "Rose in the Steel
Dust" 78–79.[45] Makes for "Emotional contemplation rather than emotional involvement." Perhaps.
    A "language of exploration."

39. From "A process in the weather of the heart."
40. From "The Wreck of the *Deutschland.*"
41. Frank Raymond Leavis published *The Great Tradition* and *New Bearings in English
Poetry: A Study of the Contemporary Situation* with G. W. Stewart in 1948 and 1950, respectively.
42. See William Harvey, *The Circulation of the Blood* (London: J. M. Dent, 1932; New
York: E. P. Dutton, 1952), 3.
43. From "Canto LXXIV."
44. Hamilcar Barca, Carthaginian general defeated by the Romans in the First Punic
War. His son was Hannibal.
45. Hugh Kenner, "The Rose in the Steel Dust," *Hudson Review* 3 (spring 1950):
66–123. Kenner argues that a concern for exact definition underlies not only Pound but

Use of colors (blue) in Valéry's "The Spinner."

Get folders for typed poems.

Experiment with breaking poetic line up at strategic points with commas and other punctuation marks: (___, _____)(example).

Poem: breaking of the light of knowledge in the mind of man. Perhaps use examples of men and "discoveries": fire, wheel, arch, etc. Or perhaps use this in another poem.

Poem: emphasis on sound: saying what has to be said and *sounding* as well as possible (intricate sound-patterns: *round* and *sharp* sounds).

"Thick(s)" as verb.

Camera and cinematic properties of poetry: experiments in controlling *distance* from imaged objects: Mulciber in *Par. Lost,* far away; Jarrell, close up.

"Breathing leap."

(He was) "loose with desire."

Cadence: "I am by blood bloodhounded out of doors."

Highway crossmarkings on sunned hill like gold ladder.

Finish Peter Yates.[46]
Do: Barbara Gibbs[47]
    James Merrill (and in *Quarterly Review*)
    F. T. Prince[48]
    Richman
    Chisholm and Maas
    Zachery
    Brinnin's commentary[49]

---

also his *Cantos,* his music, and his economics and that this precise verbal definition leads to a perceptivity where new relationships are revealed owing to "the 'motion' of the moving image." The ideogram, moreover, conveys a greater increase of emotional range and intellectual precision than the metaphor.

    46. American music critic, poet, educator, and author of books on music.

    47. American poet and educator who won the Blumenthal Prize from *Poetry* in 1949.

    48. Frank Templeton Prince, South African-born English poet and scholar.

    49. John Malcolm Brinnin, Canadian-born poet and educator.

W. S. Merwin
Margaret Avison and commentary.[50]

"Calcined to his integer" opens up a great new field of metaphor, a new way of relating things by *qualities* and *attributes* rather than by the fact that they are actually *associated* with each other in the *"real"* world.

Weber's account of "For the Marriage of Faustus and Helen": symbolism.[51]

To say that poetry is *purely* rational is a grave mistake; all we can say is that it is, in a sense, "of the mind." To deny to poetry the tremendous resources of the semi-logical, the supra- or superlogical, and the alogical is to impoverish it altogether needlessly, to thin it, to force it to conform to untoward strictures. After all, what is "rational"? This itself might be made to include a good deal Yvor Winters might dislike. The question is, how logical (or rational) or *how* (is it) logical is poetry? Or might we insist on the subsuming of these distinctions?

In Mulciber poem: sees wounds (because he can't be wounded) as *desirable,* as desirable and beautiful objects: "*calyx* of a wound," "calyxed wound," etc.

"Gentle (ed)(ing)" as verb or participle.

Troy Hauser.

Beddoes: "in any crevice of the well-built spirit."[52]

At Sara's—Sunday: middle of book?: Julian feels for George as "comic Orpheus" (he states this). Perhaps use subtilized water-image: music and muscular action (casting) correlated in metaphor: episode of "George," the harmonica, and the Christmas story.

Book: Dictionary of Mythology and Folklore: *Encyclopedia of Folklore.*[53]

Book: the Brinnin—Kimon Friar anthology of modern poetry.[54]

---

50. Margaret Avison, Canadian poet influenced by Hopkins and concerned with the total comprehension of experience.
51. See *Hart Crane: A Biographical and Critical Study,* chap. 8.
52. From *The Second Brother.*
53. No such titles are listed before 1952. Dickey likely intends the *Standard Dictionary of Folklore, Mythology and Legend* (New York: Funk and Wagnalls, 1949–1950).
54. *Modern Poetry, American and British* (New York: Appleton-Century-Crafts, 1951).

Type figure: Jean Garrigue's "gloved to air's concert." *Think* about these figures *carefully.*[55]

Imagery of cock-fighting: "gaff," "rattle," "heel," "jagger," "slasher," "king" (in this sense). Kinds of chickens: "shawlneck," etc.: "shuffle": "pit," "pitted," "pitting" perhaps used in ambiguous context.

Koestler, Meredith, Albert Cook on laughter, comic spirit.[56]

"George" episode: song is "birthday song": has nothing to do with birthdays: "Perhaps that was what was intended to be funny." Julian sides (silently) fiercely with George.

(Adj.): "haycock." "Mow," "mown," "idiate" (verb).

{Following this entry on p. 44 of the notebook, Dickey lists ten identification questions intended for what he labels a Shakespeare test but that more generally cover Elizabethan and Jacobean drama. His service in 1951 during the Korean conflict, together with the entry above regarding the Brinnin and Kimon Friar anthology, indicates that he has now returned to Rice for the fall of 1952. Among the courses he taught was English 200, "Outlines of the History of English Literature."}

Poetry: major symbol: *knight:* derision and admiration: complex attitude toward him.

Novel: fantasy transference: "also, none of (the other) images worked." Impaling self: sword driven (sat on) between legs: "ritual and shuddering (re)conciliation of steel and flesh" (linkup with impaled girl image). Eagerness and unashamedness of girl's actions: "marvellous fulfillment of self-violation." This, however, subordinate to whipping image: "tied with red ribbon (to bolts) like a gift."

Knauber: "In Eden's Skull."[57]

---

55. From "Marriage Is a Mystery of Joy," *The Ego and the Centaur* (New York: New Directions, 1947).

56. George Meredith's "An Essay in Comedy" and Albert Cook's *The Dark Voyage and the Golden Mean: A Philosophy of Comedy* (Cambridge: Cambridge University Press, 1949). The reference to Arthur Koestler is unidentified.

57. Charles F. Knauber's poem appeared in *Quarterly Review of Literature* 6:1 (1950–1952).

Mrs. Arrington (diamonds, etc.) looked "as though she might shatter, (heavily) prismatic↑(al)↓, among her ferns."

Book: *The Story: A Critical Anthology* — ed. Mark Schorer — Prentice-Hall $3.35.

"Wild" or far-fetched metaphor like Djuna Barnes' "eland" description of Robin Vote.[58]

Metaphor: —likened to the coming-to-life ↑(rising)↓ of the audience by the (carrying frenzy) of a tenor-saxophone solo.

Dynamics: improvisational qualities of poetry: Flip Phillips: wedding of jazz and traditional poetic idioms.[59]

Poem: "A Grief on ___" (after Tourneur).

At end of line: two repeated trochees ↑on same word↓: Tourneur's "...merry, merry."

Mermaid Series: Webster and Tourneur.[60]

"Had the look of one (slain) murdered by music."

Type figure: a kind of personification: Tourneur: "go . . . gray hayred *adulterie."*[61]

Rhythm: "so withered staunchly" (Graves).

Books—Alfred Knopf:
   Early Stories — Elizabeth Bowen.
   First Poems — James Merrill (2).
   Troubled Sleep — Jean-Paul Sartre.
   The Image of a Drawn Sword — Jocelyn Brooke.

Type figure: "who keeps a fairy in his upright ear" (Beddoes).[62]

---

58. From *Nightwood* (New York: New Directions, 1946 [1937]).

59. "Flip" Phillips, whose real name was Joseph Edward Filipelli, originally played the clarinet but in 1942 specialized on the tenor sax. After playing with several bands, including Benny Goodman's in late 1942, he became a regular member of Norman Granz's "Jazz at the Philharmonic" tours in 1946.

60. The Mermaid Series, published in London by T. Fisher Unwin and in New York by Scribner's, reproduced old texts of Elizabethan and Jacobean dramatists. Each volume was about five hundred pages and included an etched frontispiece.

61. From *The Revenger's Tragedy.*

62. From *Torrismond.*

The corn god: corn imagery.

Orpheus and George episodes: Radin 293: sacred clowns: "privileged to mock."[63]

Type figure: "pitch of brightness."

Before he goes to the house of Laverne to witness what he has labored to set up, he is suddenly afraid of the machinery: "but he could not but watch its operation" (alter statement).

"Vocabulary" (of acts).

"Staging" of circumstance.

Dusk: "the dulling trees."
Morning: "the sharpening ↑(whetted)↓ trees."

"Stag and raven" (Donne).[64]

The Casting: first reference: "and though the pass may hover, it must first be thrown." Word in this connection: "imponderables"—"cut down the area of imponderables."

Dropped accent for special effect in poetic line.

End line or stanza:
"——————————
. . . the king will ride."[65]

Rhythm: Donne:
    "Busy Old Fool, Unruly Sun"[66]
    Why dost thou, so and so . . .
    Shine on us.

Type figure: "or *snorted* we in the *seven sleepers' den*"?[67]

"Brotherless": read Marvell.

63. See "The Ritual Drama," in Radin's *Primitive Religion,* 289–306. Radin declares that of the four groups in the ritual drama and pageant of The Coming of the Gods, the sacred clowns, or Koyemci, are the most feared and beloved. Grotesque in appearance, they indulge in any obscenity and are adept at black magic.
    64. From "An Anatomy of the World."
    65. See the opening stanza of Donne's "The Sun Rising."
    66. From "The Sun Rising."
    67. From Donne's "The Good-Morrow."

W. M. Meredith's poems in Jan.–Feb's *Partisan*.[68]

"Vault" as verb: "vault his brain."

"Or Holland's fishing of the offal miles" (Marvell).

Rime: "they," "decay." Phonetic illustration:
    ". . . , as threshed as they
    Consume the mantles of decay."

Image of *mower*. (see Marvell).[69] Perhaps sees king approaching across meadow.

"Despondent fury": Gilbert and Sullivan.

Wave: "as it (levers) its curved and tumbling turn."

Book: *Decembrist* — Joseph Bennett — (*Hudson R*).[70]

Shaved chest: hairs were like "soldiery in shallow graves, soon to rise" (variants).[71]

Fantasy transference: The Dance in the Deserted Palace—Eleanor Clark: The Ball—Beddoes: *Outidana,* "Pygmalion."[72]

"(F)or I shall drag you through the harp, to learn what ragged and bloody music is in those chaste strings, (whetted) honed tang of razors, thumbed, (or executing) systemized torment of serenity and grace."

"A good but fundamentally insecure mind, a clear wavering, like superior jelly (gelatine)."

Explore ghostliness of Beddoes and Coleridge's "Ancient Mariner."

Alchemist and necromancer poems.

68. Meredith published three poems in the January–February 1951 issue of *Partisan Review,* "A View of the Brooklyn Bridge," "The Fishvendor," and "The Waterways."
69. See "The Mower against Gardens," "Damon the Mower," "The Mower to the Glo-Worm," and "The Mower's Song."
70. Bennett published four poems in *Hudson Review* in 1948, two in 1949, and three in 1950, all of which were included in his first book of poetry, *Decembrist* (New York: Clarke and Way, 1951). *Hudson Review* did not review the book.
71. Compare Dickey's "Drinking from a Helmet."
72. Thomas Lovell Beddoes's *Outidana* contains a section titled "Pygmalion," which concerns a Cyprian sculptor who first carves and then falls in love with a statue of a young lady.

Novel: after Laverne is beaten, goes to Arrington home, gets thin iron spike (flaking)(perhaps from fence)—[*idea* here: *chance:* dog: cocker: comes running, knows Julian: Julian calls softly to him: springs to be caught in his arms]. Julian, against the light in the Doctor's study (studies at night: 4 hrs. sleep, etc.), drives (strokes) the spike through the dog's body [previous to this: image of Julian as apprentice but assured hunter: leopard his totem animal: he uses the fact that the dog knows him, his trust, etc., "as the leopard (assimilates)(utilizes) ↑"*is*" or ("is in")↓ the innocent complicity of the shadow-clovered reed," etc.]. Goes to Dr.'s study, tells him he has last of gifts. Dr. is looking, taking last look at papers, prepared to be surprised, when Julian drives the "harpoonlike spike" with the dog on it, upside down, as if he were to be roasted, into the polished surface of the desk, "hoping to transfix the doctor's hand. But overwound by force," the dog is driven down the spike by the force of the blow, and then slides slowly, raglike head and slack tongue, down, which is pushing a new red trickle, a new streambed, etc., "to rest at the Dr.'s unmoved fingers." Julian's "ceremonial blood": his smeared face: tastes the blood on his teeth, etc. ("gilded blood").

Martyr poem: perhaps in "Thorn Tree Shade": dialogue between soul and body of heretic in which body cries, twists, screams, and pleads in pain, and the soul (mind) argues its case in cool philosophic terms, (curses) ↑demeans↓ "intellectually" his tormentors.

Beast and human in sexual congress poems.

Novel: rewrite first chapter, leaving out that atrocious, long anecdote about the statue except in a very reduced (as to length and importance) version: "She would tell me, in fact was now telling me, a ridiculous story about her love for a statue of Hector on the Sudlow campus, and of the time she had left a drinking party to take him a bottle of beer, anoint him with it, and kiss his cold lips," etc.

(Before this): "We would tell each other ↑had taken to telling each other↓ long (anecdotes) about <each> ourselves, (based on) the thinnest breadth of actuality or none. I kept thinking that someone's story *had to be,* at least once, revelatory, but I could never make sense either of mine or hers."

(My most successful): "I would deliver a long harangue on my abilities as a soft-shoe dancer, alone, atop a square-topped granite crag, with the snow floating slowly, deliver a minute description of my get-up: a checkered yellow suit from the Keith circuit, tight and small-legged trousers, a pearl ↑(sky)↓ gray derby and ↑(matching)↓ spats, a tremendous red boutonniere and a jointed cane—a dance to the ↑(a)↓ stop-and-go version of 'The Glow-worm,' knees and elbows in elaborate parabolas, Irish nose high, head tilted back, and ending with an exit into the bouldered wings by scattering imaginary daisies from my derby, the cane hung on my arm."

Whipping: setting in clover: "Jack Ketch with a bad daughter."[73]

"The (prince, king) who sketches you ↑(blocks you in)↓ roughly in coral": roughness, quickness, intuition is better (Bergson) than something worked out.

Type figure:
  "*Time,* no doubt, *has ears*
  That *listen* to the swallowed *serpent, wound*
  Into its bowels." (Lowell)[74]

A princess in a red garden, sketched by her jongleur's harp, as the strings catch on her beauty and strand themselves on pearl—unadventurous strings (wires), stranded easily on her pearls.

"Stranded" (in two <sentences> senses): ship image deliberately vague: "its marbled pale" (pale here: noun).

Perhaps have Dr. Arrington call himself "medicine man" or refer to "tribal practice" of medicine.

Reader's Encyclopedia on lion: "lounged in the seed," "the pull(ing) ↑sound↓ of drums."

The black-hooded "Immortals" of Xerxes' army at Thermopylae: "the (beating) sun," "the sea's swarming balance."

Poem on son's voyaging:
  "and sheer your cataracting sail!"
  "as of something mistrusted because long unused ↑(ill-used)↓."
  "a trumpet (splintering)↑(shattering)↓ in the mirror depths" or a splintering trumpet.
  "emblematic."

73. Jack Ketch was a seventeenth-century British executioner who died in 1686. Three years earlier he published a broadside entitled *Apologie of John Ketch Esq. the Executioner of London, in vindication of himself as to the execution of the late Lord Russel on July 21, 1683.* In it he defends himself against charges of drunkenness during the execution and of failing to deliver an initial blow adequate to decapitate Lord Russel.

74. From "Between the Porch and the Altar," *Lord Weary's Castle* (New York: Harcourt, Brace, 1946).

Rimbaud's "La Tête d'un Faune": "rigged with," "sheep-hook," "freaked with," "horn(ed) feet" for hooves.

"Has you at an immense disadvantage, like trying to follow and capture with your hand a fluttering piece (scrap) of paper (tissue)"—the will at the mercy of (pure) caprice.

Type figure: "it seemed we were submerged under a coral reef to tantalize the wise-grinning shark."

"As if a metal catch, worked on a trigger or suddenly defective, (which was) located somewhere in his breast, had slipped or been released, and he had been borne into the ancient and perpetually freshening watercourse of a river toward the distant sound of falling. It was a pleasant situation and seemed to minimize the foreboding quality" (whose pull he had felt but been held from).[75]

What I want is language seeming to live off itself but bearing an intimate, empathetic relation to the world and to men.

Novel: Julian cannot ↑(yet)↓ avail against the Squire, and so kills the dog —"although I might try that later," etc. Dr. Arrington figures women and dogs in same category. The assault on dog is a minor but substantial victory.

"The muscles of his solar plexus (clenched) ↑cinched↓ and loosened with a <soft and> random soft venom."

Eskimo poem:
  "as I release /
  A puff the ↑our↓ hell-white ceiling will not stain ↑(melt)↓."

The: "the inviolable virgin one longs for."[76]

Make symbol of "geography": eskimo and tropic poems: compass (orientation, etc.) a "permanent" symbol.

"Lying in bed, enjoying the small pains that can never harm one (impotent scouts of death), the strung nerve ↑(in the cheek)↓ plucked with

75. Compare Dickey's poem "The Falls," published in the winter 1959 issue of *Impetus* and included in the appendix of Dickey's poems herein.

76. The entry suggests that Dickey was searching for a single word that would denote the full phrase and not that he failed to delete the opening of the entry.

a sharp quill, the lower leg incased in a slow heaviness, the tremor in the side."

Figure of bullbat in several poems.

Get Twayne list: Squires, Belitt, Mayo, Weiss.

Mine is now a "poetry of (the) hypothetical situation."

With Sara on tower [Ed Van's mountain: perhaps brief mention of his former admiration for (Ed Van[77]): his desire to emulate him: disdain of whole system] on her birthday at night: climb up rotting, abandoned tower: touches her leg: this sets off cruelty to Laverne: he is impotent to kiss Sara. She calls him "Julie, darling," but he cannot come close to her. She has a diamond (or imitation tiara) and it glitters faintly there above the still town, the night wind: "it was possible to believe we were un-supported"—her compelling love of the irrational. "Boost me" ↑she says without warning↓ and he lifts her <five or> four or five feet to the first gnawed rung. Graveyard: see Agee's Shady Grove: two images. To get in gate, he says to Negro, "My name is (same as Ed Van's). My people are buried up there. I've been away," etc.

"A manifold soft peltering, (as from)(like) the flight of a herd of rabbits."

When Julian first sees Taz: "his face might have been behind a mask" or "the kind of face which one imagines behind a mask."

"Something you wish you could see, like a frozen tropic."[78]

Story about a retiring, middle-aged man who plays in a Sunday football game (as at Piedmont park[79]): "All right, *you* take it": rough play: sunny autumn day: expanses in city: sounds of children on horses.

Julian's acceptance: "an astonishingly bright day without heat" ["a qual-ity of (some) pictures"].

Julian: "my neat, cat-like face."
    "The motions made up of a warm light, as if swimming (leisurely) in honey."

---

77. Edward van Valkenberg, a high school friend of Dickey's.
78. Compare Dickey's "To the Butterflies."
79. A park in downtown Atlanta and the setting for an early scene in *Alnilam* (Garden City, N.Y.: Doubleday, 1987), 84–87.

To plunge resolutely and in some wonder into the complex prismatics of a crowd of words, to *move around* in poetry, <the> to stumble often, rewardingly, *not* to know perfectly well what you are doing all the time—that is what may produce the strong thing.

"(The jungle's)(perpetually) *hauling* sound."

"The slight involuntary leap toward impending (approaching) ruin or pain."

(On stage): "the light coming upward onto her face, making her look a little diabolical."

Poem: "Dialogue in (the) Red Garden":

   Princess and Jongleur: everything is rotting here: "rust": perhaps old, senile fauns peep through the foliage. She chatters gaily: (see "Hèro-diade").[80]

   "We are alone here": metaphor about drawing her through the strings of the harp: "to make such mortal music (from your pain)": a little "fast talk": <Princess> a modified and "usable" Hopkins. See Merrill, "Diary of Duc de L":[81] Fry.

   Princess: "Yes, I see. The light is passing because I am young. It spreads from wing to wing of the stone bird. And I, sir, am the angle at which things, gardens, wine-veined children stir."

A wedding of Hopkins, Shakespeare, Mallarmé, and Hart Crane: my *God!!*

My bias now is toward <the> "word-led," even "word-choked" poetry. There must first be something to *bring order to*. One doesn't create by the *effort* to order, except in a special sense, but by *pruning* and selecting from a ridiculous excess.

"Litter Bearers": not the jungle in the body (soul) but the body (or soul) in the jungle *of itself.*

Julian: "I sometimes think (that) the only way to teach a woman both the essence and particularities of love is to take her first to bed with a jar of vaseline and a strap and work on her with both. That way she will learn, with no diversion, no unnecessary and unhappy complication, what cruelty love entails, and what respect it deserves."

---

80. By Mallarmé.
81. Merrill's poem, "The Diary of the Duc de L***," was published in the winter 1949 issue of *Accent*.

"The future in the face of the seagull": "engine": "grot": "alabastering water"! (emphasis on becoming: here: color): becoming a *thing,* the qualities of which are given over to the noun modified.

Type figure: "*bright* logic."

Barbara Herman's account of "Lachrymae Christi": symbolism.[82]

"Litter Bearers": end: for, compelled, (com)plighted, "the forestarred christening toils."

My poetry now is "scenic," "situational," "allegorical," and, I hope, "symbolic" to some degree. It is, or may be, "hypothetical," and "problematic," and, I also hope, "dramatic." I wish soon to try "abstract," "a poetry of ideas," "concepts," soon.

A good poet must have "the *exploratory* sense of language." This does not mean the wild, desperate striving for originality of, say, Leslie Fiedler, who has no talent for poetry at all, apparently.

"Red Garden": "lutanist."

"The spangled and cautious king / ↑Line here↓ Move out across the burden of his field."

Julian's weightlifting: "seemed always to be preparing for an unknown but exacting (and important) physical trial": "its demands were undeniable."

Kenneth Rexroth's book of dance plays: see *N.Y. Times* book section.[83]

Work on a song for the jongleur to play:
    "(My merry) thick brocade ↑(only sound)↓
    O my merry lady."

Poem "Angel Embattled" to be called "Mulciber."

"May seem to you
A twangling of razors in my ↑your↓ happy (shade)."[84]

82. "The Language of Hart Crane," *Sewanee Review* 58 (winter 1950): 52–67.
83. *Beyond the Mountains* (New York: New Directions, 1951). William Carlos Williams's review, "Verse with a Jolt to It," appeared on January 28, 1951.
84. The entry's second line originally read "The twanglings of razors," which Dickey then abandoned in favor of the new wording but did not delete.

Poem on (Malebranche's) theories: intervention of God in human action (and gradually sensuous statue: who learns grief last?). This statue poem in *rigid* stanzaic form: *Condillac, not* Malebranche.[85]

"(A) ↑(the)↓ twangling of light razors in the shade."

In the garden: an iron (wolf)hound.

"The boxwood beast /
(Is) becoming mangy with excess of air."

W. Stevens' concepts of "major" and "minor."

Sudden pain: "the (swifting) of a comet through (the waist)."

"To behave, in a poem, as though you really believed you saw, in a close rose garden, a bower or trellised arbor at night, *with all his physical properties,* a white winged horse."

Fear: "a falling(-)away under the ribs."

Geographical directions as recurrent symbols.
    "South Becoming": perhaps Rilkean identification here.
    "Prayer Becoming": see Fuller on Plato,[86] Plato, *Radin,* Jung, theoretical anthropologists.

Sweeney's introduction in Thomas' *Selected Writings: sound* strategy in "Marriage of a Virgin."[87]

Sound:
    "admit no scaping ↑scraping↓ carol
    To the pick and fall of love."

Riding in train: "as though a figured silk screen were drawn swiftly (under) past the window, and the furtive motions were only the

85. Étienne Bonnet de Condillac (1715–1780), French philosopher whose theory of sensationalism argued that all knowledge derives from the senses and that no innate ideas exist. His *Traité des sensations* supposed a statue internally organized like a human being and animated by a mind lacking all ideas. The marble exterior precluded the use of any sense. Beginning with the sense of smell, Condillac then progressively opened the statue's senses to inquire about the mind's acquisition of knowledge.
    86. B. A. G. Fuller, *History of Greek Philosophy* (New York: Henry Holt and Co., 1923). The book was a text in Dickey's philosophy courses at Vanderbilt.
    87. John L. Sweeney, "Introduction," *Selected Writings* (New York: New Directions, 1946), ix–xxiii.

(prerogatives) of motion, its off-hand and illusory gestures, the self-indulgence of the millionaire's bed-chamber furnished with the rocking and noise of rods."

"My shadow has caught up with me."

Running across the fields and fences at Clemson to see the paratroop demonstration, Rothell[88] with his bullock's red face: gray uniforms, green woods: "toward a terminus (terminal) where resided (dwelt) a ↑(some)↓ singular aspiration": "a kind of flight—over misty bushes," etc.

Books: *At Swim-Two-Birds* — Flann O'Brien — Pantheon.
    Follow Me Ever — Charles E. Butler — Pantheon.
    From Here to Eternity — James Jones.
    Conclusive Evidence — Vladimir Nabokov — Harpers.
    The Age of Longing — Arthur Koestler.
    A Diary of Love — Maude Phelps Hutchins.

"Red Garden":
    "whose nail /
    Capers lyricly among the strung / <embrasures>
    Embrasures, and <makes> contrives
    A twangling of light razors in the shade."

Look up F. S. Flint's translations and read both the translations and works in original.

Poem: "Were You This (Word)(Field)[(Sea)][(River)]."

Highway: various and innumerable shades of gray: browns, silvers: surprising innocence of green pines. Girl in white in attitude of waiting at edge of highway. Illusion of man crucified on side of moving freight car: seen through young pines and brush.[89] Clock in roadside cafe where swinging girl is pendulum: background scene of house and garden: girl in plaster—blue dress, unpainted hair, crossed feet—holding (to) threads of swing: small mechanical agitations in semblance of play: strict: gives illusion of duty, compulsion rather than play: endless Sisyphean play whose play is hung on time.

    A filament in a clean bulb, high in a narrow room, glowed like a perpetually tightened (held) and cautionary pulse.

---

88. Claude Rothell. Two years ahead of Dickey at Clemson, he was a blocking back on the football team and was later killed in World War II.
89. Compare Dickey's "A Folk Singer of the Thirties."

Taz and Laverne in bowling alley: "the (cold) geometric(al) flight of arrows close(d)(ing) over her"—the geometric *close* of arrows *flighting* over her.

Perhaps in fantasy trans: have her dance on the cloudy white floor in a dimly perceived, rotting house, a "festering mansion" (subtilize this), moored face down by an (ornamental) red sash to two, glittering silver bolts.

Sara: I used to think, perhaps dream, of love as an old man in a study, a single light crusting (over) a spill of books on his table, (the) books in their cases out of sight toward the high ceiling, and this study was what I called his "lore" and I was his daughter. He would say to me, on a sum-mer('s) night, "Take your clothes off, my child," and I would do so, and strip to my barest veins in the wind fluting under the door, and turn in the throw of light slowly under his dying cackle and the pop of his learned knuckles. He would speak a long time of spring and the rose-tree under the straight star and the wanton weed. <I> "You are young. Your skin is stretched on the <metal> bright metal twine and gum of youth (which I am dying into)."

Book: *Nones* — Auden.

"Son and heir": "fret" in two senses, one musical.

The *family* as microcosm of the world.

Type figure: Lowell: "our prime, at best, is passion's season."[90]

Poem (about Moses?): "and ↑(or)↓ wrap ↑(rap)↓ your knuckles on the gangling staff(?)"

"On the solid edge of a cliff no nearer death than if you stood in the center of an endless plain."

Barker: "My minotaur life lost in London's maze."[91]

The waves' crush (against the shore): poem on wave-womb.

90. From "The Wood of Life," *Land of Unlikeness* (Cummington, Mass.: Cummington Press, 1944).
91. From George Barker's "Elegy No. 3," *Lament and Triumph* (London: Faber and Faber, 1940).

The hero—protagonist of long poem—American? Phelps Putnam? Matthiessen on Putnam.[92]

Radio: "I like my terrors quieter."

Type figure: Thomas: "Adam's wether (that is, *bell*-wether) in the flock of horns."[93]

Read poetry more closely. Let your mind run through it daringly and carefully.

Lion-lover in "Red Garden": "The ruin a blue stockade," "motley man." Symbol of *map* becoming important—direction. "Walnut-colored" (green).
    She: (on his notes): (are they) "a floral shaping of ___."
    He: "A twangling of light razors in the shade."
Have the dialogue center, at least in part, in a dialectic on *what he plays*: "Alexander's Feast" kind of thing, but ironic, tangential, language-ridden, and bitten.[94]

Sara to Julian (?): "(You have) a face like a cat looking out of a well, ↑(fiercely)↓ dedicated to repelling his rescuers."[95]

Negro in elevator: angle made his blunt nose appear like that of a worn-away statue, timeless and weathered: timelessness of all weathered things.

On looking at, assembling old army records: <You> They suck the individuality out of you, so that any activity which is not recorded as having been engaged in by you seems implausible, absurd, if not quite impossible.

The way dreams of a person alter your waking intercourse with the person.

"Complex miracle": use in several places of "miracle" image.

"These are perhaps imitations, but *living* imitations."

---

92. F. O. Matthiessen's essay, "Phelps Putnam (1894–1948)," appeared in the winter 1949 issue of *Kenyon Review*.
93. From "Altarwise by owl-light."
94. Dryden's poem, which celebrates the power of music, consists of seven stanzas resembling either a recitative, aria, or ensemble. Each stanza concludes with a chorus that repeats the last lines of that stanza. In the poem Timotheus, royal musician to Alexander, arouses his master to various passions by singing and playing in several musical modes.
95. Compare Dickey's "The Underground Stream."

"Plunged (the) heart in stone": "as though stone fled the (eye)(heart)"—
"as though the (heart)(eye) fled stone."

The profoundest concept of poetry is the correlation of *insight* with
point of view. A thing may *mean,* may symbolize, may suggest an infinite
number of other things, insights, connotations, etc. Thus, to the citrus-
grower the young orange-tree may indicate profit, to the botanist a
combination of natural circumstances, to Rilke and Agee "painless
wealth," to the painter color-values, etc. Objects, things may *mean* a great
many other things than what they "scientifically" *are.*

Joy: "the (a) soaring in the throat."

Concept of ↑making↓ poem as the forging of an iron ring, or a chain.[96]

The *necessity* of a poem's being tied in with a world (ethical, religious,
epistemological) view.

Increasing importance in poems: the *necessity* of hardship to faith: suffering as *prerequisite.*

Sex: one of the ways not to be dead.

"_____, a (the) bright swilling of energy (from) in a crucible."

Sexual image: "(bestride, bestrode) a sword."

2nd novel: wedded: the preoccupied inanity of modern life, Florida
(science can't *function;* it can only *work*) and the paradoxical apocalyptic
vision which proceeds from it. See *Revelation* (parable), Kafka, surrealists,
Thomas, Melville, Joyce (night-town), and Blake (*Thel, Jerusalem*).

2nd novel: wedded:
　　1. *Journey of the Brothers* (South).
　　2. old man (Florida)—*King.*
　　3. war (air).

"Make of fire a changeling's shroud."

She bent over me in the buried (bodied) dark, the battling world peltering ↑way↓ over us, (in) a rush, the soft flight of a herd of rabbits, and
went at my throat like a dog. I expected her to raise her <head> thick

96. See Dickey's detailed discussion of what he termed "the building of the rational
poem" early in Notebook III.

neck conclusively and shift her teeth on a morsel, and ↑to↓ hear the click there of (my) ↑a↓ bone.

Julian and the masks: wears "a shirt with a great dragon." Try for an *incisive* and real dreaming quality in his ride in the back seat of the Arringtons' car (orphanage).

Lion in "Red Garden": "The bantering paw, the bloodspring in the sun."

"Your body an instrument of praise."

Work into the thing Julian's (as mine) <of > ↑fondness for↓ masks: the consequent tension between "putting the mask over" and the anxiety of its success thus.

In Julian I must recover the callous egotism of the child and of Hobbes' "perpetual state of war" which the <individual must> individualist must engage in: (kindness), love, etc., is simply *afforded* by society, *allowed*.

The passion to "do everything right" is responsible for many good works of art but no great ones—work is robbed of individuality (re. Timothy Dwight, Kames, and *The Conquest of Canaan*).[97]

Syllable movement:
"who, (a)roused through calf and halter,
Staggered up to see
The bearing and regarding tree,
The tilth and commerce of the earth."

Word usage: Yeats: "the *uncontrollable mystery* on the bestial floor."

Books: George Santayana — *Dominations and Powers* (Scribner's) $4.50.
    Syntax — Curme.
    Time and Free Will ⎱ Henri Bergson.
    Matter and Memory ⎰
    Realms of Being (entire) — George Santayana.
    Whitehead — complete works.

---

97. Dwight's *The Conquest of Canäan; a poem, in Eleven Books* (1785) recounts the battles between the Israelites and the peoples of Ai and Gibeon and concludes with Joshua's victory over the Canaanites. The biblical account, occupying only four short chapters, fills eleven books because Dwight includes lengthy speeches, protracted battle scenes, epic devices, tributes to American heroes, and a love story. The three-volume *Elements of Criticism* by Henry Homes, Lord Kames, sought to identify the fundamental principles of fine arts. His psychological system focuses on the reader's emotional identification with the images presented in a work.

Malraux's three books: *The Psychology of Art*—send to Maxine.[98] Also, if we can afford it, the three Skira books.[99]

Type figure: Empson: "tribe-membrane" or "*tribal* membrane."[100] This ushers in a concept of society, mankind, and all kindred associations, which is quite enough to build a poem about.

Experiment (*vide* "Atlantis"[101]) with dissimilar illustrations of a single thetic metaphor. Do not be hamstrung enough by the figure itself to make the poem conform to it mechanically. Metaphors, like the atom, are in some cases more valuable if fractured.

"The mowing violence of that stride."

Story (or character) about the young flyer whose (as *he* conceives it) whole career is a preparation (he has been told of wrecks, etc.) to meet himself in the center ↑crater↓ of the flame of a burning aircraft: death by drowning or freezing. Contrast romantic beginning of this notion <to the> with its gradual overtaking of the young man as a real obsession—or perhaps he feels cheated or substitutes drink or sun.[102]

Image of sprinting[103] (wish-fulfillment never attained) of Julian: in terms of concealed (tangentially revealed) predatory intent: "legs a (furious) and compelling (assertive) wheel, (worthy) opponents falling (symmetrically) back on either side like the wings of a diving bird, whose beak is thus at one movement freed and directed to strike": "legs, appearing a little bowed, because of the tremendous sacks of muscle outside and above each knee, mapped with veins."

A poetry, or some poems, dealing with significant events out of history, *instressed,* seen personally and through fresh and unusual perspectives. Hart Crane tried this specifically and Perse more or less generally.

---

98. Maxine Webster Syerson Dickey, whom Dickey married on November 4, 1948.

99. André Malraux, *The Psychology of Art,* trans. Stuart Gilbert, 3 vols. (New York: Pantheon Books, 1949–1950). The books originally appeared in French as *Psychologie de l'art* (Geneva: A. Skira, 1947–1950).

100. See Empson's *Some Versions of Pastoral* (London: Chatto and Windus, 1935; republished as *English Pastoral Poetry* [New York: Norton, 1938]), esp. the chapter "Proletarian Literature."

101. By Hart Crane.

102. The projected story, which Dickey details more thoroughly in Notebook IV in the context of a novella he titled *The Romantic,* anticipates the narrative of *Alnilam.*

103. Compare Dickey's "The Sprinter at Forty," "For the Running of the New York City Marathon," and "The Olympian."

Book: *Poetry Explication: A Checklist* — Swallow-Morrow ($3.00) — eds. George Arms and Joseph M. Kuntz.

"Looked as though something were retreating far back in his eye(s)" or "coming forward."

"[Or swim(ming)] (in) the blind hut": the child before birth.

Novel: in his room, Julian has, in addition to the picture of the Aztec, a picture (photograph) of Sara. Intimate that he likes the picture better than he does her. This ties in with the "effigy" theme. Her face intent and smeared with sun—the look of acceptance people get when they look into cameras.

Divisions of book:
I. The Casting
II. The Effigies
III. The Casting.

Poetry: write in as many styles as you can cultivate and will be useful or that seem attractive to you. Try to use what seems appropriate to the general intent of the poem. Your own "style" will develop out of this. (Though there is reason to hope that it won't!)

Birds landing: flutter: "a subtle parody of disintegration (desperation)."

What I want in "The Red Garden": "Fragonard with blood." [104]

Novel: the exquisite perversity of electing the homeliest and the most popular boy (in school) the "handsomest" (Julian supposes *himself* this).

Type figure: Thomas: "hear by *death's accident*," etc. [105]

Poem in the cleverest of poetry's styles: "The Lady in the Statue." 3 or 4 short, cleverly-phrased stanzas: rime "nose" and "rose": Condillac.

Epitaph for the worst modern poetry: "Sacrifice everything to the unique comparison." Like O. Henry stories.

"The Dead": "Thin sails of his channel voice," "colorless as bait."

104. Jean-Honoré Fragonard (1732–1806), French painter esteemed for his brush technique, the vitality of his portraits and landscapes, and his virtuosity in depicting the character of gaiety and charm in the age of Louis XV.
105. From "It is the sinners' dust-tongued bell."

Fast and slow pace of poetic line: Eliot on Tourneur.[106] Experiment with pacing poems at breakneck speed and at "drag" tempo, and their judicious admixture. Bring a fast poem to a brake, a cliffhang, precipitous.[107] Run a fast <line's> poem's *meaning,* development in *sense,* rapidly through several lines to give the effect of breathlessness.

She was thin and intent, and looked like an amorous and engrossed, even amused, bird of prey.

"Red Garden": lion "ranged among rocks." The poem to be an "exercise" in the manner of Valéry or Mallarmé.

Ways the poetry-making mind operates:
  1. Paradox
  2. Analogy
  3. Antithesis
  4. Logic
  5. Personal association
  6. Sub-basic and remembered rhythms.
Book or article on this: see Philip Wheelwright, Valéry, F. S. C. Northrop.

3 or 4 short, cleverly-phrased stanzas. Condillac's hypothesis about statues.
  "Nothing
  Is so whole or here
  But I may (numb) it,"
  (Is) ↑Goes↓ her plaint.

"Lady in the Statue":
  "she (knows)(has)
  No hurling forth of door,
  No healing ↑(weeping)↓ home."

(End line):
  "and I, searching for what she may imply,
    through a thousand gardens, find only the flamed and (sumpy) ↑(the flaming deserted)↓ summer
    Taking its stance from her ↑(Takes its stance from her)↓."
She is imprisoned in her senses,
  "finds that having one sense only, employed in one ↑sweet↓ scene
  Is deepest cage," etc.

---

106. See "Cyril Tourneur," *Essays on Elizabethan Drama* (New York: Harcourt Brace and World, 1932).
  107. Here in the entry Dickey scans a two-foot line as an example.

"The Poor Girl('s House)":
　　"If I should ever come there,
　　If I should come."
The (her) old house in the country (Agee):[108] "the house like an up-
ended grate": Elizabeth Bishop—"Jeronimo's House," "Songs for a
Colored Singer."

You know rebel angels better if you have known The Poor Girl.

"The Poor Girl": (change ending): "Lamar" (the boy).

My work a curious mixture of fearful cruelty and compassion.

May I not work from two strategic angles:
　　1. Language-led (Graham, Thomas)
　　2. Objects in "real" world (Jarrell, Bishop, Williams). Where will these
then coalesce, or will they? I don't want a "writing-up" of common
objects. Keep these types separate for awhile. If each develops independently, follow the more profitable. If they coalesce, ok, provided there is
vitality and not a mechanical synthesis.

"Angel Embattled": disarticulate:
　　"who is a pouring cloud　　　　　　arose
　　Blue, unlitten stone　　　　a summer's day　　　_____
to me
　　An isle."
Flower theme.
End line: male sexual theme: Lawrence and Melville: Christ is female:
　　"My anthered towers　　dark as the root　　and rising."

Disarticulate:
　　"blue to me　　arose
　　A summer's dusk　　gold on my golden　　an isle
　　Greaves.　　Our fiends decamped　　I furled down past light."

Impossible to imagine: as a crippled tiger: his deficiency is entirely
irrelevant to the fire, speed, and power he represents, not by himself, but
by being of the class of which these are attributes.

Image of fruit-pickers: ridiculous and justified grumbling on the lad-
ders: "Bring all such sweetness home."

108. See *Let Us Now Praise Famous Men,* photographs by Walker Evans (Boston:
Houghton Mifflin, 1941).

Sestina: not necessarily in this order: keep cloud and tree apart:

1.	cloud (visor)
2.	tree (knight)
3.	severance (by severance / Tried and found)
4.	plain (told)(beast, animal)
5.	effigy (viscera)(divining)
6.	pear (archer).

He enables a silence to *be,* to become profound with tellings, all in the gold-touched head.

Sex: "the star in the viscera / Comes on."

Friar Bacon:[109]
   "performed his only magic,
   The gross and gold-lit head."

(End):
   "As (when) a grailward knight,
   Unaware of the leafiest beast in the tree,
   Boosts his bright visor for the dusty pear."
(The leafiest hair-hung beast in the tree).

Pear—pair—pare (alternate).
Pair: Castor and Pollux (Yeats: Leda).[110]
"The tissues of the pear."
"A pair / Of athletes from a frost of swan(s)"—swanning ↑swannèd↓ frost.

"Angel Embattled":
   "when I fell, well-swanned
   From the (stolid) parapet, (and) there rose
   A summer('s) day to me, an isle."

"(Traced) in that air a column of sure flame ↑(certain fire)↓."

"And all that threadless day heaped up my towers."

---

109. See Robert Greene's *The Honourable History of Friar Bacon and Friar Bungay.* Roger Bacon in this sixteenth-century drama is a Franciscan friar who possesses magical powers and who endeavors to conjure a brass wall around England.
   110. W. B. Yeats's "Leda and the Swan." Castor and Pollux were the sons of Leda.

(Another poem): figure of blind angel, or one who is deaf (to trumpet) (or Michael) or indifferent.

I want more of the gore and guts of life than Crane gave, but I would like something of his language.

Second novel: deals with kingship, exile, king-killing, crossing of kingship (duties, responsibilities) with personal emotions—concept of kingship, royalty, *divine* right of kings.

Old man has cancer in the center of his forehead "like a diadem":[111] Pesewick on cancer.

War, violence theme is chivalric, symbolic, and realistic (in the good sense). Theme of fish, fishing—cannot catch fish, a "lean season." Background of decadence in which there is a *disguised* but desperately serious search for value, salvation, resurrection: a "demonic" novel. Old man: "let the sun into my wound." Read, research on king-killing. Old man, perhaps an industrialist, a "tycoon" or "emperor of finance" (be careful with this).

Informing concepts:
1. Kingship
2. Exile
3. Decadence
4. Resurrection
5. Faith
6. Quest (war theme)
7. Violence
8. Frivolity at the heart of seriousness, and seriousness at heart of frivolity (Florida).
Huxley, Firbank. Old man: Mark (?).

"Angel Embattled": end line: "Dark as the root   and (climbing) rising."
        Conspiracy: "voice   edged my phosphor cheek (face)."

Second novel: the sailor's (soldier's) hornpipe in the shoddy sitting room (see similar scene in *The Free and the Lonely*).[112]

---

111. The entry describes Frank Cahill, the diabetic protagonist in Dickey's *Alnilam*, who sees in his blindness only a shuttle of gold sparks.

112. Leonard Ehrlich projected a historical novel titled "The Free and the Lonely." Excerpts of the book, which was never finished, appeared in *Cross Section, 1947: A Collection of New American Writing,* ed. Edwin Seaver (New York: Simon and Schuster, 1947).

"A pair / Of athletes from (the) god-charged swan."

Charged with white (or other value, natural or imputed).

The leopard is "the (shadow, fire) clovered beast."

Poem: "The Change of Philomel" or "So Rudely Forced":[113] end line:
"Sleeved
Straight up in chaos; spiring the law of the ↑dumb↓ world,
But to be heard."

Poem in two sections: (from) "The Poor Girl":
   1. "The (Old) House in Fannin County ↑in the Country↓"
   2. "The Deserted High School"
Library: "patched with words beyond my element."

Julian's "playing at having emotions": these are often compellingly strong, but always false: "I had long since acknowledged that the only true feelings I <had> possessed were pride and vanity" (jealousy).

"The Kingly Lover": lion and girl: human and beast congress poem: picture by Leonardi or Dali or Berman or Chirico:[114] the well-cool walls (ruins): (your)(his) gross and gold-lit head.

After, or before, or in the middle of "The Kingly Lover," she wakes in her bed "in the tree," or wind.

End?: "dusts a strong (stone) daylight with the sands of (lust.")

In third person: "she thinks," etc., "it is her (hand)."
Sphinx:
   "and that she was also born
   Of that congress, (and stretched a stone gaze) ↑and propped on her abrading paws,↓
   Stretched stonely a gaze on the river's greening."

"Stands on the combed hill ↑(dome)↓ at fall of night,
Equal(ly) of passion and delay (dismay) in the vertical(s) of light ↑sun↓ ↑(noon)↓."

The lyrical exile the sea makes (of) you.

---

113. See Eliot's *The Waste Land,* lines 99–100.
114. See Dali's *Accommodations of Desire,* a 1929 oil on wood panel, 8⅝ inches by 13¾ inches.

Novel: shaving and shaving off hair: an attempt at rebirth: likes it: ceremonial (ritual): stress this obliquely.

"Rain that appears to have in great weariness and at great sacrifice detached itself from the sky, but for this reason is impossible to prevail against."

Type fig: Bergson: image cut out of pain (anxiety), smoothly or raggedly, archetypal.

"The Kingly Lover": two versions of the same poem: 1) as I originally intended to write it; 2) "subconscious," Graham, Thomas, Crane, Lorca.

"Three Crowns and the Crooked Shade": references: W. S. Merwin, "Carol": Vernon Watkins, "Three Harps": Elizabeth Bishop, "The Hermit."

"Three kings in southern glade $\left.\begin{array}{r}\text{glade} \\ \text{shade}\end{array}\right\}$ rime.
(Sometime), swap crowns like comics, though slowly, "and never smile": trade "by the weather's wish." Rime: feathers.

Poem: "The Hillside": Bacchic rite: Russell on Bacchus worship:[115]
Orphic tablet at Peledia: possible title: "Bacchanal."
     "And keening tore him wine and thigh."
Muriel Rukeyser, "Orpheus": Crane, "Lachrymae Christi."
     "The pearling grass."

1. And spring the God from goat and wine.
2. Now the goat climbs in their ↑our↓ wine.
3. And are the goat (we) ↑they↓ tore for wine.[116]

"The Hillside": changes of day for parts of ritual. Goat: 1) sacrificial animal; 2) Satan.

Short penultimate line: "me ↑(you)↓, even."

Question: can the poem rise through my hacking?

"(As) the gull balances, (delicately), his feathered and offal shores."

---

115. See Bertrand Russell, *A History of Western Philosophy* (New York: Simon and Schuster, 1945), esp. chap. 1, "The Rise of Greek Civilization."
116. Dickey labels these projected poetic lines for "The Hillside" as "good" in a parenthetical note.

"Suite: (from the Outside)":
  1. The Sought
  ", and with civic laugh
  Wind(s) his last dim alley on a thumb."
  2. The Accused: he has brought them all to cage.
  3. The Convicted: who has won?
Think out what each section is to do: short: 3 or 4 stanzas apiece.

References: Blackmur's "Before Sentence is Passed."[117]

"(Creep) on the fiend-(laid) ↑reared↓ bridge": Whitehead on Milton's Satan's voyage: *Process and Reality*.[118]

"For the Accused":
  "Go(es) in to judgment
  As into sacrifice."

Type figure: "unholy of works ↑(days)↓" ("Piers Plowman").

Type figure: "such and such *will* happen": cf. Eaton: "The Garden Party."[119]

"They shook hands manfully, like children doing it for the first time."

Second novel: figure of Hotel: *The Hotel*.[120] Instead of the castle, the hotel: power, riches: archetypal figure of "vacationland paradise." Perhaps end novel in or around the hotel.

Transcribe both navigation notebook and small red one.[121]

"The Poor Girl": "The Old House," etc.

---

117. The poem appeared in *Kenyon Review* 3:1 (1941) and was collected in *The Second World* (Cummington, Mass.: Cummington Press, 1942).

118. Alfred Lord Whitehead's *Process and Reality: An Essay in Cosmology* (New York: Macmillan, 1930), esp. 146–47. Whitehead comments on Satan's journey across Chaos in *Paradise Lost,* arguing that it "helped to evolve order" by providing a path for the damned.

119. Charles Edward Eaton's poem was published in the February 1950 issue of *Poetry* and collected in *The Greenhouse in the Garden* (New York: Twayne, 1955).

120. Dickey's capitalization and underlining do not make clear whether he intends this as the title of the second novel or whether he is merely emphasizing the type figure.

121. The navigation notebook, which contains technical aviation information, is among the Dickey collection at Emory University. The small red notebook is unidentified.

—I said (")About that dancing, (about) that dancing beam (shaft),
Under the loft."[122]

A (robe) of haws: mitred cellar: the grub s(hined) on the (under)wood:
mason (bell)jars:
    ", in the rafters played," etc.[123]

To be *caught up* in a poem the way Barker is in "Calamiterror": no one
more tired than tired Barker, no one more alive than alive. Some of
Barker's fireworks devices.

A "flash-out" of Hopkins in the "ordinary" rhythm of a poem: (and) "fall
elver, whip sap in loose-lashed rage" (on God).

If the wilderness were set with mirrors, (all) the animals would stare
themselves to death or die of self-murder.

Book: *Selected Poems* — Richard Eberhart.

Juxtaposition of mythology and present in Robert Lowell.

Second novel: old man: "except for his face, a collocation of (blues)
↑veins↓." He "goes among them" (like) a (dying) peasant.

"The (smooth) brute
Anopheles."
    "(the sibyl)(who)
Moves off to greet you, in tearful gold."[124]

My life is a perpetual proof, proving nothing.

Julian: shaving: close shave is at least a temporary conquest; halfway shaving is not even that.

Football game in novel, or practice: "all this gaiety on a sad autumn
night. It made the cheering (and the players) seem physically more
distant, so that the sounds were too loud for their causes, and gave the
scene the air of a too-persistent revery."

---

122. See Dickey's "Patience: In the Mill." Among his papers at Emory is the unfinished typescript of a short story originally titled "Reeds, Shadows" that he subsequently
calls "Through the Loft." Although the poem and the story are quite different, the image
of a loft clearly had significance to Dickey.
    123. See Dickey's "The Rafters."
    124. See Notebook IV, n. 36 and the entry to which it refers.

Poetry is yourself, your personality, whatever things peculiar to you as a human being, smashed, forced, and bled through whatever poetical techniques you have mastered. Enough of the technique should stick to the utterance to make it say itself most effectively, but not enough to allow the utterance's individual quality and its essential humanity to be destroyed. The question of technique is pertinent here. How much is *found, clarified,* by grappling with (purely) technical problems? Good and bad modifications proceeding from the "discoveries" inherent in technique.

Julian: "(all) my futures (situations, *et al.*) were slanted toward recollection" (memory).

Bum, hobo, crime poems: a world of freight sidings and cruelty: sense of Villon, not Crane's "The River."

What to write is not hard, but *how?* Jeffers' introduction to the Modern Library *Roan Stallion.*[125]

"Time," he squeaks, "and time,
And time."
    "The Confession": confession in two senses: criminal (murderer) and theological.

"Cell": priest's and criminal's. Make this a great thing, not localized.

Type figure: not necessarily a "tongue of blood" but Lowell's "*blood licks the Greek cosmetics with its tongue.*"[126]

Read up on *confession:* Catholic.

George Grosz's pictures of "questionings" in Nazi Germany.[127]

The literature of "analysis," brilliant as some of it is, is not generally great literature, which makes the analysis implicit in the events and does not pause to explain.

125. Robinson Jeffers, *Roan Stallion* (New York: Random House, 1935), vii–x. Jeffers relates his struggles, against the then prevailing modernist trend toward poetic reduction, to achieve originality when he felt himself so much an imitator of past writers such as Milton and Shelley. Dickey's effort to discover his own style and his attitudes toward originality are revealed in the first chapter of *Self-Interviews* and in *Sorties,* esp. 101–15.
    126. From "Dea Roma," *Land of Unlikeness.*
    127. Born in Berlin, Grosz became famous in the twenties for his satirical paintings of the military and the wealthy class. Disturbed about the rise of Fascism, he emigrated to New York City in 1933 and became an American citizen in 1938. World War II compelled him to create a symbolic series of ravaged figures.

"Don't tell 'em, show 'em"; or at any rate, show 'em more than you tell 'em.

Swimmer: "luxurious crawl."

The poets: "(as) they sleeve ↑(palm)↓ their syllables by the hoarded wave."

"Sarpedon" (the *Iliad*).[128]

"The Kingly Lover": girl: monologue:
  "from me (my loins)
  White towers (rise)
  And the order ↑graven tables↓ of a race ↑(people)↓."
1. Present: common, shabby.
2. Dream sequence.
3. Prophecy.

End:
  "(left one) much fraught by signs
  On (by) the signless (water) ↑(sand)↓."

"Blood of his fierce ease"—"whispers, hot with meat."

"The king is come, and the combed hill pours."

"He saw his daughter in the garden, and her dark brown hair fell away from her (brow) ↑forehead↓, deep and clear and white, as she raised her eyes to him, and he turned into the house and drank glass after glass of brandy in commemoration, in an effort to preserve the look she <gave> had given him, the feathery leaves and the shaded sundial" (Dr. Arrington).

"She lay in his arms, her heart and the insides of her veins bleeding heavily."

The king as god-head:
  1. The conception of a new king.
  2. The giving of the laws: bound up in the person of the king.
(Perse, Thomas).

Four, short, counterpointed, unpunctuated lines that lead into the next section.

128. In the *Iliad,* Sarpedon leads the Lycians against the Greeks in the Trojan War. Killed by Patroclus, he is carried back to Lycia for a hero's burial.

Novel: vomiting scene: reflections on vomiting: purge: "a purely physical holiness."

Novel: I must work for the overall conception, that it may be enriched by the minor (incidental) insight and not be impoverished by it. See Mann.

My work—a statement of joy and longing.

Kingship, animals (lions, panthers) in *Golden Bough:* "soul (under) ↑(over)↓ my soul."

Thomas Mann: a great, heavy, warm mind.

Maud Bodkin's *Archetypal Patterns in Poetry.*

The rhythmic structure of the lines of "The Red Garden" is not good; the method by which it got composed is not good. Instead of letting the lines fall more or less as they will, try to *feel* and *hear* what you want, *what will do,* what the thing needs, *must have,* both in each line and in the overall stanza. Let your ear forge the thing *all of a piece.*

I sate myself on romantic notions of poetry and love, that I may return purged to the classic.

"Unto": "And I am dumb to mouth *unto* my veins," etc. (Thomas).[129]

"The hand that <stirs> whirls the water in the pool
Stirs the quicksand; that *ropes* the blowing wind
Hauls my *shroud sail.*
And I am dumb to tell the *hanging man*
How of my clay is made the hangman's line." (Thomas).
    (Note word order of last line—*meter* and *word order: both* stress important syllables).
Note here the *kind* of relation that is introduced. There does not have to be a *total image* of hanging, an execution, but the relation of *rope* ↑(verb)↓, *shroud* ↑(adjective)↓, and (participle) *hanging,* these three words in different contexts but related in the stanza through connotation, atmosphere, and tangential reference. They refer specifically to different things, but pull toward each other emotionally and supra-logically.

"Your *calm* and *cuddled* is a scythe of hairs": Thomas.[130] *Adjectives as nouns,* denoting attributes as possessions.

129. From "The force that through the green fuse drives the flower."
130. From "When, like a running grave, time tracks you down."

Type figure: Thomas: dry breast as "the hanging famine."[131]

Shock of surprise, strength, when the poem switches from the third to the first person as though a revelation to the poet himself.

"The sight of his (her) own body drove him (her) mad with the passions and rages of another."

"I name it with your name."

Auden the example of the poet who uses everything he can get his hands on. He *systematizes* this, finds a meaning or meanings in and through it, and there, with a few elaborations and a genuflection toward technique (usually not impressive), is his poem.

The depersonalized, the abstract, the general in Auden irritates me extremely.

"The Kingly Lover"—a kind of dream poem, subjective extremely.

The will and <vanity> the ego are inextricably linked.

If I keep a journal, it will not have the same kind of interest as Gide's, for I am not (yet?) a first-rate literary man. But I am a man.

Mann: *Faustus* 132:[132] "The gold kitchen"—"the golden kitchen(s)."

Music: "the finding, the taking-up of a theme already in the air, as the sculptor liberates the woman from stone." It should *seem* so, at any rate.

To be a great writer, it is necessary to go strongly and break things. What to be: an alienated artist working craftily (pun) at his art (Joyce), the natural force, full of cultism and spontaneity (Lawrence), the regressive, the recessive, the mountain-blaster, the lapidary, or what? *How* can one go one's way, when there are so many commanding precedents? Mine is a *cultivated* spontaneity, operating rigidly within sharp bonds; the cage is its own wild freedom. Is it impossible to combine W. S. Graham, Thomas, and Valéry? And have something of Jarrell's humanity also?

---

131. From "From love's first fever to her plague."

132. Thomas Mann, *Doctor Faustus* (New York: Alfred A. Knopf, 1948). Dickey's intensive reading of this novel becomes more apparent in Notebook II, clearly revealing that he was using both notebooks simultaneously.

Must "rhetoric" and "truth" forever pull apart the poor string (thread) of the poem? Or is there a cannier, wilder spider than these?[133]

How to read poetry: inspect every line to see how *and why* it was done, and done that way, and then the stanza the same way (how the lines are integrated, and *if* they are, and if so why, and if not why not) and then the poem.

Each line, each stanza, each poem is infinitely rich and suggestive. The greatness of them is in their luck or skill in *channeling* the suggestiveness effectively. Any line, closely read, reveals multitudes of possible uses. Any good line reveals these also, but at times fewer and more striking ones. A good line always drives you toward the dangers of imitation precisely because of <their> its peculiar *way, manner, prescription* of *organization,* of organizing and directing emotion significantly. Empson is wrong; good poems do not open out into infinities of meanings; they clamp shut on two or three (or one) overpowering ones.

The Crane rhetoric as engineless aircraft: from "The Cloud Juggler":
  "Expose vaunted validities that yawn
  Past pleasantries."

Type figure: Crane: "Extinction stirred on either side."[134]

Broaden out, learn other figures from other poets. Your technique is pitifully meagre.

Take the lines (Crane):
  "The anointed stone, the coruscated crown
  The drastic throne, the
  Desperate sweet eyejet-basins of a bloody foreign clown—
  Couched on bloody basins, floating bone
  Of a dismounted people."[135]
These are not entirely successful (why enjamb on "the" except that the next line is so long?), but embody a method which might be useful in other circumstances. It is couched in terms of sacrifice, but instead of having a sacrificial *scene* (priests, witnesses) as I most likely would have had, there are several components of sacrifice given as well as the underlying and embodying causes (throne). The atmosphere *in large* is

---

133. Compare Dickey's Introduction in *Night Hurdling* (Columbia, S.C., and Bloomfield Hills, Mich.: Bruccoli Clark, 1983), in which he equates the essays, conversations, and other literary efforts to threads all spun from the same body, all aspects of his Self.
134. From "Enrich My Resignation."
135. From "The Circumstance."

created, and a "people" (abstraction) is caught up into the initial figure. People—sacrificers are people—sacrificed. Neat? Yes. Useful. Probably. Good Crane? Not very.

My novel is not a "perfect" one like *Gatsby*. I want to get under, *down into* more, and though I genuflect to "form," I had rather the book created its own.

I would like more solid, stationary objects in my poems than there are in Crane's.

Flattering letter from Ransom today. I am fairly launched. I am on the right road to writing like I should. I am breaking through.

Rilke: "Und er gehorcht, indem er überschreitet."—"And he obeys, while yet he oversteps." (The poet).[136]

The eighth of the *Sonnets to Orpheus:* a little like Keats' "Ode to Melancholy."

Rilke: "the endless song welling out of silence."[137]
    "The high achievers."[138]

I enjoy reading poetic theory, but it does not touch my practice. Some of it has been instructive.

Rilke's interpretation, his intellectual and animal *relation to* his material, or, if someone will, his *vision,* extremely important.

Poem: "Sennacherib."[139]
    "On the Head of an Assyrian General."
(Durant).[140]

George Barker's calling upon all history and projecting himself into it with pride and violence and with odd *personal* twists is extremely effective, but there are times when it seems terribly flat and forced.

---

136. From *Sonnets to Orpheus,* part 1, #5, trans. M. D. Herter Norton (New York: Norton, 1942).
    137. Ibid., #1.
    138. Ibid., #25.
    139. King of Assyria from 705 to 681 B.C., Sennacherib spent most of his reign fighting to maintain the empire established by his father. He was killed by two of his sons, who were jealous of their brother.
    140. William James Durant, American historian and essayist whose ten-volume, comprehensive *The Story of Civilization* (New York: Simon and Schuster, 1935–1967) ranges from prehistory to the eighteenth century.

"I am Sir John on the Patinos of my heart.
I hang my hand on the Haman tree—
Babylonian gardens do so and so."[141]

Poem: "Sennacherib at Babylon": A. T. Olmstead: *History of Assyria.*[142]

Poetry is the sensitive, skillful man's defense against all men's essential inarticulateness.

Books: *Collected Poems* — Marianne Moore.
   Selected Poems — Basil Bunting — The Cleaners' Press.

"(I think of) that cruel king
Sennacherib,
Whose head speaks boldly from the rotten gate,

And then I see
How far you are, in what kind empery,
Your stretched hand written well with gaffs,
The summer uttered golden at your feet."
   Needs much complication.

"Bursts like a throat
In joy or pain
On country summer,
The rind and sough of autumn at its (wheels.)"
   "On country summer, the rind
   And sough of autumn at its wheels."

"Can I, (while) ↑for↓ the not-Assyrian bull
(Broken) ↑Breaks↓ in pieces among the swelling leaves
Hand out ↑(Hold)↓ the petal-bloody source of cries
Of my awak(en)er?"

Sennacherib: his two sons "shipt from his thunderous loin and slew."

Mozart's "Overture to the *Abduction from the Seraglio.*"[143]

141. From "Holy Poems," *Lament and Triumph,* pt. 4, sections i and ii.
142. New York and London: Charles Scribner's Sons, 1923. Sennacherib captured and destroyed Babylon in 689 B.C. Angered, Olmstead declares, by the city's continual revolts and by its betrayal of his son to the Elamites, he burned Babylon to the ground and put nearly all its inhabitants to death.
143. The opera concerns the fate of two sets of lovers imprisoned by a pusha and his majordomo. Threatened with torture unless they declare their love, the two women remain defiant. When the pusha learns that his bitterest enemy is the father of one of the men, he frees his captives, declaring that he refuses to stoop to the kind of revenge his enemy would demand.

("The sun /)
[Step(s) through the golden kitchen(s) with a ↑(its)↓ ↑(his)↓ knife."]
   Bad: use only "golden kitchen(s)."

Book: *Thomas Merton's* latest: *The Ascent to Truth* (I believe the name is).[144]

I would like *vitality* for my poetry, and a certain deep, free-wheeling strength.

Memory: "that salt shrine."

"The (orphic) roots of water."

"That self-perpetuating tragedy, my family."

I need a collected Goethe: letters, critical writings, in the best translation I can find.

"He (leaps) into his image in the dream" (variation of Marianne Moore's "The Plumet Basilisk").

Poetry is not a *purely* verbal construct. See R. P. Blackmur's essay on James in *Accent,* Summer 1951:[145] not *pure*<ly> technical accomplishment.

I have been fairly successful in cutting down the narrative elements in my poetry.

My best poetry is tending toward the "rhetorical," I hope in the good sense.

I finally see what the end of "The Templar's Dream" is about. Abel, the "innocent" (hence self-righteous, "justified" brother, i.e. the Templar, convinced of the *righteousness* of his killing), slays the "guilty," i.e. he who has been designated as "evil," much as the opponents of an army are so designated. Thus, "innocence" of this perverted kind assumes the guilt which it is supposed to repudiate.[146]

The poet is one who, because he cannot love, imagines what it would be like if he could.

---

144. *The Ascent to Truth* (New York: Harcourt, Brace, 1951).
145. "The Loose and Baggy Monsters of Henry James."
146. Compare Dickey's commentary on "The Firebombing" in *Self-Interviews,* 137–39.

Croce on history and aesthetics.[147]

For a good *book* of poems, it is necessary that a fundamental, control-ling, <and> formulating and informing attitude be expressed. Berryman is right in this respect on Darley and Keats.

Work for awhile on the theory that poetry is *consciously* created, willed into being. Explore detachedly various communicative devices. "What will best get this said." Let the deep springs work for you. Or make them.

Device: begin a poem in apparent utter confusion. Clarify, give the set-ting in the middle part, or toward the middle. Define what you are going to say before you begin, or be sure you do as you go along. Be sure the poem has an intellectually justified relational structure.

Fall of man: machine (aircraft): "terrible metal": similar to Graham's shipwreck poems: his water my air: man created from unstable ribs, large ↑(great)↓ body (air): dying in a great (sustainingless) body: vowels of the air: <"conversation"> "lean whirling": "↑(the)↓ air / as obstacle, aflow with all its ribs."

America compared to the *military* empire of Assyria: basic metaphor: winged *lions* and bulls. Involve this metaphor deeply. Nineveh: under the bull's hoof.

Bull, the sun behind his head: gold, purple: figure of regal destruction:
    "And he in the glass cage, his fear
    Minting in skills his fabled sight."

Under the bull's hoof: Chaldea: the first and last watchers. *Look up chief city of Chaldea.* This is where he is.

Why is it that Emily Dickinson's meters are so perilously close to the mechanical, and yet manage to say so well what she would have them say? Emily Dickinson is a little like John Donne in the formal (and some-times mechanical) method she uses to align her figures in metaphor:
    "Two bodies therefore be;
    Bind one, and one will flee."[148]

147. Benedetto Croce (1866–1952), Italian philosopher, historian, and critic whose system of philosophy is related to the idealistic school in that spirit, monistic in mani-festation, is the only reality. The work presenting his system, *Philosophy of the Spirit* (1902–1917; trans. 1909–1921), is divided into four parts: *Aesthetic as Science of Expression and General Linguistic, Logic as the Science of Pure Spirit, Philosophy of the Practical,* and *History: Its Theory and Practice.*
    148. From "No Rack can torture me" (#384).

Emily Dickinson is the poet *par excellence* whom one does not wish to read in her entirety, whose poems are better individually than collectively, whose virtues dwindle and defects magnify in bulk. In a few pieces she is superb; in the main she is "cute," mechanical, *diligent,* and thoroughly small. The north: "so adequate its forms."[149] This is in her best vein.

Yvor Winters likes Emily Dickinson because her lines are so *scannable,* because they are so *easy* to interpret metrically that he can belabor the smallest point for hours and have the audience get his meaning. In more difficult and better poets like Crane he never attempts metrical analysis, though he does with Hopkins because of Hopkins' own metrical theories, which give him a point of departure.

Emily Dickinson's neatness is rather irritating; she turns to you and says sadly, but with a perfectly bright face, "Isn't *that* an insight!" But she is good at times; there is no mistaking <this meth> her practice when successful. It is the fate of all good writers, when they don't connect, to sound like their imitators, and their worst ones, at that.

One of Hardy's greatest assets is that he perfectly seriously believes the platitudes he builds his poems on, believes them structurally, and *believes* them. Cf. first stanza and the rest of "The Convergence of the Twain." In this poem the Fate metaphor works wonderfully until "The Spinner of the Years" is introduced. Stanza VIII especially good.

In "Channel Firing,"[150] 1st line, "unawares" especially well-placed and effective.

Any poem comes to life by
   1. Subject matter
   2. Attitude toward this: definition of attitude
   3. Examining what technical means, images, metrical practices will best get this said
   4. Experiment
   5. Revision.

The wonderfully right *sound* of "*Stourton Tower.*"[151]

Parson Thirdly wryly obvious, humorous. I now think he is necessary to the poem.[152]

149. From "Of Bronze—and Blaze" (#290).
150. By Thomas Hardy.
151. From Hardy's "Channel Firing."
152. See Hardy's "Channel Firing."

"As though by laboring all-*unknowingly*":[153] *good here.*

4th stanza of "Nature's Questioning"[154] good: the thing is well-conceived, the attitude is explicit, and the stanza is well-said.

The study of *attitude* in poetry important. Why has this been neglected? It is the necessary prologue to all technical devices, is what calls them into play, or even *into being.*

3rd, 4th, and 5th stanzas: different points of view. It is well this was not carried on any further. It is the kind of mechanical device that, so to speak, exposes itself as mechanical, and becomes therefore tiresome. All good poetry preserves the illusion of spontaneity.

"An Ancient to Ancients":[155]
    "worms have fed upon
    The doors."
Why "doors" here? It seems good. Perhaps "there are no more entrances here."

"The Darkling Thrush":[156] how can "dregs" make "desolate" a "weakening eye"? Figure of an (old) drunkard? Memory ("dregs")? Winter theme? Old age as "winter"? An "*aged*" thrush? "Broken lyres" ("fled is that music").

There are certain things you cannot sacrifice to sensual gratification.

I cannot help noticing how much better my notes and reflections on poetry are than the poems I write. I hope eventually this will be reversed.

It seems to me that, in effect, most (good) poetry is saying not "This is the way it is" but "this is the way it *can be* regarded, seen," or "it is possible to regard, see, it this way, and I choose to do so." Poetry is in this sense a pure construct, built out of associations both personal and literary and techniques partly personal but mostly literary, an imaginative construct to satisfy both hope of insight and desire for form, mutually moving, completing, and calling forth to view.

"For His (Supposed) Mistress": tetrameter couplets:
    "a saint /
    Sparkling like Venus, in the ragged snow."

153. From Hardy's " Ἀγυωστωι θεωι."
154. By Thomas Hardy.
155. By Thomas Hardy.
156. By Thomas Hardy.

Novel: notion of "control": controlling lives of others. Protagonist's name: Julian Glass.

Rewrite "To My Father": rework symbols: articulate better: work for better sound combinations, rhythms.
   "As the Star ↑(Moon)↓ of Sires[157]
   Burns in the nostril of the exiled (circling) fox,
   I shake my (head)(blood), the feathers flow ↑(all)↓ one way
   Under the bladed ball and fist."

The terrible struggle between "art" and "experience" seems to be beginning to resolve itself. When I look back on the significant "experiences" I have had, there always occurs a terrifying sense of loss and desolation: "these things must be replaced." Consequently, I feel I must go through the world holding out my hands for "experience," a terribly wasteful procedure, considering the fact that for every memorable ↑meaningful↓ experience there are thousands of hours of boredom, wandering, and frustration. A work of art is an achievement in a way these things are not. You look again and it has not escaped.

The fascination of the past a strong thing in most artists: where can we find the past recreated? In novels, the arts, artifacts, etc. Yes, but where visually? Museums, perhaps. Yes, but where *moving* visually, living? In a carefully researched cinema. That is an astonishing phenomenon. The beginning of *The Golden Horde* was tremendously effective, as were the "games" scenes from *The Black Rose*. I would like to see a well-researched movie about Assyria or Babylon.

The search for the illusion of promise is what shapes and falsifies my life.

Poetry (or a kind of it): the gathering of meaning into a moving inarticulateness—for the poem ultimately cannot be said.

The emphasis on crime, catching the criminal: a childlike hope that evil may be embodied and dealt with so easily. To evade the man within.

Fill notebook on notebook with analyses of poems. Devote an hour or two a day to this.

Novel: "I sat back in the iron chair and put my laced fingers behind my head, the muscles in my upper arms cramping comfortably, and let the soft wind blow past my head and for a moment or two was happy, or

---

157. In the notebook entry, "Star," "Moon," and "Sire" were originally lowercased. Dickey then capitalized the first letter of each word.

enjoyed an illusion akin to happiness. Or <was> is there <any> a difference? I was not disposed to argue the point."

A poet begins as an imitator almost invariably (how else is he to begin?). It is only gradually that he builds away from this. The poets (granted that eventually they are to achieve some idiomatic individuality) who seem "pure" or "sole" imitators are simply those who have seen fit to publish their early imitative poems. This a drastic oversimplification.

I feel constantly that I am at the edge of hysteria, and would welcome it.

The most terrible thing to me is the forehead of the future.

I wonder if the discipline of writing can hold me together.

Second novel: new device: abrupt shifts within the sentence: method of poetry: suppressed simile: "The old man's eyes, where hundreds of bats hung from the walls." Figure of ruined castle: "crenelations," "archerless, though manned."

Second novel: may the slain young man not comment lyrically-analytically on certain scenes, these sections to be placed strategically throughout the book. Learn *cautiously* about counterpoint and recall from Joyce—a thorough study.

Novel: as Julian sizes up situation by Laverne's house (evening scene), have him make geometrical designs with a stick or something: represents a (desperate) striving for *order,* control.

Get four ledgers: label: work in them.

Novel: "the sun struck soft and cruel (from) on the tops and hoods of automobiles parked in the lot opposite."[158]

"Bush quivered (in the wind) with furtive, desperate motion" (with a furtiveness seemingly proceeding from desperation)—random, intense gestures.

Novel: investigate the possibility of having Taz Lighthorn fill in his off-time with singing on one of the local hill-billy programs. Good place for satire. Show the cruelty and inarticulateness beneath such sentimentality. Tie in with watermelon-stand scene.

158. Compare Dickey's "The Flash."

"The sea the shady fiddler's scales": *Creation poem:* Pythagorean, Darwinian, *Genesis:* "mucked ↑(cast)↓ gills and (cast-on) ↑uncast↓ head. Refrain: "my great dark laugh to(ward) the fiddler's shade."

Look up Croce on aesthetics—*Aesthetic as Science of Expression and General Linguistic*—New Directions #13.

A good part of the time I write I feel as though I have my foot on my imagination.

Poem:
"Father, Self, Son
. . . threaded all
On one blue eye."
Father, chickens; me, bad knee.
"An odd blond hand
Stretched over a willow bush."

Chris:[159] longest section: catches up others. Try for strong end.

In "The Siege," study castles and courtyards and use several technical terms: i.e. "corbels."

Books: *The Myth of the State* }
   The Problem of Knowledge } Ernst Cassirer — Yale U. Press.
   The Dead of Spring — Paul Goodman.
   Light on a Dark Horse — Roy Campbell.[160]
   Let It Come Down — Paul Bowles.
   Book on music — Hindemith — Harvard Press — *A Composer's World*.
   Book — Francis King.[161]
   A Season in England — P. H. Newby — Knopf.
   The Lost Childhood and Other Essays — Graham Greene —Viking.
   Praise to the End —Theodore Roethke.

Poem: "Owls and Satyrs": "owl-light."

Books: Omond on *metrics.*

159. Christopher Swift Dickey was born August 31, 1951.
160. Chicago: H. Regnery Co., 1952. The notation is the first conclusive entry that Dickey was writing in Notebook I in 1952. See note on p. 27 to indicate the earliest probable reference for entries in 1952.
161. Possibly *The Dividing Stream* (London: Longmans, Green, 1951; New York: Morrow, 1951) or *Rod of Incantation* (London: Longmans, Green, 1952).

Saintsbury's *History of English Prosody.*
See about getting a collected *Darley.*

Books: *The Portable Melville* —Viking.
  Totem and Taboo — Freud — Norton.
  A Treasury of French Poetry — (Harper's).[162]
  Winged Chariot and Other Poems — Walter de la Mare.

I don't see how Kenneth Burke has missed the significant analogy between machinery (its emphasis in America) and the American critics' emphasis on the machinery, the *mechanics* of literature, especially of poetry—the "let's see how it's put together" aspect of the work, as though its mode of expression were entirely the work in question.

Great Russian Short Novels — ed. Philip Rahv — Dial.
Short Novels of Colette — intro. Glenway Wescott — Dial.
Ghost and Flesh — William Goyen — Random.
The Brigand — Giuseppi Berto — New Directions.
Thelma Jo Wells — McFerrin.
Syntax — Curme.
Letters — Henry Adams.
Mont St. Michel and Chartres — Henry Adams.
Reflections on the Theatre — Jean-Louis Barrault.
Poems — Christopher Smart (2 vol.) — Harvard University Press.

Poetic form is the means by which a unique <original> mind arrives at its own uniqueness.

"The child snatched into time."

From radio:
    Mickey the Weasel: What—what are you laughing at?
    The Shadow: At you, you ridiculous little man.

Latest poem: "Meditation for One Fallen."

Is there nothing but the raw well of emotion? And all meaningless?

I would like my life to be a sustained orgy of sensation, ratiocination, and recording.

162. Comp. and trans. Alan Conder (New York: Harper and Row, 1951).

Type figure: "*brow,* so *stormed* with *other wandering*" (Graham) and "the *pacing white-haired kingdoms* of the *sea*" (Graham).[163]

Books: D. H. Lawrence's *Letters* (complete).
  Gerald M. Hopkins' *Letters* (complete).

Novel: (to Julian): "You spend all your time trying to be what you're not."
  Julian: "What keeps ↑a↓ man alive is the belief that through persistence <and> or luck he may someday become what he's not."

The terrible feeling that one is not available to experience.

The *developing* sense of the poem, the sense ↑of encounter↓, *discovery, occasion,* of *coming-upon.* To rig this is the ultimate poetic skill. If the hand is seen moving the scenery, the feeling of having been cheated is inevitable and destroying, as it should be.

For a *large* fiction: *archetypal fantasy*: fantasy or dream on a large and *consistent* scale, and yet with a distinct correspondence to reality, so that the reader may go, with a little effort, *wholly* one way or the other into reality or pure dream. An extreme degree of subtlety and skill here to be required—requires a great amount of thought and planning and above all *execution*: *The Cloud Hotel.* Read fairy tales, myths, and fantasies of all descriptions: should move on a *theory* of fantasy evolved from these.

Keith Douglas: his gentle poise.[164]

Book: *The Creative Experience* — ed. Brewster Ghiselin — U. of Calif. Press.
  Regnery: An Age of Criticism — William van O'Conner.
  The Rise of Short Fiction in America — Ray B. West Jr.
  Men, Ideas and Judgments — Grey, Brodbeck and Metzger.
  Ezra Pound and the Cantos — Harold H. Watts.

New Directions: *Who Walk in Darkness* — Chandler Brossard.
  The Man Outside — Wolfgang Borchert.
  Intimacy — Sartre.

Story: I stood in for Nettles.[165] These things (Manila episode) happened, or something like them did.

---

163. From "The White Threshold," *The White Threshold.*

164. British poet killed in 1944 at age twenty-four during a bombardment at Normandy. His *Collected Poems,* edited by John Waller and G. S. Fraser, was published in 1951 by Editions Poetry London.

165. Nettles is the principal character in the typescript of Dickey's unpublished story "The Eye of the Fire."

Poetry: the investing of the mind with new ↑(rhyming)↓ ↑(rhythmical)↓ grammars.

Originality plus force produces the archetype.

The importance of the confrontation scene to fiction: the forms this may take.

"The confrontation was intolerable, and for him ultimately impossible, like trying to stare down a (young) child."

"His hair had some of the erratic force of fire."

Loosen up and straighten out your syntax; the strangest things may be said, the densest symbols communicated, by means of simple sentences.

The grimace of the athlete: analyze.

Ubi Roi — Alfred Jarry — New Directions.
New novel by Anthony West.[166]

Poetry is the use of certain techniques to make the imagination accessible.

Every tree, every blade of grass has its own motions.

One finds so seldom in American women the ↑capacity for↓ "head-longness" that one longs for, the ability to *create* within the conventions of the love affair, and almost never the whole-souled submission to sex one might expect of a people seemingly so obsessed by it. Instead there is a furtive, hang-dog, niggling, shrinking-violet quality about these women. One longs for complete lust with nostalgia.

Research on Druids, Druid mythology.

That ↑feeling of↓ sickness and dread that comes on us at any display of fury or violence.

For Weiss:[167]
   1. "Orpheus"
   2. "The Sea Sacrifice"

---

166. *Another Kind* (Boston: Houghton Mifflin, 1952).
167. T. Weiss was editor of *Quarterly Review of Literature*.

"The Mouth of the Flint"
   3. "For My Son"
(Possibly) "The Hunter." Revise, correct all.

The scene ↑inventing itself↓ taken ↑driven↓ ↑broken↓ ↑(adverb)↓ into my head.

The luxury of effort.

Lamiel — Stendhal — New Directions.

A good theme for the novel or stories (*The Casting*) is <that of the> the belief of some persons that others are somehow in league with them secretly: to have this dissolved in a strong scene ("The Eye of the Fire").

Technique: second novel: part empathy with fish (shark?) in *Journey of the Brothers.*[168] Work on prose: types of sentences: "teeth passed softly through <his> the hand."

Study of poetry: read part of poem, then stop and see if you can *anticipate*. If the "structure" is good, you should, after a certain amount of the poem has been traversed, be able to do this; the "inevitability" of good poetry should begin to make itself felt. This is almost entirely untrue of the greatest poetry, however, which seems to me to be creating an entirely new thing with each word. Try "anticipating" in *The Waste Land*. Housman and Marvell are amenable to this; W. S. Graham <is not> and Lorca and Hart Crane are not. Perhaps, however, this is only a distinction between *kinds* of poetry and is not necessarily indicative of quality. It seems to me to *be* so, nonetheless.

On meter: why has "this" a ↑(slightly)↓ heavier emphasis than "the"?
   Ăbóve thĕ trée
   Ăbŏve thís trée
Everything else is equal but the two words. This factor seems to me to be an important and neglected one in the study of prosody.

The World's Fair[169] <has> had something of the parable in it—the fine, bright, logical things wrought by the scientists, and, stumbling delightedly among them, the uncomprehending hordes who will use them.

---

168. Compare with Dickey's "The Shark at the Window," "The Shark's Parlor," "Pursuit from Under," "The Movement of Fish," and "Winter Trout." "The Shark at the Window" appeared in *Sewanee Review* 59 (April–June 1951): 290–91. The remaining poems are collected in *The Whole Motion.*
169. The World's Fair was held from 1939 to 1940 in New York City and occasioned newspaper tributes in the early fifties.

Second novel—during *Journey of the Brothers:* aquatic gardens, the water nymphs (Rhine Maidens): Kafka: great nature theater of Oklahoma (*Amerika*) base on Weekawatchie Springs and swimmers there: animals (and trainer: jodhpurs, pith helmet: theatrical looking: black mustache, whip).

The serene unconsciousness ↑mindlessness↓ of a great work of art. None of them proclaim their greatness. *You* do that. The *contrived* masterpiece almost never has this serenity: *Finnegans Wake, Paradise Lost.*

End of a poem's stanza: "mate through ↑(in)↓ the needle's eye."[170]

A good poem, immediately it is written, seems to move away from you and establish itself.

The frustrations I have accomplished!

It is not the athlete I was <who> that will not let my body disintegrate, but the athlete I was not, nor could be.

That all I have to do is sit down with a pencil or a typewriter to open up that miracle.

Novel to be conceived and written (and perhaps presented) on several different levels. Instead of having it levelled in time (as in Philip Toynbee's *Prothalamium*), have it apportioned in depth: "Level #1," "Level #2," "Level #3," etc. If not *presented* in this manner, the work may first be written out, (the same events) in ↑(the)↓ several parts, and then interwoven.[171]

The (good) poet, if he senses something lurking in it, ought to be willing to write years of nonsense to unearth his own voice. John Peale Bishop is one who could not do this; he did the most he could with a second-hand instrument played with intelligence and discretion. He is not a great poet.

The inner surface of ↑along↓ ↑(within)↓ ↑on↓ ↑upon↓ reality.

170. Compare Dickey's "The Voyage of the Needle."

171. Toynbee's *Prothalamium: A Cycle of the Holy Grail* (Garden City, N.Y.: Doubleday, 1947) is paginated according to the period and events described and according to the narrator, so that page A7 covers the same time period as pages B7, C7, and so on, with a different narrator relating each experience. The speaker always begins his experience at his point of entry and concludes with his departure. Narrator B is present throughout the book.

The two types of (great) work: ↑(dependent upon)↓ form or vision.

Finnegans Wake: what (would be) ↑is↓ so remarkable about writing a novel (work) in cryptogram?

Novel: birthday party: "inscaped" description of doing imitations, "impersonations" by Julian.

How much cleaner, sharper, and in better focus your face is if you have shaved recently.
    Face: unfocussed (because of his) beard.

Modern literature: a literature of complex attitudes, techniques, conclusions, or complex attitudes proceeding from and revolving about a central one—"the spray defines the fountain" (mine).

"The collected hysteria of orgasm."

Next poem: "The Structure of the Fish": break feathered bread (loaves and fishes).
    "of no less miracle."
    "darting the withered tooth."
    "nor less his feathered bread."

Syntax: Graham writes not "and put into speed as green kindles quickly into a flower," but "and put into speed as green *kindles into quickly a flower.*"[172]

I like poetry which shows a loosening up (of language) toward (to) the possibilities of (the) vocabulary. This is part of Graham's appeal.

Novel: rewrite the arch parts: Julian is, at best, an acute *non-literary* sensibility. He may use figures of speech, but no high-falutin' ones. He is a sensibility attached against its (unconscious) will to the events of the story. Rewrite carefully for this.

Rational Poem: "Peccary (Javalina)"[173]
    "Where
    Place him / at all,
    Under a broken marble, a fallen arch

172. From "With All Many Men Laid Down in the Burial Heart," *The White Threshold.*

173. The collared peccary, or javelina *(Tayassu tajacu),* is the more common of the species of small, wild pigs native to the Americas.

Or under the plumb of nothing,
The letting blood of a wave
That his anger rot the gods."
Teeth, humped back.

The secret of stanzaic form in poetry is to let a stream of sounds crystallize in the ear (and on the page), and then rework the overall pattern
selectively until nothing can be changed. If you are lucky, the changes
will enhance, facilitate, the overall "chiming together" of the first solid-
ification of sound. If you are unlucky, it will disturb, ruin it.

The uses of the participle—explore: "this misseling."

"Or war on swans."[174]

(Variation on a theme by John Wheelwright):
    "anent the pointed shape."
    "The god's face littered ↑propped↓ the wave, most endlessly."
    "his knuckles webbed,
    Spreading the dies of his net."

{The last entry occurs at the bottom of page 152, the final page of
Notebook I. In the left-hand margin is a listing of names and scores for
a class designated Eng. H-2 (Dickey does not identify the course). The
notation indicates that as he reaches the end of the first notebook, he is
teaching at Rice Institute after completing his service. A reference to an
upcoming football game between Rice and Louisiana State University
suggests that it is still the fall semester of 1952.}

174. Compare the scene in Dickey's *To the White Sea,* 94–96, where Muldrow slaugh-
ters part of a flock of swans for their feathers.

Notebook II

The second notebook includes ninety-five written pages in a bound ledger and centers on Dickey's detailed reading of Thomas Mann's *Doctor Faustus,* Marcel Proust's *Swann's Way,* Kenneth Burke's *A Grammar of Motives,* and W. H. Auden and N. H. Pearson's *Poets of the English Language.* It also includes efforts to create long, original poems. Internal evidence indicates that Dickey began writing in the notebook during 1952 and that he likely continued these entries into the following year. Certainly, he commenced reading *Doctor Faustus* in 1952, as the first notebook indicates, and he quotes liberally from Mann's novel throughout this notebook, beginning on page 3. In the notebook's final entry, Dickey declares his intention for "Utterance I," his poetic contribution to the 1953 anthology *Soundings: Writings from the Rice Institute,* which the English department dedicated to Dr. Willard Thorpe, a visiting professor from Princeton. He states, "I wanted to write a poem with some *believing* in it." The use of the past tense suggests that the poem was completed or perhaps already published. Since this notebook continues his creative efforts both in poetry ("The Kingly Lover") and fiction (*The Casting*), it acts to complement what he began in the first ledger. However, because this second journal also examines outside readings and incorporates attempts to create new, more extensive poems, it extends the understanding of Dickey's literary apprenticeship. He was utilizing his critical readings to focus and determine his own philosophic and poetic attitudes and efforts.

Dickey directly quotes or summarizes specific passages from Mann and Proust with which he feels an emotional affinity or which address immediate critical interests. Excerpts from *Doctor Faustus,* for example, reveal now-familiar Dickey concerns—the individual personality, physical love, the poetic sensibility, the relationship between the Self and what is not Self, and a belief in images whose impermanence does not mitigate their efficacy. Dickey discerns in Mann the same sensitive yet analytic mind he considers himself to have, and he sees in Adrian Leverkühn, the novel's central figure, an artist whose efforts to achieve great art involve understanding many of the dilemmas and questions Dickey also is confronting, including an attention to past phenomena whose significance extends into the future. This attention likewise explains his interest in *Swann's Way,* specifically Proust's focus on memory and the manner in which the sight of some object or the recognition of some smell may call up an entire series of past associations, long forgotten, but which now totally involve the consciousness. Memory, Dickey understands, becomes a means for one to enhance the present and redeem the past, though he nevertheless realizes its impotence in countering the passage of time.

Dickey's interest in Burke is philosophical, while his reading of Auden and Pearson (and, to a lesser degree, Mark Van Doren) derives from his search for poetic understanding, that is, his effort to establish a general basis for good or great poems. The majority of the passages he transcribes from *A Grammar of Motives* involve Aristotelian and Platonic views of reality, reflecting, in one way or another, the empirical or the ideal world. His extensive notations yield the sense that, in critiquing Burke's analysis, Dickey is working through an understanding of concepts such as perception, knowledge, and form and determining his own attitudes toward them. Nowhere, however, does Dickey systematize these philosophic concerns into an organized pattern of beliefs. At the heart of this effort is his need for a unity that exists not so much in spite of the physical world's essential diversity but because of it. His Platonic idealism, the separation of form from matter, conflicts with his Aristotelian duality, the idea that matter, while distinct from form, is nevertheless immanent in it. Such tension explains, for example, his interest in certain quotations from Burke, as when he cites this passage and then underlines for emphasis: "a thing does not 'simply' exist, but 'takes form,' or is a record of *an act which gave it form.*" The search for unity also underlies his focus on Burke's discussion of act or motion and on Burke's explanation of a joined duality, such as in the Minotaur. Both motion and duality are physical properties but, more important, both reflect a process of actualization, the beginning or state of essence or awareness. The lack of motion or the failure of such a unity denotes death or stasis, and Dickey therefore summarizes part of Burke's commentary by noting "a thing's *essence* or *quiddity* can become identical with its principle of *action.*"

Dickey's interest in poetic criticism developed simultaneously with his interest of philosophy. He read Auden and Pearson's anthology, *Poets of the English Language,* and Mark Van Doren's *Introduction to Poetry,* determined to understand how the conscious manipulation of technical devices such as meter and rhyme reinforces narrative intent or dramatic situation. In good poetry, he concludes, manner complements matter. These concerns, what Dickey calls the "given" in a poem, enable the poet to present "the poem behind the poem," to render the intent "more *actual,* evocative, expressive." His readings facilitated his experimentation with his own poems and broadened the types of poetry he was writing. "The Kingly Lover," for example, which he was writing in both a "rational" and an "unconscious" version, now becomes a poem in which the two styles are integrated and alternated. He also realizes that he writes better if he "blueprints" the poem in advance and then allows the material to assume its own direction. Worried that his poems might become "image-bound," he decides to study Emily Dickinson and E. A. Robinson, whose works also deal with abstractions but without the overuse of imagery. However, images are not Dickey's only poetic concern. Although he suspects individual images are archetypal and must be induced to yield their mystery or meaning within a poem, he also involves himself in creating what he terms "a *driving* lyric." He cites Burke's discussion of the lyric and specifically notes not only how the physical arrangement of lyric stanzas contributes to the narrative but also how the lyric mood reflects a culmination or state of arrest that is "a beginning and an end, for all action."

As if *A Grammar of Motives* becomes a springboard by which he exposes himself to and involves himself in relevant philosophic and poetic ideas, Dickey also quotes from and comments on Burke's discussion of historical process. While he questions whether Burke is "more ingenuous than profound," the focus on history as a process—that is, as cultural development initiated by an individual or human collective acting within time and place and identified by a pattern of symbols— appears in Dickey's poetry and fiction, including later works such as "The Performance" and *Alnilam*. Moreover, many of the abandoned poems in the second ledger testify to his decision to present, in poems where style contributes to subject, a hero acting within history to determine the course of events. Dickey acknowledges that the notebook is "littered with the corpses of poems," but because "[t]he past is furnished with bad tracks," he believes the future offers greater poetic promise. He works particularly on poems such as "Now Float the Shells of Air," "The Saviors," "The Warrior's Birth," "Theme from de la Mare," "For a Ballet," and "The Crusader's Dream," all depicting larger-than-life figures engaged in heroic struggles that threaten to overcome them. There is pageantry about the efforts of his personae, a grandeur that distinguishes both the heroes and their struggles. However, the language is not so much abstract as general; neither the protagonist nor the narrative or dramatic situation assumes distinction. Such generality, for example, evidences itself when Dickey writes, in "For a Ballet," "The Knight danced onto the captive stage / Hung round with chains and rosemary." He has not yet acquired the ability exhibited in *Into the Stone* (1960) but more pronounced in *Drowning with Others* (1962) and *Helmets* (1964) to depict an archetypal act within a specific historical setting. He has not yet discovered, in other words, how to mythologize a personal memory. Interestingly, he does attempt an untitled poem about memory, which lacks narrative but retains mythical elements. The poetic lines here and elsewhere consist of short, declarative sentences or phrases that anticipate Dickey's early published works and reflect his interest in music. "Lines like the slow tolling of gongs—even, measured, and deadly certain," he writes, seeking to bring musical qualities into the poem, and in another entry he admonishes himself to listen more often and more closely to musical chords and progressions.

Dickey struggles in the second notebook to achieve a self-discipline, attempting to better his writing by segmenting his time each day rather than alternating days by genre. However, few entries in the second notebook pertain to *The Casting*. When he does focus on the novel, he tries to keep the entire work in mind, advising himself to revise specific scenes and by being concise to limit the overall length to no more than 275 pages. He also cautions himself to enhance the narrative details, broadening the principal thematic concern of casting and elaborating on the dance motif. The absence of detailed entries on *The Casting* reflects not only a partial loss of interest but also the fact that Dickey originally intended the notebooks to focus on particular concerns. He clearly wants the second ledger to focus on his readings and not on his fiction. Although that intent is evident, Dickey never consistently fulfilled it.

Because he devotes much of this notebook to his poetic efforts, he also begins, not surprisingly, to assess the abilities of other poets, though the analysis of specific poems that characterizes the first ledger is absent. The entries possess a directness and conviction that anticipate his critical statements in *Sorties* (1971). For example, in one entry he asserts that the work of Jean Stafford, Elizabeth Hardwick, and Eleanor Clark contains "a terrible, clever sterility." Other entries declare that Richard Wilbur's poems possess "a kind of weak, well-meaning, and ordered vapor" and that John Berryman's poetry is "full of tricks, 'craft,' and purely mechanical effects." Dickey also disposes of Randall Jarrell, James Merrill, and Anthony Hecht. However, artists like Robert Horan, W. S. Graham, and George Barker receive praise. He calls Horan "quite an imaginative poet," a writer who "thinks naturally in images," and he acknowledges Graham as an influence on his work.

{Dickey began writing in Notebook II in the fall of 1952. He had re-turned to his teaching duties at Rice Institute.}

There is a perfect and diamond clarity about the fact that my best and profoundest asset is my analytic refusal to be hoodwinked; my best quality is my faculty for analysis. On this depends my best poetry, the best character-searching I do, the deepest convictions I have. This may depend at least in part on intuition (perhaps not), but most of it is con-tained in the stubborn "not-to-be-fooled" principle which I exercise even in looking at someone. There is that in me which cherishes, yearns for, a sincere and self-negating (but *is* it this?) delusion, but my analytic faculty will forever prevent this while I am worth anything. A good delusion (while one is *aware* that it is a delusion: Walter Armistead,[1] etc.) is a pleasant diversion, or an intense one, a sort of gentle and deep lay-ing of the ghost of one's youth, but the delusion must not become a *principle* of contemplation (except as an *exploratory* device) or action, must never supplant.

There are hundreds of *images* that crowd one's mind. These seem in a sense *sequential* and should be noted, explored, correlated, and used. Warren has a good evocation of this in *All the King's Men*—image of Ann Stanton swimming in the grey waters with a gull flying over. These things are, to the individual, archetypal, and their meaning awaits, per-haps until deathly revelation. Images predominantly sexual occur to me, but there are a great many which are not of this type. These memories are useless unless they are *symbolic* in a literary work, unless they are overtly or *secretly* (another *kind* of overtness) made to yield *insight* into character, situation, etc.

Spender's concept of the "poem behind the poem."[2] This is what the "given" in the poem evokes—the power of "giving" the "given" so that the poem behind the poem is made more *actual,* evocative, expressive, etc. This is what constitutes poetic talent, genius.

A "nice" mixture of pictorial and non-visual poetry. Try poetry of "statement" (abstract or no), even of syllogism, logic, induction, deduc-tion, etc. Try poem based on sorites (J. V. Cunningham, Jonson's "To Heaven," etc.).

1. A high school friend who was shot down during World War II and spent time in a prison camp. Recalled for the Korean conflict, he was subsequently killed in a train-ing accident. His imagination as well as his enthusiasm for the swing music of the forties provided Dickey with a sense of what genuine ecstasy might be.

2. See *World within World* (New York: Harcourt, Brace and Co., 1951), esp. 52–55.

To bring from Atlanta: Kafka's *Diaries,* Rilke's *Letters* and *Poems,* Gide's first three *Journals.* All *Partisans, Sewanees* and, above all, *Hudsons.*

I must have at least three notebooks:

1. Notes for poems, remarks on poetry, more or less formal. Also for novels.

2. Jottings as they come. To be carried at all times.

3. A journal of readings, wherein all I come across that is important to me is noted and, if need be, discussed. Where I preserve my readings.

I should like:

To read (carefully) an hour a day.

Every other day to write poetry for three hours.

Every other day to write on the novel for three hours.

Exercise a half-hour a day.

Pascal: "adorned with mirrors and chains."[3]

Symbol: Mithra: grotto on Capri: Tiberius (Montaigne?).[4]

Are the mythic and the "true-to-experience" (as in Jarrell) irreconcilable? Are the archetypal and the "true-to-experience"?

It is the task of poetry to find and articulate the archetypal, individual (or possibly racial) vision, examine it, determine (or arrive at a tentative, or even assign one) its meaning, and make this meaning available.

Mann: whores as "daughters of the wilderness."[5] "Daughters of the garden."

"Kingly Lover": alternate the kingly with the human lover (Lamar)[6] and alternate rhetoric with plain statement.

Human L.: "and, hearing the cricket whimper,
        Turned back into this house."

3. From *"Pensées" and "The Provincial Letters"* (New York: Modern Library, 1941). The quotation is from #33, which concerns poetical beauty.

4. Mithra was the principal deity of Persia in the fifth century B.C., the god of light and wisdom, closely associated with the sun, who imparted to his worshipers the blessed hope of immortality and who was the fearless antagonist of the powers of darkness. Mithraism found its widest favor among the Roman legions, for whom Mithra was the ideal divine comrade and fighter. Tiberius, the second Roman emperor (A.D. 14–37), retired to Capri in A.D. 26 and ruled thereafter by correspondence.

5. From *Doctor Faustus,* 147. Dickey's earlier citation of Mann (see Notebook I, n. 132) suggests that he began Notebook II in 1952.

6. "Lamar" appears in Notebook I in reference to another poem, "The Poor Girl." See p. 46.

Adrian's flight from the brothel:[7] the merest touch of sin (flesh) works its own brute, elaborate snare *through* the personality of the ensnared.

Mann: "one must have command over what has been achieved even though one no longer finds it essential."[8] Is this true, absolutely? I should think that there are instances in which this would be fatal or disastrous.

Listen more to chords and progressions in music.

Sense of being *infected* with the past, tradition: Freudian view of art.

Mann: "a sense of the deadly extension of the kingdom of the banal."[9]

Lines like the slow tolling of gongs—even, measured, and deadly certain: chorale.

Mann: "naïvete lies at the bottom of all being."[10] Northrop's "undifferentiated aesthetic continuum."[11]

It is blasphemy for one who knows no more about poetic technique than I to attempt to write poetry—and yet, and yet—the ear is perfectly naked, and hears, and the eye sees, and the hand flows, and the good thing comes occasionally, and now more frequently.

Figure or symbol: "the man in the well."

The beginnings of symbolism, the symbolism of beginnings.

I do not know whether Thomas Mann is a great novelist, but I do know that he is a great mind.

I am at last learning to *read,* thanks to my *concentration* on *Dr. Faustus*— my refusal to let therein my concentration lapse.

There is not *enough* in Henry James; his work is a triumph of (sometimes) revealing mannerism. If this is the ascendancy of craft (the other denotation of the word occurs to me, and I dislike it), we would do well

7. See *Doctor Faustus,* chap. 17.
8. Ibid., 141.
9. Ibid., 152.
10. Ibid.
11. From F. S. C. Northrop's *The Meeting of East and West* (New York: Macmillan, 1947).

to use only enough of it so that the work is left comparatively free from its supercilious corruption. There are crafts and crafts, of course. Even the abandonment of technique is a strategy.

The conscious effort to *remember* is an integral part of good reading (what an advantage I have here!!). A notebook preserves this.

The writer's (poet's) greatest difficulty is in letting experience come through his learning *virginly,* as experience, *not* as material. *Then* letting, at his leisure, the shaping flood fall and make meaningful! This is what Wordsworth meant by "emotion recollected in tranquillity" (What a truly strong, deep utterance this is! Professors!! Would Wordsworth love you?). But first there must be emotion, and prior to emotion there must be experience, and prior to experience there must be *involvement.* This secures the common bond, the feeling-into of experience, the being caught-up-into-it, which enables a writer to enter the arena of man, wherein his voice begins to break, in <a> the strange, warm language of art, tragic as it flows, as is that arena.

On quotation: one should not say "Mann, Goethe, say (so and so)," but "Mann, Goethe have *taught me* to say it."

Dusk: the birds: "their wings like many rapid blinks of the eye."

Figure: Crane: "wine talons build."[12]

Mann: *Faustus:* on Rüdiger Schildknapp: "That he could have as many love-affairs as he chose seemed to satisfy him, it was as though he shrank from every connection with the actual because he saw therein a theft from the possible. The potential was his kingdom, its endless spaces his domain—therein and thus far he was really a poet."[13]

Leverkühn: "The lust after strange flesh means a conquest of previously existing resistances, based on the strangeness of I and You, your own and the other person's."[14]

The lust to *possess* a good writer, to make his virtues and even defects yours, and to improve ↑on↓ his virtues and refine his defects.

---

12. From "The Wine Menagerie."

13. *Doctor Faustus,* 169. Rüdiger Schildknapp in the novel is the Anglophile poet who befriends Adrian Leverkühn. His enthusiasm for Shakespeare results in Adrian's decision to plan an opera. Dickey's interest in the quotation lies in its description of the poetic nature.

14. *Doctor Faustus,* 187. Adrian Leverkühn is the central figure in Mann's novel, a German composer whose life and career are described by his good friend Serenus Zeitblom.

Leverkühn: "Every sensual act means tenderness, it is a give and take of desire, happiness through making happy, a manifestation of love."[15]

Discussion of *form* as "magic square" in Chapter XXII of *Faustus.*

Leverkühn: music and Ptolemaic system of cosmology and astronomy: form, order. Note cluster order as "constellation."[16]

Leverkühn: "Most interesting phenomena probably always have this double fare of past and future, probably are always progressive and regressive in one. They display the equivocalness of life itself."[17]

Mann: *Faustus:* correlative of the Cow Trough:[18] a little obvious, but oddly effective: "Cold."

The *subtlety* of the correlative important. Subtlety not to be <corre-lated> equated with ambiguity. It should be (the meaning, or perhaps two or three self-reinforcing meanings) lightly hid and concrete, thunderous and piercing when discovered. It must display a "will to discovery," a "small clamoring for the light," but must come to the reader only after he has reflected, probed a little, and so got the snake to flash at his stick.

Ambiguity not to be considered an end. This notion (Empson's)[19] is merely a product of materialism, the desire to "possess" everything, the wish for *many* things. No materialist ever possessed anything.

I am never happier than when thrusting, or when I have just thrust, toward a goal, toward writing something I think good. The conflict (I saw it once as a searing, unendurable, and unending conflict) between "art" and "experience" is beginning to resolve itself. For what is the "experience" for which I sacrificed so many good writing hours? A bad movie, a pair of buttocks on a girl no more intelligent than a stone, browsing around bookstores thinking that by the painless expedient of paying for books I could acquire what was in them. There is a great deal of work to be done, and I will do it now, more or less without interruption. There is no question of talent, sensitivity. All that is needed is technique, and a making *available* of the mind. A life like Gide's, Flaubert's, James's, Joyce's

15. Ibid., 188.
16. See ibid., 193.
17. Ibid., 193.
18. See ibid., 194.
19. See William Empson's *Seven Types of Ambiguity* (Norfolk, Conn.: New Directions, 1940; rev. ed., 1947).

without the hermeticism of these. *Control the daemonic.* Let it come, and *use* it. "Use" here has <the> reference to technical capability.

There is a terrible, clever sterility about the work of Jean Stafford, Elizabeth Hardwick, and Eleanor Clark. What *could* I have admired in them?

The insight and strength and essential unhealth of D. H. Lawrence: a *man* writing: consequences of this.

Pocket Book: *In Tragic Life:* Vardis Fisher. Essay on Fisher: J. P. Bishop.[20]

Taz Lighthorn: perhaps wears shirt (T-shirt, sport shirt) with the "irrelevant" figure of a man with a flyrod on it. Another sense (symbol) of "casting" connected with the "proxy-wooer" and object of (semi-) wishfulfillment.

Sex and marriage: woman's part is to have found; man's is the perpetually renewed act of finding.

Devil on inspiration and technique: Mann: *Faustus* 239–243.

"Hell is at bottom only a continuation of the extravagant existence." (Mann).[21]

The devil changes ". . . as clouds do, without knowing it, apparently."[22]

Music, poetry as *incantation* (ties in with daemonic).

"Kingly Lover": perhaps inset different parts.

In second novel: here is where I can use something of the hallucinatory technique of *Finnegans Wake:* nightclub (or entertainment center of some sort) here to be enacted a shipwreck scene with frantic (seeming) chorus girls, etc. This something like Kafka. Or, enacted the decline of Rome or Sardanapalus or some such: Pompeii, *Ecbatana.*[23]

---

20. See "The Strange Case of Vardis Fisher," *Southern Review* 3 (autumn 1937): 348–59. Bishop argues that Vridar Hunter, the protagonist in Fisher's novel, struggles against a fear of life by asking how one should conduct himself so that his soul does not sicken and die.

21. *Doctor Faustus,* 246.

22. Ibid., 247.

23. Sardanapalus, or Ashurbanipal, was an Assyrian monarch who lived luxuriously and under whose realm the country reached its climax of wealth and prestige. After his death, Assyria fell into exhaustion and decay, ruined by forty years of intermittent war. Ecbatana was the capital of Media, captured in 550 B.C. by Cyrus the Great and plundered by Alexander, Seleusus, and Antiochus III.

"Full of vision and nausea."

Mann on wedding of "advanced" and "popular" art: "an intellectually winged simplicity."[24] Not badly put and a sound goal *if* it can be accomplished. Can it? Is it possible?

Mann: "↑(a society)↓ which will not *have* culture but will *be* a culture."[25]

Zeitblom: "Art is mind, and mind does not at all need to feel itself obligated to the community, to society—it may not, in my view, for the sake of its freedom, its nobility. An art that 'goes in unto' the folk, which makes her own the needs of the crowd, of the little man, of small minds, arrives at wretchedness, and to make it her duty *is* the worst small-mindedness, and the murder of mind and spirit. And it is my conviction that mind, in its most audacious, unrestrained advance and researches, can, however unsuited to the masses, be certain in some indirect way to serve man—in the long run men."[26]

Little Negro boys leading the blind beggars home for the night.[27]

The Mark Van Doren anthology of poetry: *The Reading of Poetry* or some such—*Introduction to Poetry.*[28] Collected Frost.

Music: the effort(s) to speak, cry out, of a tongueless angel.

"Shaman," "shamanistic."

Place names (and proper names) in poetry, as in Milton and Pound's "Alchemist": Columbia one-volume encyclopedia:[29] Ecbatana: find who (besides the Assyrians) worshipped lions: (Beelzebub, as in John Collier's story).[30]

Mann: *Faustus:* remarks on Sorel: 366–370.

24. See *Doctor Faustus,* chap. 28.

25. Ibid., 322.

26. Ibid. See Dickey's commencement address, "Guilt as Blackmail," in *Night Hurdling,* and his comments in *Self-Interviews,* 68–74, on the role of art in society.

27. Dickey's treatment of blindness appears in poems such as "Why in London the Blind Are Saviors" and "Reading *Genesis* to a Blind Child" as well as his novel *Alnilam.* "Why in London the Blind Are Saviors" appeared in *Poetry* 102 (August 1963): 284–86. "Reading *Genesis* to a Blind Child" is collected in *The Whole Motion.*

28. *Introduction to Poetry* (New York: Sloane, 1951).

29. *The Columbia Encyclopedia* (New York: Columbia University Press, 1950). The first edition was published in 1935.

30. See "Thus I Refute Beelzy."

Analysis of Leverkühn's *Apocalypse* 370–380, especially the "instrumentalization of the voice" and the "vocalization of the orchestra" as symbolic reversals of spiritual and material surrogates.

Mann: "calculation raised to mystery."[31] Leverkühn's *Apocalypsis cum Figuris.*

Novel: some of it (my novel) is intolerably embarrassing, but some of it is good enough, and some of it is quite good. Go through and cut out all unnecessary polysyllables. Revise the conversation between Julian and Sara in the first chapter. Work hard and write three or four pages a day, revise them at the end of the day's work, reread them at the beginning of the next day. See how what you have written "stands up" over a period of time. It may be you can, by great compression, confine the thing to 250 pages or, at most, 275.

I find that when I cut myself off from the outside world and concentrate on literary matters, technique, etc., I am a great deal more satisfied with myself than at other times. At these other times, talking to people, walking the streets of a city when I could be working, I tend to assume a Byronic attitude toward myself and others which is more a defense mechanism than anything else.

"Kingly Lover": instead of "two versions of the same poem," integrate the two. Play the dream-kingly off against the actual-human, and alternate *styles* as well.

Poem in square "block" stanzas, like Marvell's "The Garden."

Archaism: "*make* the *tears to flow*": perhaps useful.

". . . as, after a dream-affair with a beautiful and admiring woman, one feels, among mundane affairs, a distinct superiority because of that secure and unrepeatable relationship."

I seem to write better poetry when I give myself a framework to begin with and then let it be altered if the poem expresses itself better through alteration.

Leverkühn: "Idealism leaves out of count that the mind and spirit are by no means addressed by the spiritual alone; they can be most deeply moved by the animal sadness of sensual beauty."[32]

31. *Doctor Faustus,* 379.
32. Ibid., 414.

Leverkühn: love: "an amazing and always somewhat unnatural alteration in the relation between the I and the not-I." [33]

Study Emily Dickinson's poems wherein she deals with abstractions ("pain," "fear," "love," etc.) without images and without adjectives.

The Van Doren anthology on meter: [34] he seems to me to have the essential approach, not the fastidious, "button-examining" examination but judicious, passing comments which tie the metrical practice in with the rest of the poem rather than isolating it as an end.

Or perhaps it would be better to work for a certain time (say, 2 hours) on the novel and the same time on poetry *each day*.

Pay more attention to sound, the sound of syllables in words in the poetic line, and from line to line. Example: "lime-bright" for "i" sound, in connection with light-effects.

The ease with which you can change the style of your poetry from poem to poem, under or not under "influences."

Mann: "The past was only tolerable if one felt above it, instead of having to stare stupidly at it aware of one's present impotence." [35]

"To set limits already means to have passed them." [36] (Mann). Also, Nietzsche said it.

Mann: ". . . Adrian, who was no schoolman but an artist and took things as they came, apparently without thought of their proneness to change. In other words, he gave to impermanent becoming the character of being; he believed in the image: a tranquillizing belief, so at least it seemed to me, which, adjusted to the image, would not let its composure be disturbed no matter how unearthly that image might be." [37]

"Now Float the Shells of Air"
     Now float the shells of air, the silk sails run

33. Ibid., 415.
34. Van Doren's *Introduction to Poetry* analyzes thirty poems, explicating their narrative or dramatic situations and showing how form and structure enhance meaning.
35. *Doctor Faustus*, 454. Compare Dickey's comment on the past in *Sorties*, 55.
36. *Doctor Faustus*, 457.
37. Ibid., 467. Compare Dickey's comments on the importance of the image in his essay "Lightnings or Visuals," *South Atlantic Review* 57:1 (January 1992): 1–14.

Upon the coruscant scattered strait;
The mailed wave sets them home for joy.

Here, along this blowing beach,
A brave beard (flags,) ↑flutters↓ picked and scorned

By tattered ibises, and a prayerful boy
Hacks with his childish sword the dunes:
The last red infidel, among his rages.

Mann: "all expressivism is really lament."[38]

The kind of insight I very much am drawn to: Mann: "The echo, the giving-back of the human voice as nature-sound, and the revelation of it *as* nature-sound, is essentially a lament: Nature's melancholy 'Alas!' in view of man, her effort to utter his solitary state."[39]

Mann: *Faustus:* discussion of freedom, form, expressiveness, lament: 487–488.

"The speaking unspokenness given to music alone."[40]

"The Kingly Lover": nails: "stuck (round) with nails and hammock-screws." *The playground at dusk by Brookwood Hills swimming pool—here she waits for her lover.*[41]

Work out the several levels of action of "The Kingly Lover." Be satisfied with from 5 to 10 lines a day, and <at> a total of from 50 to 100 lines.

"Battle-spring, a caged people break,
Tents flow over the waste, gongs,
Hands, mouths (waste) drink in terrific hope,
(The)(As)(the) green towers shoot—
(Out of) [(From)] whose loin(s)!
                                        He stands
In the orange moon, on the combed
Hill."

38. *Doctor Faustus,* 485.
39. Ibid., 486.
40. Ibid., 490.
41. A swimming pool in Atlanta where Dickey worked as a lifeguard.

Now: *other section:*
  1. Pathos: hopelessness.
  2. Majesty, submission in hope.
  3. *Significant* fusing.

Novel: in the dance scene ("from the Keith circuit"),[42] have Julian "demonstrate" a little of it. "Around the glass coffee-table I went, scattering daisies." (Or some such). Then she begins. "I was in hopes she would continue the dance figure, for I (most) often thought of her as a dancer, although to my knowledge she had no such talent. Instead, she went into an involved story about," etc.

James: Marcher and May Bartram: "It <she> [her face] affected him as the sequel of something of which he had lost the beginning."[43]

"Perseus": first stanza:
  <Andromache> Andromeda my cloudy shield
  Has shored. To cypher ease
  I pluck it bold from groaning doves,
  Buckle and stare. My forearm slung like a nerve to war
  I make twining stare to glitter and go
  Back five thumbed sights past ↑(from)↓ the grainy altar
  Danaë tops, hair swirled in answered harp,
  In what ↑(such)↓ chord coifed.

"The Warrior's Birth"
  Others past as rain
  Set in their live fields
  Easel and clavier.
  The string trembled featly,
  The world knew its colors.

  As this light stills
  You sweat for the trident,
  The barb, the fuse,
  For the Hanging Dog
  Borne past your window.

  The desert awaits you
  The men ranged on horses

42. The Keith circuit, named for Benjamin Keith, who opened in Boston the first American vaudeville house in 1883, consisted of a series of theaters in cities such as Providence, Philadelphia, and New York. See another reference to the Keith circuit in Notebook I, p. 31.
  43. From Henry James's story "The Beast in the Jungle."

The goatshair and brazier
The anvil for shaping
The whetstone for sharping.

Here at your cradle
The earth's wells are stricken:
You crow in your pleasures:
Your dam is (hardy) ↑forsaken↓
And bloody your sire,
Guiltless as you.

"For a Ballet" ↑Figure for a Ballet↓
  The Knight danced onto the captive stage
  Hung round with chains and rosemary,
  Circled the lights of the Spider's House,
  Clanked and called his Lady.

  Her strains of gauze snared thick his heart,
  His gold greaves fixed in their raptures;
  The drinking light from underneath
  Devilled her claiming features.

  Her crimson nostrils sore aflame,
  She slid into his knotted whirl,
  And he in the frozen wood, his joy,
  Turned with his narrow ↑(turning)↓ girl.

I am acquiring a good sense of what poems *not* to go on with. I have
wasted much time trying to redeem unredeemable stuff.

My whole childhood rose crying to me.

Capitalism works its "miracles" (bathtubs, "high standard of living," etc.)
by appealing to all the worst instincts of men.

"The Crusader's Dream"
  I lay full shorn on the plains of Hell,
  My sword like a graven flake;
  The mullioned towers shone like walls
  And rose with the singing Snake.
  He <fled> ↑laved↓ ↑(nursed)↓ me in his (silken) ↑(golden)↓ toils,
  My jewelled wounds he sped,↑(;)↓
  <(>He<)> (And) bade me conjure the (glittering) <(shreved)>
    ↑sunken↓ blood
  Where my Holy Wars had fed.

I flashed my blade, I crowed with ire,
The Samite Warrior slew;
I sank to the sand with a giddy phrase
And rose with the ringing dew.

The Snake slid glistening round the Tree
Where the Hanging Man was slain;
I wiped my blade on the golden ↑(silken)↓ ↑(silver)↓ grass ↑(weeds)↓
And slew my brother Cain.

Archetypal images:
   1. The battle in the desert.
   2. The battle for the home fields (harvest).

"I saw a way to put the world together."

The purely American reaction to genius as to one who has found a
"gimmick," a *new* way, or has *invented* some means of expression. Tie-in
(unconsciously) with quickening interest in exploitation in terms of
artistic value rather than money. This is one reason why we are a nation
of imitators. An artist who has "invented" a new means of expression
is, in the world of the arts, the equivalent of Henry Ford or the Wright
brothers.

On Memorial Avenue:[44] the overgrown stone stairs.

"The dark entrails of America" (Locke).[45]

The wish or compulsion to armor myself in muscle basically fear.

I must get a more systematic way of writing in these notebooks.

Although the impulse is more or less random with me, its *systematiza-
tion* is the only way it can get on paper.

Readings

G. of M.: K. Burke[46] "The great departures in human thought can be

44. A street in south Atlanta that Dickey occasionally visited.
45. From *An Essay Concerning Human Understanding*. The quotation is from book 4,
chap. 17, titled "Of Reason." In this passage Locke discusses the difference between the
use of syllogism, which he calls "the Art of fencing with the little knowledge that we
have," and the use of reason, which provides the means to discover "that Mass of
Knowledge, which lies yet concealed in the secret recesses of Nature."
46. Kenneth Burke, *A Grammar of Motives* (New York: Prentice-Hall, 1945).

eventually reduced to a moment where the thinker treats as *opposite,* keys terms formerly considered *apposite,* or v.v." (vice versa).

G. of M. 193: on empirical, transcendental and transcendent realms: "As soon as one considers things in relation to other things, one is on the way to dissolving them into their contexts, since their relations lead beyond them."

195: whole argument on realms of motion and action: Kant: "I must abolish *knowledge* to make room for *belief.*"

Many young poets' ground for a poem: "Have someone doing or saying something *unusual!*"

Auden-Pearson anthology—Vol. I: [47]
    xvi–xvii: on the peculiarities of various languages for poetical use.
    xxx to end: the modern writer's search for a unifying principle.

I would in part return to the exceptional character, perhaps through the (trials of the) ordinary.

Books to have sent:
    Both Céline.
    Journals.
    Tate: *The Limits of Poetry.*
    Patrice de la Tour du Pin: *The Dedicated Life in Poetry.* [48]
    Muriel Rukeyser: { *The Life of Poetry* / *Selected Poems.*

Books ordered:
    Jarrell: *The Seven-League Crutches* (Harcourt Brace).
    The Notebooks of Samuel Butler (Dutton).
    Selected Poems: Basil Bunting (The Cleaner's Press).
    Collected Poems: Marianne Moore (Harcourt ??).
    Poems and Prose: W. S. Landor (Oxford).

Burke's mistake in making Marxism "idealist": he has previously attempted to demonstrate that idealism is necessarily grounded in "agent."

---

47. *Poets of the English Language,* ed. W. H. Auden and Norman Holmes Pearson (New York: Viking, 1950). The entry also highlights other pages in the anthology's introduction. See Dickey's more extensive reading and analysis of Auden and Pearson's book in Notebook IV.
    48. See Dickey's comments on de la Tour du Pin in "The Poet Turns on Himself," in *Babel to Byzantium: Poets and Poetry Now* (New York: Farrar, Straus and Giroux, 1968), 278–92.

He maintains that Marxism stresses the individual and collective human agent as a primary factor in social action. He thinks that he is justified thus in calling Marxism "idealistic." But obviously the process is incapable of being reversed.

Hegel: "The History of the World is none other than the progress of the consciousness of Freedom . . . the *intellectual* comprehension of what was presented in the first instance to *feeling* and *imagination*."[49]

Burke: "The patterns of communion, sacrifice, and transcendence involved in party loyalty give Marxism, on the Symbolic level, the great value of a profound social drama, quite as Christianity was formed about the patterns of drama, though the typical Marxist prefers to stress the rational elements of Marxism, while discountenancing explicit recognition of the dramatic rituals implicit in the Marxist eschatology."[50]

210: "So far as our dramatistic terminology is concerned, the Marxist philosophy began by grounding *agent* in *scene,* but by reason of its poignant concern with the ethical, it requires the systematic featuring of *act*."[51]

Dickey: is ↑not↓ this juggling of terms and crowding of philosophies and political movements into <them not> categories more ingenuous than profound?

216: on "animal faith": "we posit the existence of the external material world by taking it on *faith*" [from agent (positor) to scene (what is posited)].[52]

216: "The objects of the material world are thus seen to *transcend* our knowledge."[53]

218: on spirit and its grounding in the animal psyche (Good).[54]

---

49. Burke, *A Grammar of Motives,* 204.

50. Ibid., 209.

51. Compare Dickey's discussion of the poetic self in "The Self as Agent," in *Sorties,* 155–64.

52. Burke's wording reads "in taking it on faith." The quotation is on p. 217.

53. The wording reads "are thus found." The quotation is on p. 217. Compare Dickey's essay "The Green Mountain Kid" (in *Night Hurdling,* 204–7), in which he relates his inability to know the wilderness.

54. Santayana, Burke argues, grounds spirit in the material yet locates its actuality in its freedom from material conditions. In so doing, he celebrates the ability of spirit to transcend the mechanical flux of nature while simultaneously stressing its location in the animal psyche, which depends upon the conditions of material existence. Burke's discussion anticipates Dickey's interest in uniting Platonic and Aristotelian views.

218: on Santayana and pragmatism: ". . . his application of theological thought to the realm of poetic imagination and intuition."

219: on "appearance" and "essence." Any *appearance* is an essence, although every appearance (or essence) does not *exist.*

220: on the infinity of essences, the "indelible background" for all the transitory facts of nature.

221: differences between Plato's "forms" and Santayana's "essences" (Good): Plato's forms the agents of *generation,* familial; Santayana's essences individual, without progeny.

221: "As matter is the realm of flux, or motion, the corresponding dialectical role of essence is that of *rest.* And since this orbit of mechanical motion is also ambiguously called 'the field of action,' the kind of rest here indicated is ambiguously both the cessation of motion and the end of action."

224: Stevens on the Minotaur: "The hybrid [Minotaur] represents a joined duality of motives, and here apparently symbolizes the union of a labyrinthine imagination (the 'unconscious') with the rationality of a poetic medium developed by deliberate conscious sophistication" [Dickey: This figure (and its type) delights me].[55]

227: Aristotle: form is *actus,* the attainment, which *realizes* (the) matter (in scholastic realism, derived from Aristotle). St. Thomas: "A form is an *act.*"
    Existence is "the *act* of essence."

Dickey: Burke is more a *categorizer* and *characterizer,* a parer and fitter, a kind of academic Procrustes,[56] than anything else. He solves most of his problems by seizing on a particular phase of a philosophy, emphasizing it according to his needs, and slanting it to fit.

228: a thing does not "simply" exist, but "takes form," or is a record of *an act which gave it form.*

55. Burke discusses Stevens's essay in the autumn 1944 issue of *Sewanee Review,* "The Figure of the Youth as Virile Poet," in which the latter stresses the merger of imagination and reason. Compare Dickey's comments on the poetic imagination in *Sorties,* 26–27.
    56. In Greek mythology Procrustes was a cruel highwayman who forced travelers to lie on a very long bed and then stretched them to fit it. If they were themselves too long, he sawed off their legs.

230: "Socrates, approaching the world as a moralist, necessarily considered it in terms of action."

230: Aristotle's God as the *end* of *action*. Paradox of Unmoved Mover.

231–232: on Aristotle's centering of *act* being different from Plato's, from which it was derived.

Dickey: the method of the later poems of Weldon Kees: the body of the poem deals (somewhat disjointedly) with history, a specific period or periods: tradition, ceremony, violence, belief. The end of the poem is in the *here, now,* and the poet regards the contrast gloomily, ironically, with the enforced passivity of the 20th-century man of feeling. It is a simple method and takes off, I imagine, from Eliot's "contrast of the ordered, meaningful past with the disordered (or *disorderly*), meaningless present."

234: "The realm of motion is now *par excellence* the realm of instruments. No instrument can record or gauge *anything* in the realm of *action* ('ideas'), except insofar as the subject-matter can be reduced to the realm of motion."

I mine eventually to be a *mystical* poetry? It is possible. Must it thus be vague? Can there be a hard, glittering, *precise* articulation of mysticism?

Memory poem:
    One green ware for morning
    One <black> white ware for the sea
    One ware for the earth sustained in bells
    One overhead
    One for the salt of shrines.

    By this exchange a bloody crow
    Orbits the ↑(chill)↓ (grave bride's) ↑(spinster's)(bridal)↓ barge,
    Withers and, shaken, rings
    Impossible you and me
    Laid bare ↑(there)↓ in seed and shrine.

    Bird, tiger (or) ↑and↓ mineral kiss
    We held in stitch and <froth> cloth
    Or chimed in singled music from the nails
    Of lutanists, where were
    Let down to <salt> speak the garden by the leaves,

    The green gifts of the morning
    The wild pearls of the sea

The soft earths of those bells
The proud crow overhead
The heaping up of salt to make a shrine.[57]

238: "The sense of self" is developed as the individual learns to foresee the kinds of resistance which external things will put forward if he acts in certain ways."[58]

238: dialectics of assertion: subject and object: "The individual becomes aware of *himself* in terms of other people. [*Very true.*] And *his* attitudes, being shaped by their attitudes as reflected in him, modify his ways of action."[59]

239: Korzybski on "unspeakable level": "He would systematically sharpen our awareness of that silent moment from which we may derive a truer knowledge, in transcending the level of automatic verbalizations that hide reality behind a film of traditional misnaming."
    (Dickey: "silent moment": Poetry? Or does it make poetry impossible? Or is it what poetry tries to utter? Rilke's "endless song welling out of silence.")[60]

240: on "Korzybskian analysis of poetic forms": "For semantics is essentially 'scientist,' an approach to language in terms of *knowledge,* whereas poetic forms are kinds of *action.*"
    D: Burke is assuming a great deal here. There is no poetry without "knowledge" of some kind, in that communication *necessarily* involves a *transfer* of knowledge.

243: on Aristotle's <terms> dialectical terms "actuality" and "potentiality," and the ambiguous nature of "incipient action": "That which is capable of being may either be or not be."
    "The scientific concept of potential energy lacks the degree of ambiguity one encounters in the potential as applied to the realm of living beings in general and human beings in particular."

243: on parallel between "incipient action" and "symbolic action": *important paragraph.*

57. See entry on memory in Notebook I on p. 60.
58. Burke's quotation appears on p. 237. The statement resembles Dickey's discussion in "The Self as Agent" as to how the poetic persona, or I-figure, develops and how it relates to the poet.
59. Burke's exact quotation appears on p. 237.
60. See Notebook I, n. 137.

243: para#3: "Images can *have the force of attitudes.*"

243: para#2: on structure of lyric poem (*important*).[61]
    Parallel of *narrative* poem: "pre" and "post" abysmal character: narrative *told* in lyric suggested physically by arrangement of stanzas and by having the (physically) middle stanza somehow abysmal.

244 para#2: important: on lyric and dramatic "ends": "State of arrest."[62]

244-245: these are "different" from "lyrics"; they are "the depiction of such personal situations as *most acutely need* resolution in the lyric state, but drive to action precisely because such resolution is missing."
    "Intense moments of pre-action."[63]

244: Wordsworth's "Composed Upon Westminster Bridge" analyzed as an example of "the perfect lyric mood." It is "marked by the state of arrest in its *culminative* aspect." On "crossing": transition (poet bridge).
    "The very process of transition is made motionless." It is not a retrospective summary. "It just *is*, . . . It encompasses. We are concerned not with its *potentialities,* but with it as an end in itself. . . . It envisions such rest as might be a ground, a beginning and end, for all action."[64]

Richard Wilbur is not a very good poet. He is skillful; he is gracious, graceful, charming. He means well. "But where's the bloody horse?" All his poems are metaphoric "examples." In essence very mechanical, the blueprint of "how to write a poem that is gracious, skillful," etc. The poetry has gone or was never there. His poems are a kind of weak, well-meaning, and ordered vapor.

249: para#1: on the *creative* and *generative* features of *act* in both Plato's idealism and Aristotle's realism (nominalism).

249: para#2: on scientist emphasis on nouns <(things)> (*particular things*) and the dramatist emphasis on verbs (*abstracted* or abstract, general *acts, actions*).

249: para#3: how a thing's *essence* or *quiddity* can become identical with its principle of *action.* "He has a *way* with him." The "way," if we can define it, *is* the *essence,* in any given case.

    61. Burke's discussion occurs in the third paragraph.
    62. The discussion occurs on p. 245.
    63. Both quotations occur on p. 246. Burke discusses lyric poems on pp. 245 and 246.
    64. Burke's discussion occurs on p. 246.

Materialistic bias of modern American mind: "I'll *buy* that" for "I'll accept that."

Poem to be constructed point by point, image by image, and word by word. To be logically worked out, image, meter, syntax. Start relatively simply, complicate, and rise to an obscure (impressive!) fury at the end. See notes in other notebook.[65] Assyrian (lions and) bulls, Chaldea, bombardier, fallen aircraft, fall of man: when man fell, he fell into war: "from leaves and fruit"—"from leaves and bitten fruit / Into the eye of the bull." "Into the stretched gaze of the bull"—"Into the red rays / Of the blazoned bull"—"From leaves from the core of the bitten fruit / Into the eye of the bull." "The lean blades (stir)," etc.

Be satisfied here with 5 lines a day. See Empson: *emotionalized* rather than intellectualized;[66] see Whitehead's final distinction between the intellectual and emotional interpretations of life.[67] Or one line a day. This poem is a structure: revise. Don't be afraid of your intuitions, but don't depend exclusively on them either.

Nietzsche's epigram about "fighting with monsters" for "Perseus": the one from Pericles for this one—(epigram 146) *Beyond Good and Evil*.[68]

My poetry is carrying its best efforts now in broad, clumsy patterns. The subtleties will come later.

Really to explore my youth—what would it take?

On Randall Jarrell's latest book, *The Seven-League Crutches*:
It is a little tiresome to read (of) the ecstasy of reviewers over Jarrell's poor poems. The worse he gets, the higher the comments pile up. You read the book. It is like nothing so much as listening to a garrulous, self-pitying, thoroughly untalented <woman> old woman tell the same

---

65. See Dickey's "Sketch for the building of the rational poem" in Notebook III, dated February 12, 1952.

66. See Empson's *The Structure of Complex Words* (London: Chatto and Windus, 1951; New York: New Directions, 1951), esp. the chapter "Feeling in Words."

67. See Whitehead's *Process and Reality: An Essay in Cosmology* (New York: Macmillan, 1930), esp. part III, chap. 5, "The Higher Phases of Experience." Whitehead argues that both interpretations involve feelings; however, the difference lies in their "emotional patterns." In intellectual feeling, this pattern reflects the close connection to the logical objects being judged. With imaginative feeling, the emotional pattern reflects the initial disconnection from the objects.

68. "Whoever fights monsters should see to it that in the process he does not become a monster. And when you look long into the abyss, the abyss also looks into you." Dickey is referring to Pericles's funeral oration, related by Thucydides in *The Peloponnesian War*.

tiresome, sentimental story of her tiresome, sentimental life over and over, poem by poem. She has three or four devices, three or four subjects. By means of these she can go on forever, and damn near does.

Poem: "The Casting" [:(Two) Aspects]:
    1. Casting of lots for the Assyrian victims.
    2. Casting of snakeskin.
    3. The live day under the withered scale.

The seed of a good stanza: make more conceptual: less imagery:
    "From Ashur's mouth, the (snake) ↑red↓
    Fang of lion towering up (the) ↑a↓ town,
    Swell the hordes of Elam
    To the great tear carved like a general's head
    Fallen on the King's Feast, a scattered lamb
    Runs through the rotten war and crown.

In second novel: have long, Larderesque lists of things eaten, clothes worn, material about automobiles and things *owned*.

Slochower on Cassirer's concept of art—gives "life as she is lived: offers *interpretation,* not analysis."[69]

If my poetry becomes image-bound, a study of E. A. Robinson should work to generalize and abstract it.

This book is littered with the corpses of poems. I feel this to be a good. The past is furnished with bad tracks.

Blueprint the poem on Assyria. Should be around fifty lines. Sidon and glass, glassblowing: "dye," "our purple hold."

My lines are not *dense* enough, nor heavy enough with meaning.

I am more interested in the verse-paragraph than the line: the working from the whole *back down to* the parts which compose it. You begin getting the sound of the *whole* first.

Stanzas 1. Introduction: king, victims, head, wars, tortures.
    2. A world of cruelty: shark, trade (Sidon).

---

69. See Harry Slochower's "Ernst Cassirer's Functional Approach to Art and Literature," *The Philosophy of Ernst Cassirer,* ed. Paul Arthur Schlipp (Evanston, Ill.: Library of Living Philosophers, 1949), 631–61. For Cassirer, Slochower argues, art comes closest to combining the universal with the particular because it communicates through an immanent symbolism that has both specific individuality and sensuous form.

3. Only out of such terrible spiritual conditions can peace come, more or less as a last alternative.

4. The comet (meteor-headed) shark has circled home: trade again. The victims scream, but less. They have invented martyrdom.

5. Trade, war, and the possibility of kindness "in a cage": the head— crisp and rotten head: the King's Feast (capitalism).

This is a good process for "structure." Now let the "imagination" operate *within this.*

"Reference": implication in the poem of "I make a weapon of an ass's skeleton" and "The Marriage of a Virgin," and analysis of this last by Sweeney.[70]

Spender: the American poet as a *"machine* of sensibility."[71]

End:
  "In the threads and thorns of their perilous cage
  Will lie, lie shorn, and keep the light to die."

Robert Horan is quite an imaginative poet. He thinks naturally in images, and his rhymes are easily managed. However, the poems are not individualized; a facility like his usually tends to cause the poems to blur and overrun into each other, and this is what happens here. He is going to be very good, though, eventually.

Decorative poets: Wilbur, Merrill, Hecht: work proceeds by "illustration," extended metaphor, usually drawn from subjects in the arts, literary figures, (domestic) animals, birds, gardens, etc.—essentially minor stuff. Best one can say of it is "charming," "apt," "graceful," "skillful." Worst is "trivial," "mechanical." But where's the bloody horse?

The best poems I have written: the last section of "For the Accused" and parts of "Perseus." "Orpheus" is also rather good. "Suite from Crime," "Andromeda."

Poems beginning with "Because" are usually unsuccessful.

Too often the poet's attitude in writing his poem is that of the builder of fortifications. He believes he has it as his task to <build> construct *an edifice to keep off criticism,* that will be invulnerable to attack under any

70. See Introduction by John L. Sweeney in *Dylan Thomas* (New York: New Directions, 1946), vii–xxiii.
71. See *World within World,* esp. 82–87.

or several of the (current) criteria of criticism. The poem is conceived in a negative rather than a positive sense; it is not an utterance but a defense. This is meant not as a rule of procedure on how to write (or not write) poems but as a comment on what seem to me contemporary trends. To use Hocking's phrase, the poet has cut himself off from his own conceptions, prejudices, idiosyncrasies—in short, <his> from most of his attributes as a human being in the action we call life. He has no "points of accepted vulnerability."[72]

Are not my recurrent fantasies about running and football images of *flight*? Struggle and flight? Release?

Hocking on Whitehead as man responding and as man reflecting: discrepancy and relation between these two.[73]

"The Earth Gate"
    One by the ridden willows rides into the earth, furiously,
    the horse deep as fire, and the chidden thongs of his legs—[74]
    [Thong(s)] and skequered willows, by the fastidious and simple
    (nude) dancers in the grove—in pursuit of his women.

He is Orpheus and Adam: Orpheus to hell and Adam to the flesh: Ryderesque picture.[75]

Proust: "The quality of a direct experience always eludes one, and only in recollection can we grasp its real flavor."[76]

The novelist's first task is to *surrender* himself to his experience. His second is to evaluate it. His third is to invent corroborative material. His fourth is to write.

Ancient cities: recurrent theme of some of my poetry: Sodom, Tyre, Sidon, Nineveh, Ashur, Babylon.

---

72. See William Ernest Hocking's *Thoughts on Death and Life* (New York and London: Harper and Brothers, 1937).

73. See Hocking's *The Self, Its Body and Freedom* (New Haven: Yale University Press, 1928).

74. The entry has an arrow drawn from "chidden" to "ridden," indicating Dickey's deliberate effort at internal rhyme.

75. Albert Pinkham Ryder (1847–1917), American painter who consistently experimented with oils to produce works dominated by moonlight and the sea and that evoke a lonely, poetic mood by expressing the mysterious forces of nature in rhythms and solid masses.

76. Dickey's statement summarizes motifs in the opening chapter of *Swann's Way.*

Proust: "Memory reveals its impotence at the same time that it seems the only instrument against Time that we possess."[77]

W. S. Graham has shown me that poetry *need not be* essentially decorative, proceed by "examples," à la Merrill, Wilbur, Hecht, *et al.* His is full of *big* things, pity, terror, and not merely mincing and "apt" metaphors. It *means* rather than "illustrates."

Jot down happenings, things which seem important at the time, enough to recall an incident significantly to memory. Then recollect and ponder the meanings.

I am absolutely prostrated by any kindness or beauty directed exclusively my way, or even that I am allowed to witness. It is painful beyond words; <and> it is what I live for.

Dewey's theory of art as consummation, movement toward repose, reunion.[78]
    You might say that art is <both> a ↑separation from, contemplation of↓, reunion with, purification of, insight into, and understanding (ultimate) of experience. You *might.*

It is necessary at all times to think and feel clearly, to clarify and *explore* everything, as well as to react to it in an essentially <irrational> instinctual way. Feeling is a state of being; reflection is the act of a god, timeless.

Christopher: before such ↑(that)↓ innocence everything is helpless.[79]

Type figure: rather than "the seas *like a* nut," Dylan Thomas' "nut *of the seas.*"[80]

The *object* is to the poet both a thing in its own right and the (possible) receptacle and vehicle of *meaning.*

The greatest broadener of poetic technique: to ask yourself, when you read a poem, *How is it done?* This is why criticism is important. Also, *what* has been done, or what is being done perpetually, and by what means?
    How is it done: imagery, meter, line-length, stanza—all the components. *How?* Ask it with every poem you read. Tremendous vistas of achievement and fulfillment open up.

77. See *Swann's Way.*
78. See John Dewey's *Art as Experience* (New York: Minton, Balch and Co., 1934), esp. chaps. 1, "The Live Creature," and 14, "Art and Civilization."
79. Dickey's son, Christopher Swift Dickey.
80. From "On no work of words."

Type and figures: (Graham, W. S.):
"*bright / In a girdle of grief . . .*
The *haft Remembers heaven.*"[81]

When you read George Barker's prose, you think, "Why doesn't he write poetry?" Then you read his poetry, and it is just what you would have suspected. How strange. Poets' prose writings are usually withdrawn and academic.

Barker has a busy, thin kind of inspiration. He is a good deal like Shelley. He is completely a poet, however. He has the one essential attribute—he thinks *instinctively* in images, analogies. This results in the absurd poetry in which he tries to force all kinds of material into his headlong lyrical impulse, but it also makes his best work absolutely distinctive.

Metaphysical poem in several parts on the building of the Hanging Gardens of Babylon: "fresh."

I like the period when, arriving in a strange town, you drift about like sediment before settling into the first of your new relationships.

It is true—I know almost nothing of poetic technique. I know a little about imagery, a very little about meter. My rhyming is strictly hit-or-miss. I should study these things more.

"The Earth Gate": also the vulva: earth as fruition, etc., fertility. Horse: *mare.* Comfort: "and I shall ride her thighs' white horses": union with Earth.

"The Earth Gate" should catch up all these meanings and transcend them all. Sex: "riding into the earth."
    "The mare deep as fire": earth "turned on a wet hinge"—"soared on ↑down↓ ↑flat↓ a (wet) ↑damp↓ hinge": tends toward repose: action: "the red rag hill."

Feel for the *implications* of words in reading poetry. Why, for instance, does Crane say in "At Melville's Tomb," ". . . beat on the *dusty* shore and were obscured"? Because of the familiar connotations of dust with death and oblivion. And yet I had never got that from <it> the line. Pay more *attention* to what you read. Let (or *make*) the words *operate* on you.

Thomas' success stems in part from his being able to relate a great many disparate images and types of figures to his central theme.

81. From "To a Tear," *The White Threshold.*

You can't imagine a person other than he is until memory gets hold of him. Then you can't imagine him as he is.

Today there are so many careful and expert scorners and no great tongues or hearts.

The secret of poetry imagery is the controlled penumbra of association.

The young poets in their lairs of sensibility.

There is not enough real arrogance in letters today.

(The weaving of) "reed shields": (*Our Oriental Heritage* — Durant).[82]

In novel: Jack *Herlong,* rather than Jack Corbett.

John Berryman's poetry depresses me; it is full of tricks, "craft," and purely mechanical effects. He literally has nothing to work with but "the art of poetry." There is nothing moving in his poetry; it is far more dangerous than the poetry of tricks of Dunstan Thompson[83] because it purports to be something entirely different, more "serious." You do say "Well said," but grudgingly; this too is irritating. The man simply is not a poet. Neither is Randall Jarrell, but it is easier to tell about him, for he <makes a point of employing the "forms."> does not make a point of employing the "forms," as <of> Berryman does. One longs for a commonplace in Berryman's poetry, but it doesn't seem to make much difference.

My poems are becoming too dependent upon metamorphosis, antithesis, circularity. <It is bec> These devices are becoming habitual and therefore mechanical.

What I would like is to write a *driving* lyric. "The Last Song" is not a bad example, but I would like to do better.

Movie: *Across the Wide Missouri:* Clark Gable's stomping, thumping dance in which is shown both his increasing age and his enormous vitality: "gesture as language."

82. The first volume in William Durant's *The Story of Civilization* (New York: Simon and Schuster, 1942).

83. An American Army corporal during World War II, Thompson was one of the founders of *Vice Versa,* a verse publication of the late thirties; he had published two volumes of poetry, *Poems* (1943) and *Lament of the Sleepwalker* (1947). Dickey discovered Thompson's work through his poem "Largo" in *A Little Treasury of Modern Poetry* (New York: Scribner's, 1946), ed. Oscar Williams, and was affected by Thompson's technical abilities.

One reason sex ↑gratification↓ is so universally prized and practiced is because it is so perfectly easy. It entails no effort of whatever kind; even the emotions are furnished. Sex seems to promise great returns for a small, or no, investment.

If I really worked at writing instead of seeking every conceivable excuse <to> not to work, I could really do something good, if not great. Writing is enough of a world in itself. One needs but few excursions to the outside. Proust knew that.

It is better not to possess, but to preserve the illusion of the value of the thing desired.

Life with no sense of direction, a mere sensual drift, is inconceivable hell. Don Juan in Hell knew this, as do Sartre's people.[84]

Poem: "Three Variations from Stephen Crane":
    I. The Hunter
    II. The Dwarf
    III. The Sleeping Man.

Stephen Crane's poems, when least conscious and therefore least obvious, are a hall of mirrors of limited suggestibility.

Cultivate sensibility in every occasion, strongly and penetratingly. Cultivate, cultivate! *Look,* hear, see, *feel,* act, do, *reflect, write!*

The moment when you are beginning to be drunk, and a strain of music or the heatened working of the brain invests something you hadn't remembered for years with incredible nostalgia and loss, is the greatest time of one's irrational life. This to me is dangerous and wonderful.

The stone face of Lust, somehow humorous and perfectly dreamlike, but undeniable when it rises—let this not be taken from me.

The impulse to "begin again," to "start over," is one of the most powerful and dangerous of human motivations. It means really, "If I could only weave a *new* set of confining conditions."

More Burke: 252–253: on Plato's and Aristotle's notions of universals.

---

84. At the height of his licentious career, Don Juan seduced the daughter of the commander of Seville and killed her father in a duel. When he later visited a statue of his victim and jeeringly invited it to a feast, the statue came to life and dragged Juan to Hell.

258: on "surprise" as an element of aesthetic value:

"The present ease of printing, which makes it almost a necessary condition of the publishing trade that readers turn avidly from one novel to another, without pause for rereading, has led to a corresponding set of esthetic values. Hence the overemphasis upon the element of 'surprise' <despite> as a factor in esthetic appeal, for 'suspense' is now universally conceived in terms of 'surprise,' despite the fact that one can feel 'suspense' in hearing a piece of music with which one is perfectly familiar; and Greek audiences underwent 'suspense' when witnessing dramas whose plots were traditional. But suspense is formally more substantial than mere uncertainty of outcome, even when one has 'identified himself' with the characters of the fiction. There is a fundamental difference between art on the one hand and competitive sports on the other.[85] For we would resent the thought that the outcome of a game might have been settled in advance by collusion among the players. And we would be just as resentful if the outcome of a play depended simply on the toss of a coin or on a last-minute decision of the actors. Even when the ending of a play has been changed, we are satisfied only if the new ending is felt to grow 'inevitably' out of the preceding action."

260: on Heisenberg:[86] "Statements about the nature of the world's substance can never be established any more firmly by instruments than they can by words."

Much too heavy a burden placed on language here. Notice that he says "statements about," thus clinching his case (because "statements" necessarily involve "words"), rather than "knowledge of."

260: Burke knows nothing of physics. He thinks the physicists are reading the inadequacy of their instruments back into nature.

261: on Aristotle's entelechy: "Everything that comes into existence moves toward an end. This end is the principle of its existence; and it comes into existence for the sake of its end."

263 ff: on unity in diversity: ". . . the 'high orders of abstraction,' when *personalized,* can become replicas of the 'unchanging self,' hence a delight insofar as one is pleased with oneself, and a bondage insofar as one would be reborn."

85. Burke's exact wording is "competitive sports and games of chance."

86. Warner Heisenberg, German physicist, announced the principle of uncertainty (or indeterminacy) in 1927, which states that it is impossible to determine simultaneously the position and velocity of an electron in motion because of the presence of the observer.

264: on Japanese propagandists and "action–passion" configuration: not *passively* suffering attack, but *actively* drawing the enemy in for the counterblow.

265: on Gods, Furies, tribal and individual motives: "In proportion as men's sense of *tribal* identity is uppermost, a supernatural vocabulary of motives (either divine or Satanic) is felt adequate."

267: on Hegel and "world–historical individual": ". . . one who, in consciously following the lead of merely personal interests and ambitions, unconsciously furthers the designs of the Universal Dialectic." This something like Caudwell's idea of the Hero (essay on T. E. Lawrence).[87]

267: "But modern freedom, as the slogan of an upstart middle class, was polemic, propagandistic, a doctrine of partial slaves in partial revolt, as with its stress upon service and utility. In proportion as the social values of this rising class became the norm, the original upstart aspect of modern libertarianism was transferred to socialism and anarchism. . . . The development of business had so circumscribed the concepts of practical or moral utility within monetary limits, that the original religious and moralistic vocabulary of bourgeois apologetics became more and more like a sheer Rhetorical evasion of the Grammatical realities."

"For it had become too undeniably obvious that political actions and passions [clever!!] are a major aspect of 'reality' as now constituted. [from Thos. Mann, I believe] Where motives are vigorously actual, these are the themes of art."[88]

Burke, the great *Categorizer.*

269: Burke says by means of showing his grammatical terms to underlie all psychologies, ancient and modern, he can point up the resemblances and disresemblances (but mostly the resemblances).

Sure, you can make anything jibe with anything else if your categories are broad enough; "action" and "passion" are pretty broad.

You would think scientists and artists had spent their time over hundreds of years attempting to do nothing but "conceal" Burke's terms and categories.

273: on Aristotle's concept of the third principle, or ground, which makes possible any given dialectic. Burke believes this is the principle of "potentiality."

87. Christopher Caudwell is the pseudonym for Christopher St. John Sprigg. His essay appeared in *Studies in a Dying Culture* (New York: Dodd, Mead and Co., 1938).
88. The quotations occur on pp. 267 and 268.

273–274: on terms "active" and "passive," and the possibilities of a third *linguistic* voice <when> to resolve them: problem of linguistic voice (active, passive) in different languages: of third resolving "*voice.*"

278 #1: "Beauty" (Emerson): "Nature disciplines the will."[89] Such tripe.

On Dewey's and Mead's "biologism" as linking system between "purpose" and "agency": *The bodily organs are means to ends.* Each organ carries out "purpose" for which it was designed, and it serves in furthering the survival of the organism.

Read poetry with an eye to structural principles—the principles of organization of rhythm and image.

Writing poetry: find what the limits are within which the poem's invention shall be circumscribed.

"Utterance I": I wanted to write a poem with some *believing* in it.[90]

{The general emphasis in this journal on critical readings and the lack of otherwise convincing internal evidence make dating the end of Notebook II difficult. It is likely, however, that Dickey continued entries into 1953, given the use of past tense in the final entry and the publication date of the poem.}

89. The quotation occurs in the second paragraph.
90. Dickey's poem was included in *Soundings: Writings from the Rice Institute,* published by the Owen Wister Society in 1953.

Notebook III

The briefest of all the bound ledgers, the third notebook contains seventy-three written pages and provides the first material that Dickey specifically dates. The initial entry is dated February 5, 1952, and subsequent notations also are dated within the same month. Because he remained on active duty for the Korean conflict until the summer of 1952, Dickey wrote part of the third notebook while in the service. The final journal entry is dated November 14. The year likely is still 1952, after he had returned to his teaching duties at Rice, partly because the ledger is not completely filled and partly because the extensive plans for his fiction, which constitute the majority of the entries, exhibit little development in style or subject matter, which one might expect if the notebook spanned two years. Then, too, no internal evidence conclusively indicates that Dickey continued writing in the notebook into 1953. Neither the publication dates of the books he cites nor the dates of critical essays he is reading suggest with certainty the later year. Dickey does mention Erich Auerbach's *Mimesis* on page 28 of his notebook, a translated edition of which was published in 1953 (though he incorrectly lists the publisher as Yale University Press instead of Princeton). Yet two chapters of Auerbach's study had appeared in separate issues of *Partisan Review* in 1950, and *Kenyon Review* had published another chapter in 1952. Moreover, on page 45 of the ledger, he suggests using parts of a poem titled "Harp Quartet" in a then-unfinished poem, "The Anniversary," which was published in the June 1953 issue of *Poetry.* It is possible that Dickey finished "The Anniversary" early enough in 1953 for *Poetry,* a monthly literary magazine, to print the poem in June, but it is more likely that it was completed in 1952.

Attempting to use the journal more efficiently, Dickey drew a line across the top of the final written page and began a section devoted exclusively to *The Casting.* He labeled this part "Journal of the Novel." Its lone entry cites the work's lack of detail as its principal stylistic difficulty. That *The Casting* receives so little attention here suggests that Dickey's interests had turned elsewhere.

Those other interests include a detailed outline for what Dickey labels "the building of the rational poem." His distinction between two types of poems—poetry of "form" and poetry of "release"—leads to an extensive and systematic analysis of how to create or build the former and his projected use of a pseudonym when writing the latter. He hopes that if he writes both kinds, a cross-fertilization will occur, similar to what Dickey intends in later published volumes such as *The Strength of Fields* (1979) and *The Eagle's Mile* (1990) in which he creatively translates poets such as André Frénaud, Vicente Aleixandre, Pierre Reverdy, Lucien Becker, Michel Leiris, and others. The notebook establishes an internal debate, as it were, between, on the one hand, poetry that utilizes traditional techniques of stanza, meter, and rhyme and that the poet methodically plans in advance, and on the other hand, poetry that derives essentially from the unconscious and that is word-centered and word-led. The debate will continue, for both *Sorties* and Dickey's essay "The G.I. Can of Beets, The Fox in the Wave, and The Hammers over Open Ground," published in 1983 in *Night Hurdling*,[1] clearly reveal the same concern. Later, as here, Dickey's interest lies in creating a third kind of poem that melds the other two types, allowing the mind unrestricted play with language that the poet then confines through a self-determined set of restrictions, what he labels in a notebook entry "the situation as it utters itself through me."

As with the previous notebooks, Dickey is reading extensively—essays in literary journals such as *Partisan Review;* philosophical works such as Werner Brock's translation of Heidegger, *Existence and Being;* and artists such as Wallace Stevens, Rainer Maria Rilke, and Hugo von Hofmannsthal. He rigidly patterns his day from noon until bedtime to focus his efforts more effectively, using a schedule that he often fails to follow. He also struggles to make succinct statements or pronouncements on what poetry and fiction must be or must accomplish, believing that a thorough understanding of the nature of each art form is necessary to better his own creative efforts. A poem, for example, should require the poet to become something, should capture the essence of a thing, and should always anticipate the final line as it develops. In fiction, actions or episodes convey meaning; they become symbolic. In poetry, however, "symbols are usually *objects,*" which explains why poems do not inherently require action. Yet more than anything else, the third notebook centers on Dickey's projected short stories and novels, which he lists and on which he elaborates to the extent of planning the manner of their publication.

Dickey projects a collection of nine short stories titled *Sennacherib and Other Stories,* while additional entries present ideas for almost a dozen other stories. Although notation regarding these stories is uneven, the principal thematic concern is the failure of relationships, whether in warfare ("The Eye of the Fire" and "Through the Silver Log"), within

---

1. *Night Hurdling,* 124–40.

a family ("The Porpoise," "The Hawk," and "Reeds, Shadows"), or between men and women ("The Spring Garden," retitled "Dialogue," and "Sennacherib"). These stories generally depict an individual separated from that which might vitalize him. In "The Eye of the Fire," for example, an Army Air Force recruit experiences a sexual reaction to a low-level firebombing, an intensity of sensation that reveals the inadequacy of other daily experiences. Robert, the central figure in "Reeds, Shadows" and the illegitimate son of a Jewish New York broker, meets his biological father but fails to achieve a camaraderie that would recapture the sense of identity he previously felt with other soldiers during World War II. The married recallee in "The Spring Garden" cannot reestablish the closeness he once experienced with a Louisiana woman. Their chance affair during his visit to New Orleans, and the deceit that permitted it, causes her to react "conventionally" when he calls her again two months later while being shipped to the coast. Because he inexplicably cares for her, he senses loss. Unlike *The Casting*, these stories exhibit no mythology and little history. Only "Sennacherib," which involves an affair between a waitress and a history professor, displays aspects of history, as she learns the names of ancient rulers at a tourist court called The Assyrian Kings.

Although the narrative details of other stories remain problematic, many also involve the inability of the protagonists to achieve meaning or consequence in their lives. They search for someone or something to enhance the present or redeem the past but do not succeed. For example, an untitled story focuses on an old or "perpetually young" artist (Dickey's model is E. E. Cummings) who attempts to "reconstruct the past" by writing "fresh" love poetry. While he almost triumphs in writing the poem that captures what his now-dowdy wife once meant to him, he compromises on "cleverness," and she never suspects his near-success. Another untitled story involves a young man who begins to date an older woman, his high school idol. However, she is demoralized because of the failure of another relationship, and he remains unable to do anything but reiterate his love. In "The Grotto" Dickey uses Hemingway's "The Three-Day Blow" as a precedent to present two young recallees, one of whom is Polish. He talks bravely about Polish history and heroes, attempting to achieve an importance commensurate with what he feels the other recallee possesses. In the end, however, this effort fails to elevate him.

In addition to *The Casting*, Dickey identifies or elaborates on almost a dozen other novels that he contemplates writing. Most are untitled, but like the short stories, they suggest a search for integration. *The Snows of Brothers*, for example, concerns two men who should be devoted to one another but who remain estranged because of previous misunderstandings. As with poems such as "The String," "The Underground

Stream," and "In the Tree House at Night," its genesis owes to the death of Dickey's older brother Eugene from meningitis. Another projected novel depicts the efforts of a mother to raise her son according to the imperatives of a sensitive yet dictatorial father by having him read music, philosophy, and literature. The son "loses himself" in the Army; at the conclusion, he is writing for pulp magazines, hoping finally to arrive literarily where his parents had him begin. Dickey also discusses another untitled novel, tentatively a hundred pages in length, about Air Force recallees, that would portray their inability to establish meaningful relationships with women and the consequences of this failure. Interestingly, he also projects a character called The Pistol-Shot for a future allegorical novel.

That Dickey seriously worked at his fiction and considered it a possible career is indicated by his beginning a work titled *The Entrance to the Honeycomb,* which concerns the problem of maturity, specifically the issue of how one attains such growth if others do not recognize one's being mature. As the fifth notebook reveals, an editor from Doubleday, Lee Barker, read the manuscript in the late spring of 1953, though he declined it. Dickey's commitment to fiction is also indicated by his plan to "yoke 'by violence' together" four of his projected works to produce what he calls a "Big novel." This tetralogy of sorts was to consist of a work about Florida and old people; a shorter work titled *The Journey of the Brothers* that centers on an elderly historian; a novel called *The Repossession of Assyria,* in which this old man attempts to recapture Assyria in his imagination; and a work titled *Figure,* which presents the aftermath of the Pacific campaign in World War II. Dickey wanted these fictions to be published in four separate volumes, an ambitious project for a writer who had not yet published any fiction and who had published only two poems in respected journals.

{Dated entries in Notebook III establish the period during which it was in use. When Dickey began this journal, he had been recalled to duty because of the Korean conflict and was stationed at Connally Air Force Base in Waco, Texas.}

5 Feb. 1952: tomorrow try a more <conceptional> conceptual poetry rather than the allegorical. Two or three fair poems completed, ready to go. My thought seems to run entirely in images rather than propositions. These come later, if they come.

6 Feb.: good poem—"The Love." Written quickly, very easily. Talk with Col. Couser. Interested in teaching: some intelligence, honest, conscientious. Other lieutenant, Nelson, too assertive, one of these "I'll have to disagree with you, etc." people. Read "Many Thousands Gone," James Baldwin, *Partisan Review:* good on American Negro, rather rapt, some extremely penetrating insights.[2] Read "Joyce's Dublin" by Joyce's brother Stanislaus.[3] Gene Hairston—Villemain fight. Good, close.

I must organize my time better. There is a quality in observation which makes it more than observation. I must insist to myself on this. Look intently, think, think of all possible meanings. Weed out what the best emotional (or *felt*) ones are and what the best intellectual are, and explore.

Not much interested in my novel but will complete it more or less as an apprenticeship and in an attempt to salvage what I think <might> may be several good episodes.

Barrett in *Partisan* on American fiction and values. Barrett here good, as usual.[4]

Galsworthy on Conrad. Conrad's feverish working habits. Read more Conrad.[5] Especially letters.

---

2. *Partisan Review* 18:6 (1951): 665–80. Baldwin argues that the dehumanization of the Negro is indivisible from the dehumanization of America and that the loss of American self-awareness stems from the annulment of black identity. Paradoxically, moreover, Americans are unable to allow blacks to forget their past. They "re-invest" Negroes with their guilt because of "an unrealized need to suffer absolution." Compare Dickey's essay "Notes on the Decline of Outrage," in *Babel to Byzantium*, 257–78.

3. *Partisan Review* 19:1 (1952): 103–9. This essay reviews Patricia Hutchin's *James Joyce's Dublin*.

4. See "American Fiction and Values," *Partisan Review* 18:6 (1951): 681–90. The essay is a review of John W. Aldridge's *After the Lost Generation*. Barrett suggests that the United States has not produced a great work of literature in the past decade because American life tends away from "the emotional and organic depths" from which great literature has sprung.

5. See H. V. Marrot's *The Life and Letters of John Galsworthy* (New York: Charles Scribner's Sons, 1936).

11 Feb.: plan of a kind of action:

Explore a kind of poetry in which I am most interested; under the name "Virgil Shawker" build poems word by word: "build the word to release it." Tradition is unconscious and shapen, Graham's "poetry of release." Forebears are Perse, Thomas, Graham, Herbert Read, Hart Crane—all those word-led men. Also, under your own name, continue in "the forms," one every other day: Lowell, Valéry, Bridges, the metaphysicals, W. S. Merwin. Cultivate side by side. The exchanges should be interesting. Tomorrow I begin to go earnestly into poetry instead of fooling around. I would like to know and use "the forms" before discarding them. Ern Malley a good forebear as a hoaxer.[6] In this sense the hoaxer <was> revealed some of the depths of the kind of poetic construction I would like to do: philosophy, politics, and metaphysics of the hoax, the hoaxer: Poe. The hoaxer's art reveals the essentially serious core at the center of the <essential> mechanical frivolity of the (mere) <mechanics> technics of poetry. To a mind which cultivates words and images, the poem will seem to leap into them, as an animal creates his own shape in the net that confines him. The net is nothing without the beast, but perhaps it would be better were he free. Richard Wilbur's "genie in the bottle" a terribly tame creature.[7]

"So cleft, half in that light
Gate, bright head's (anointure) anointment
Knows, all under every angel lies a lust
Crossed, bearing a red love sight
Crossed round and passaged as ↑(in)↓ a raging font." Etc.

What I want from these strange poems is contrast, burden, the sense of lifting an angelic weight obscurely, in darkness and a breaking confusion.

6. Ernest Malley was the fictional creation of two Australian poets, Donald Stuart and James Macauley. Intent on debunking modern poetry, they wrote sixteen poems during the course of an afternoon and, posing as Malley's sister Ethel, sent them to Max Harris, editor of *Angry Penguins*. Believing their story that Malley had died at age twenty-six of Graves' disease, Harris put out a special issue of his journal as well as a first edition of Malley's extant poems titled *The Darkening Ecliptic*. Dickey used one line from the book's epigraph in *Alnilam* and attributed it to Joel Cahill: "Do not speak of secret matters in a field full of little hills." Stuart and Macauley finally exposed the hoax. Dickey became aware of the controversy while in combat during World War II.

7. From Wilbur's essay "The Genie in the Bottle," *Mid-Century American Poets,* ed. John Ciardi (New York: Twayne, 1950). The essay presents Wilbur's responses to questions involving a poetry's aural intent, audience, language, allusion, irony and paradox, subject matter, imagery, rhyme, and structure. Wilbur concludes by asserting, "In general, I would say that limitation makes for power: the strength of the genie comes from his being confined in a bottle."

Work out of this procedure. Let it become of its own accord complex, and work out the several themes.

Boxing a staged clash of wills really bent on destruction. That it is done for money is a comment on the crowd's unformulated <desire> belief that they can pay for the <sublimated> sublimation of their inmost personal and collective desires.

In this new poetry, begin with *a set of terms* and work through sounds. Really *listen* to the sounds the words and lines make.

Terms suggestive, to be related.

Type figure: "the *virgin juries*."[8]

12 Feb.: in *poetry* and, to a certain extent, prose:
   The answer I want lies partly, I think, in a thorough exploration and exploitation of syntax. I shall study this: "gentle masking." Good poem: "Address." Worked well on novel. Finished second chapter, first draft.

I must stop slopping and think sharply; I must ask always "Why" and "How."

Sketch for the building of the rational poem: these must be answered: question:
   1. What is the subject?[9] What is the *general* subject? Grief, joy, renunciation, acceptance, avowal, love, lust, hatred, death, life? A combination? Antithesis? Development from, (through), to?
   2. What attitude toward the subject is to be expressed? Confusion, understanding, immersion, helplessness before or under? (Conversion from one thing to another?) Awakening?
   3. With the first two clearly defined, the *method* begins to make itself clear. The burden of the poem is thrown wholly onto an answer to the question: What ↑devices↓ will best get this said? Be most vivid, powerful, moving, and profound? This perhaps is something like the "objective correlative." The correlative, however, is only "objective" in order finally to reside in the imagination. Its "objectivity" is simply a making available of a certain ↑image or↓ train of images to the individual imagination to "mean" what it will and does.

8. From "Listen, Put on Morning," in W. S. Graham's *The White Threshold*.
9. Dickey places a small "a" preceding the following sentence. When he occasionally uses a *1* without a *2* or an *a* without a *b,* these have been omitted to maintain Dickey's intended outline format and the omission has been noted.

The questions may then be subdivided into the "personal" characteristics of the particular poem, all to turn round the considerations: what devices will *best* make available the decided–upon attitudes:

    a. Who is speaking? What voice? Active or passive? Where?
        1. First person
        2. Second person (very limited use) addressed
        3. Third person

These considerations require considerable exploration.

    b. *Why* is he speaking?

Usually[10] implicit in the poem but may be used as a deliberate device: ("Because I do not hope to turn again.")[11]

    c. What is the setting?

Some setting, to be related intimately to the imagery[12] by comparison and/or contrast, is <by definition a part of> a part of the poem. It is either stressed, to be let emerge, or implicit: ("Silk bars the road, a spider rope"). Is it a reflection, reminiscence, an anticipation? How combine these?

Now a gathering up: take stock: line up and integrate what has thus far been achieved. Follows

↑poem as rehearsal↓:[13] A rehearsal of possibilities as to imagery (or is the poem to be relatively imageless? conceptual?):[14] Kind:

    a. <Violent> Active (violent)
    b. Passive (still)
        and combinations
    c. Sight (predominant), sound, smell, touch, taste
    d. What is the *context* of the imagery; what is to *link* the images? A knowledge of the genius operative beneath mediaeval statuary? Physics (Empson)? Freud? Mythology? All men's grief, joy, common knowledge? ↑Or no context? an interplay?↓
    e. See section on "words." How may the image best be verbalized? Best be integrated with, moved *through* the language, words of the poem, best be *expressed by* them?

Setting: Something moved through? In? Or static (as a still life)? How, how much moved through or static? *Why?*

---

10. The entry has "1" preceding "Usually."
11. From T. S. Eliot's *Ash-Wednesday.*
12. Dickey parenthetically adds here, "see bottom next page 6," which refers to the section below titled "Syntax."
13. The entry has "(a)" before "A rehearsal."
14. Dickey has "1" before "Kind."

Stanza form or form in general. This is a difficult thing to determine:[15]

a.[16] May the poem best be expressed through a series a linked (imagery, concepts) and developing packages ↑(stanzas)?↓ <Or does it follow a long> Or does it *seem to want to* flow a long way at once, without conceptual or syntactical break?

b. If a stanzaic form is to be used, *which* stanzaic form? Rimed? Unrimed? How many feet to which line? ↑Rime as *organizational factor*—↓

1. If a rime scheme suggests itself, are the rimes to be full rimes, or slant or assonant rimes? Rimes as I see them are by nature "clinchers," intensifiers. The harder the conclusion is to be made, the harder the rime should be struck. (This rather a shallow notion but a fair beginning). What do we rime *for*? Simply to satisfy an essentially meaningless convention? Assonant or slant rime a kind of subtlety device, making us realize connections where there apparently were none: work "undercover." Is the rime to be feminine? What are the uses of these? Look up. Feminine: inconclusive, delicately unbalanced.

2. How may the stanza rime? Couplets? It is possible, although considerable mastery is involved, to make a convention (of rime) work against itself, to make the heroic couplet non-epigrammatic, and to express a slow-paced movement of the emotions in tetrameter couplets. Must the rime of <the couplet> the stanza recur like a memory (<a> repetition of an early line-end in a late) or must it bang closed like a gate (closing couplet, full-rimed). Must it be touched very lightly (slight slant rime, early-late repeated), a faint gong or whisper?

These things must be worked out.

Enjambment? Where? Use sparingly.

Meter:

a. What is the metric to accomplish? Is it to dance? Or plod? Shake? Be firm, conclusive? Is it to tear along (Tourneur, Roy Campbell) or be struck off slowly like bells?

b. At what stage of the game is the meter to do exactly what? What syllable is to be emphasized; what balance or imbalance of weights to be achieved? Where do we need a foot substituted, the spell retarded, impelled forward, made to sink, rise, circle, hover, stop, begin again? Dance music or dirge or any balance?

---

15. In the notebook the section beginning here on stanza form precedes Dickey's comments on setting. However, Dickey drew an arrow in the margin connecting section "e" under "Now a gathering up" with his statements on setting to indicate their continuity. The sections have been arranged accordingly.

16. Dickey placed "1" before "a."

Syntax:

a.[17] Is the poem to be expressed logically, conceptually, syllogistically (Overt, or motivating undisclosed)?

b. What syntactical distortions, if any, are justified, and why?

c. Declarative sentences? Questions? Rhetorical or really questions? Balanced or loose sentences? How do these several jibe with <the> other technical considerations (meter, stanza-length, etc.)?

Sound:[18]

What sound pattern for any given territory of the poem? An overall pealing-together of sounds? Opposition, contrast? Overall slow weaving or staccato breakage all along a given line in contrast? Sound as device <of> for congruence, emphasis, re-emphasis. As mood-establisher, dispeller. How does the sound go with <the> other considerations (meter, imagery)? A development of one kind of sound pattern (also with imagery, syntax, meter) into another? A displacement in favor of another? Why? What is accomplished?

Symbol, Allegory:

To what extent are the images to be "more than themselves," to stand for, represent, be replaced by, evoke? How precisely establish *this* degree? (Tone, emphasis by the various technical devices).

Analogy? Metaphor? Simile? Local or extensive (Metaphysicals)? Linked? Progressive? Digressive? Unravelling?

To what extent is narrative to be employed?

How is the poem to proceed, develop? By what means? Logic? Illogic? Association? Repetition? (Of what?) Dream? The subconscious? Conceptually? Train of images? Development of one central image? Metamorphosis of image, sound?

Words:[19]

What word had better be used here? Why? How much strength to give to adjectives, adverbs, etc., under the <developing> self-developing laws of the poem's problem? How do the words ride under the ↑(now)↓ existing laws?

Revision: how to take out, put in, so that the whole rides together, addles the imagination and resettles it, by its variously-wrought magics, into more permanent forms?

17. Dickey numbered the considerations under syntax. The numbers have been replaced with letters to maintain his original outline method.
    18. Dickey began the following paragraph with "a."
    19. Dickey began the following paragraph with "1."

This whole diagram is <a> directed toward developing a program of action to answer: What is to be done with the impulse, or whatever arrives from "inspiration"? It is <unlikely> impossible that a good poem should develop out of the impulse unaided.

Make a marriage between meaning and sound, and experiment with interplay. Try always to encourage the exploratory sense of language in every phase.

Out of a careful rendition and exploration of these possibles the poem <should> develops.

I wish a subtle, introverted poetry, nuanced well and strongly, subtly sensitive where Graham is heaving and rockbound.

Beginning or part of a story in which I would like to combine a Lawrentian sense of life (sensual life) in a decayed or decaying background, perhaps the aftermath of a war: nightmare and sensuality: the incipient, sensual poet on a mental jag during which the actual carnage and his mental processes become indistinguishable.

"Sitting on the stone, after he had gone on for a time and then stopped <for a while> to rest, he was for a while aware of the dull, toneless moan of the thicket of trees in which he found himself. His hair blew lightly across his forehead, <as> the breeze itself a stillness to lay across his cool head, in which any motion it provoked, as to the sleeper, was a delight and a care not to be ordered in common ways."

This too "knowing": must try for more physical *substance,* strength, "*withness.*"

To write "out of" the brute and animal nature of reality, to deal with essences, entelechies [Rilke, (Graham), Roethke] *as if I were* a stone, frond, tiger, kiss. There is too much clever, "judged" poetry, "judged and rendered" verse. I would like a poetry which proceeds naturally (or *is*) from the situation or encounter, which is the *essence* of its make-up, its being, which is the situation as it utters itself through me.

In poetry, you have to let yourself feel *in behind* what you are trying to do. You must allow the original experience, or an invented one, perhaps more original, to begin to word itself, darkly or blindingly, and to see itself in the words. The uncontributing words and the too-meaningful and so meaningless words are cracks in the mirror, ripples in the moving water, to be excised. You must allow the poem to invent itself and its meaning simultaneously: Blake, Crane, Graham, Smart, Thomas, Clare, Hölderlin. Try to implement the *natural* form: "every artist is *half a critic*" (Elizabeth Bowen).[20]

"Tiered responses."

Poetry: "to get hold of some of the *muscular certainty* of reality."

Heidegger: "Only he who is steeped in the philosophic tradition, understanding the thought of the great thinker of the past, as if it were his own, philosophising with him, as it were, in dialogue and only then criticising him constructively, would eventually develop philosophic problems in an original manner worthy of being contemplated by his own contemporaries and by posterity."[21]

The "coördinates" of different systems of poetry, and of all poetry.
   1. What is stressed.
   2. What is omitted.
   3. How the stressed is stressed.

Heidegger: "Time is the transcendental horizon of the problem of Being."[22]

Heidegger: "the-Being-Towards-One's-Death."[23]

Don't be driven to your work, even by yourself. You are a creator. Glory in it.

Story: sexual reaction to low-level firebombing:
   Scenes: 1. Recruit from airstrip: remote, very fair, his hands always in beautiful repose ("Up from Tacloban").[24]
   2. Leave in Manila after few convoy-cover: "blazing and screaming on a red couch with spikes driven through her nipples": fire.
   3. Trip to Manila with serious pilot: had boy draw wife's picture: "put that boy through art school": "and when the main gear buckled on

---

20. See the Foreword of Bowen's *Collected Impressions* (New York: Knopf, 1950): v–vi.
   21. From *Existence and Being* (Chicago: Henry Regnery Co., 1949), 7. The book, in addition to presenting translations of four Heidegger essays, also contains an introduction by Werner Brock and his analysis of the former's *Being and Time*. The quotations, properly speaking, are from Brock.
   22. From *Existence and Being*.
   23. Ibid.
   24. Besides "Up from Tacloban," Dickey also considered "The Fire Music" and "The Eye of the Fire" before deciding upon the last as a title for this story.

landing and the \<plane> C-47 slid incredibly off the runway into a ditch, he merely braced himself in the navigator's compartment, and then got up and walked out": slept heavily while the conscientious pilot sweated: the gold-toothed Filipino whore: "My little eggs," "the terrible groans of pleasure."

4. After the firebombing he volunteers: "I will," he said intently. "I will. I will." White crust on \<his> the upper leg of his flying suit, which he never washed.

Crushed abundant green and sour mud.

"Down with Japanese puppets."

Critical study: "Poetry and Attitude."

Books:
  1. *The Later D. H. Lawrence* — ed. N.Y. Tindall — Knopf.
  2. *American Literary Criticism* — ed. Chas. Glicksberg — (Hendricks House).
  3. *The Life of the Virgin Mary* — Rainer Maria Rilke — Philosophical Library.
  4. *The Man With the Blue Guitar* and *Ideas of Order* — Wallace Stevens — Knopf.
  5. *A Little Treasury of Modern Poetry* — ed. Oscar Williams — Scribner's (*revised edition*).

Blackmur and the other New Critics: the determination to work at no superficial level eliminates a good deal of explanatory material which would seem to be indispensable.

Book: *Oswald Spengler* — (20th Century Library).

Prose of Hugo von Hofmannsthal — Pantheon.

Mimesis — Erich Auerbach — Yale.

Volume of stories: \<*The Porpoise*> *Sennacherib and Other Stories:*
  1. "The Eye of the Fire"
  2. \<The Buffalo Hunters (novel)>
  3. "The Porpoise": (Vacationers) drive through wood:
      (a) At Hampton River: small boy and father on first fishing trip together. Boy and father do not know each other very well. Boy buys father hat: hard to tell whether a man's or a woman's. He has a straw sombrero. Hat makes a heart-shape of the face: peak over brows. Father explains about sun. Wears sombrero. "Valentine hat."
      (b) Fishing gear: Mr. Brady and nephew: live at boarding house: boy fifteen.

(c) Carries barefooted son over muck and oyster shells. Boat needs bailing: shrimp box. Mr. Brady rows out to drop.

(d) Advice to group by proprietor of fishing camp: "Soldier": had been in First World War. Brown skin, Negro helper "Clarence."

(e) Drop: through eye of hollow log, 500 yd. offshore.

(f) Dark day: waves move uneasily and with a sudden random violence.[25]

(g) Porpoises surface near boat: grape-colored backs: Brady's boy: "What would happen if one came up under the boat?" Father remembers beached shark. "They push drownded men to shore."

(h) Not good fishing: a few cats and dogfish: Father baits boy's hook: throws catfish[26] toward stern of boat: fin sticks in boy's leg. He starts up unbelievingly and in horror (thinks Father does not love him): sways in boat. At same time a huge porpoise surfaces with a rolling motion not five yards from the boat, his blow-hole visible.

(i) Father catches boy, who quivers with terror, very white, and takes fish off skin. Lightning like a map against the sky.

(j) Mr. Brady rows home against the tide.

(k) Boy sits silently in car. Father wonders if, <by> when they reach the shore bridge, he should replace the straw (if this would do any good).

4. "The Spring Garden":
  (a) Recallee.
  (b) North Florida: (Biloxi).
  (c) Long trip to New Orleans: has wanted to see it.
  (d) Meets girl, does not tell her he is married.
  (e) Go to (Pat O'Brien's)[27] garden. Armed Forces Day: planes go over.
  (f) Cabildo:[28] glittering costumes: poor girl's dreams of splendor, etc.

25. Following this, the notebook reads: "(g) Not good fishing: a few cats and dogfish: Father baits boy's hook: throws cat toward stern of boat: fin sticks in leg." However, in the margin an arrow indicates that the unlettered wording underneath this entry should follow "(f)." I have labeled this addition "(g)" and placed it to maintain Dickey's intended sequence.

26. Dickey rewrote the original "g" entry, which became "h" after he inserted the new entry above it. I have combined his revised entry, which begins "Father throws catfish," with the original.

27. A bar located in the French Quarter of New Orleans.

28. The Cabildo, located in New Orleans, was the ancient seat of Spanish rule and, beginning in 1789 when the colony was returned to France, the French Town Hall. The scene of the formal transfer of Louisiana to the United States in 1795, it is now a museum, one floor of which contains the story of the Carnival, displaying costumes, jewels, and men's and women's fashions.

(g) Her "office."

(h) Hotel: she wants to be seduced: liquor: thin, heron-like motion.

(i) Menstruation: "How can I?" "You can."

(j) He writes her the truth.

(k) Two months later he ships to the coast, passes through, calls her on an impulse. She reacts "conventionally." He somehow really cares for her; it had nothing to do with his wife and child. "I just felt awfully sorry for your wife."

(l) His sense of loss.

5. "Sennacherib":

(a) Told by waitress, just off. Talks to rich woman someone has sent to her. Drink beer, eat oysters.

(b) Tells of <teacher> ↑(history) professor↓ she knew: left his wife every weekend for a month. Tells her he will be divorced: "I knew his wife couldn't give him (the satisfaction) ↑what↓ he wanted. He never would have treated her like he did me." First sentence: "You ask me if I knew."

(c) "He liked to talk; we talked and drank. I was working in another restaurant then."

(d) Paper jungle (Scenic Wonderland): hillbilly music.

(e) Tourist court: palace: The Assyrian Kings: Sennacherib: he liked the sound of the name: acting out of passion: "tried to tie me to the light fixture, but I pulled it out. He beat the living fire out of me. I couldn't sit on my butt again for two weeks. ↑At first↓ I called him everything I could think of, but after two or three times I didn't. He would untie me and kiss my feet and tell me how much he loved me," etc. "And he would talk so intelligent."

(f) He leaves her: she has a terrible cold and drives to another town in rain. There is a wreck on the highway. Ambulance there: a wound under man's ear, shining in my lights. I laid down on the seat and cried.

(g) "Women are more considerate. I don't believe none of them ever mistreated me."

The day a machine can produce a masterpiece of art the human race is finished.

Story: "The Hawk":

George ↑(Jesse)↓, the man who kept Pop's chickens for a while and pulled out his automatic and fired at the hawk. He has "done time": this somehow known to children (two little boys), but forgotten by stages as they ride on horse: crystallized by moment of firing.

Told (perhaps by Jesse): stock-car races and chain-gang (Jesse Pratt and Roy Hall).[29]

Stories:
1. "The Eye of the Fire"
2. "Sennacherib"
3. "Dialogue" ("The Spring Garden")
4. "The Porpoise"
5. "The Buffalo Hunters"
6. "The Hawk"
7. "Where <Is> Lies This Stone <?> Delivered?": her furious screaming that she will not be able to perpetuate herself, that her image has been marred: idiot child passes over into real grief at funeral.
8. Story about Tom Swift and his paternity: confrontation: "he said he'd give me a job." Jewish father, etc.[30]

9. Hallucinated story about invasion: small church in old graveyard: someone has shot in at the window—a cold web, a small, stark, eloquent hole in the middle: little Negro boy: fisherman, Arlo. Confrontation of enemy officer and Arlo in eye of silvered tree concerning terms of report. Enemy: "I'm not sure ↑(yet)↓ what to report. There's no doubt but what we've got the place, but what have we got?"

Arlo: "We fish here, mostly," etc.

Question: who has tried to kill the preacher; he is mad, or almost. The Swinton brothers, gamblers, whom he preached against? The enemy? Arlo? The Negro boy?

An enemy soldier goes occasionally through the passionless (sword) grass, with a thrusting sound, etc.

The broad, low outlines of another island or of the coast: resorts, etc.: the tiny scrawl of a ferris wheel or roller-coaster.

In "Through the Silver Log": the silver log's eye coincides with web of bullet hole to fasten guilt <to> on Arlo rather than enemy.

Alex Comfort — *A Summer Campaign*.
John Hawkes — *The Beetle Leg*.

Just as there is no piece of writing wholly devoid of influence, there is none wholly devoid of originality.

---

29. Jesse Pratt was an ex-convict who did small jobs around the house for Dickey's parents, including driving the children to school. Roy Hall was a stock car driver in the late thirties.

30. Dickey's working titles for this story include "Reeds, Shadows" and "Through the Loft."

Short novel or story about a man following in the *wake* of a war, look-ing for something or someone: images of war tools as farm equipment: everything silent "and dead, not deadly":"harrow," etc. Perhaps in Africa. *Read up on Boer war: modern* war machines: vaguely Dutch or German names. Stark, simple, delicate language.

"Reeds, Shadows": illegitimate son of Jewish, New York broker <gives> has "interview" with father for job. <Another> Grandmother (father) on mother's side has reared him. After his discharge sends him to father. Mother an "entertainer" in the Twenties. Man whose name he bears a wastrel: "peed on stove," then lay down among the slanting daisies.

"You were in the war, weren't you, Robert?" "Yes, sir, <in> with the Rangers," etc. "British, you know," etc. Tells of raid. Father carries on business. Son talks on, talking to himself. Tells of lying in reeds, very full of himself: "I felt like for once I completely filled up my skin" (sense of identity).

At end of interview, they shake hands; son leaves knife—long blade, full of grease. Paper-opener. Father: "I must be sure not to cut my finger."

I would like to show here the sense of frustration the son has—that of many who have, in the violence of war, found a sense of solidarity which is dispelled by the (old, familiar) civilian world returned to.

"I wanted to pick that part of the coast up and carry it off with me" (a Southern accent).

Story about young girl (Louise Brown: poor)[31] and *old* doctor she works for: love story.

Story about an old ("perpetually young") poet (Cummings) whose forte is "fresh" love poetry and who must constantly reconstruct the past in which his now-dowdy wife meant to him what he can now say of her (in that time) in his poems, but no longer has need or wish to say. Tithonus.[32]

Here have "remarkable" passage about the "making of a poem," using the "rational poem" notes and relating them to the energetic wandering of his mind over *particular* events. The poem at last is impossible. He has

31. Louise Brown was a dentist's receptionist in Nashville whom Dickey dated while attending Vanderbilt University.

32. Tithonus in Greek mythology was a Trojan prince loved by the dawn-goddess Eos, who bore him Memnon. She begged Zeus to bestow immortality upon Tithonus but forgot to ask also that he grant him eternal youth. Consequently, Tithonus grew ever older and more decrepit until Eos, out of pity, changed him into a grasshopper.

almost hit it but must compromise on cleverness. His wife does not suspect his near-triumph.

Story: "Mary" or "The Divers": (Murphy Park Pool).[33] She: flat-faced, good figure, good diver. Two young wastrels. End: "and I (have no) ↑don't↓ doubt that in a couple of days they were going at it like minks."

Story: "The Intercessor(s)."

In poems you read, classify by
    1. Type figure
    2. Locution (how it is said: means used)
    3. Syntax
    4. Meter
    5. Tone.
Practice for discipline.

Try for *wonder*.

In "Dialogue" try to get the desperate striving after the sense of discovery of being in love that married men, wearied by its familiarities, believe they have lost. (End line): "I love you," he said. "Oh, I love you, I love you, I love you."

Two schools of novelistic thought: (1) The novelist sees that his characters go through a series of actions; they are *gears* that mesh in *situations*. The engine is *meaning, import*. (2) The novelist tells a story that has impressed him but whose meaning he cannot divine. He must assume that the events which impressed him, unfathomed as they are, are yet ↑the↓ important and vital ones.

How one man may embody history: "A personality is made up of *select excerpts* from his cultural history and that of his race." *Third novel* or fourth novel: how to *embody* this in a novel.

    1. *The Casting*
    2. Aftermath-of-war novel (dream novel)
    3. Florida and war novel
    4. Man-out-of-history novel
    5. *Sennacherib and Other Stories*.

---

33. A swimming pool in Atlanta. In the notebook this entry immediately follows "Tithonus," above, but a marginal arrow indicates Dickey intended the present arrangement.

To understand is everything; the effort to understand is more than everything.

Novel: don't overdo "wit," epigram.

Rilke: use of words: ". . . the belovèd *lost in advance.*" Practice akin something to Graham's. "*Told* into *law* by imagination's *error*" (mine).

One of the more important elements in <fiction is> structuring fiction is to pause at each place and think: "Given the terms of the story <here> at this point, what do I *need* here? What do *I need to have happen or said to get accomplished what should be accomplished here in the way* ↑in which↓ *it should be accomplished?*"

Reading novels and poems critically and carefully, taking notes on them, and thinking about *means* should go a long way toward giving me the technical skill I need. Motto: nothing slipshod, neither observing nor feeling nor thinking nor reading nor writing.

"The crown of images."

Where might one reach the "norm of clumsiness"? Where are its limits? A pointing-away from this seems at least as important as achieving "perfection" in technique.

The central problem for the poet is not so much form itself, but how form is to be achieved and known when it appears. *What* form is *appropriate,* and *why?*

Story: about a (young?) boy who takes out an older (girl) woman who was the idol of his high school years. She is demoralized because (of an affair?); he is helpless to do anything but reiterate his "love" (Martha Frost).

"Still half-drunk, staggering craftily toward <redemption> resurrection."

"He had (the kind of) a face [(this was especially true of the mouth)] that seemed precariously fastened to the front of his head, sagging and trembling of its own <weight> perilous weight."

Name: "Fever" (Fever Mims): "Hello, Fever," said Jack (Herlong), so called because of my light, bright-red complexion.

"The fever-bright (despondent) landscape."

"The landscape of the dancer."

How the dancer's motions transfix and transform her surroundings—
create her landscape.

"The mind rising toward its own surfaces."

"The crown of images in the darkening brain": story about poet
(Cummings): the slow, dark mind fading from the images, receding from
their perilous lack of weight, their undiscovered meaning.

Novel: I thought of myself as a strong, fair, open-faced (blond) boy, who
had just "discovered himself" saying to a girl: "I'm so sick of all this
niggling talk, everybody going around saying what they should. You're
a human being, aren't you? You must have some things you really like,
some you really hate. Let's get a few of them out in the open, in the sun,
where I can see them with you and talk about them (with you) and
maybe love them and you."

Psychological, moral, didactic poem on girls, soldiers, Biloxi, etc., in
(heroic or tetrameter couplets):
    "the meat-hooked shark
    (Has danced to clasp the wenches in his dark.)" ↑Dances among
his wenches in the dark.↓ Samuel Butler (1), Louis Simpson, Roy
Campbell, Pope, Dryden, Rochester, John Manifold, Saintsbury on
Pope and Dryden.[34] Try to rise past Lowell at the end: savagery, elo-
quence, and a (confused) delicate, against-my-will tenderness for these
exploited by themselves and others.
<Cyril Swift> Full or almost-full rhyme.
    Dual exercise: (1) This one ↑ as myself (even send to Spears).[35]
                   (2) "The Anniversary"—Cyril Swift.[36]

Yvor Winters' poetry: he's got his well-made clothes on, all right, but
you wish he would get up and move around in them a bit.

34. George Saintsbury published a volume on Dryden for the English Men of
Letters series, ed. John Morley (New York: Harper and Brothers, 1881). Both Pope and
Dryden are included in Saintsbury's *A History of English Prosody*, 3 vols. (London:
Macmillan, 1923 [1908]), which also contains a discussion on the use of the couplet.
    35. Monroe Spears, Dickey's professor at Vanderbilt, whose specialty was eighteenth-
century British literature. He became editor of *Sewanee Review* with the autumn 1952
issue, later accepted a poem Dickey submitted ("The Ground of Killing"), and invited
him to apply for a fellowship, which Dickey won. The arrow in this line points to "al-
most-full rhyme" in the line above.
    36. A pseudonym Dickey proposed to use for poems derived from his unconscious
or that he felt were not rationally conceived. See the entry for n. 42, below.

Problem: to be aware of the various *possibilities, directions,* linkages of images, etc., *to what purpose* of the poem. This has heretofore been my biggest difficulty. I have worked mostly with antithesis, metamorphosis. Simple notion, but fundamental:

1. *What* is to be said: content.
2. *How* is it to be said: form. This embraces all technical means.

A study of the metrics of common speech.

Two children (girls) running as fast as they can without falling, one trying to grasp the other's hand.

Guitar:
  "the ↑irrelevant↓ fingernail
  Borne in relevant images ↑figures↓ over the stream."

"Movement two ways" (music and water).

Poetry: make bold statements, or make statements boldly, and *let them ride (as though* you believed, and your belief compelled assent) to the round end. See how boldly Thomas steps into his poem.

In "The Anniversary" use whatever of "Harp Quartet" you can. Suggest *scene* of this in one or two stanzas: "my shirt / Softer than Hades."[37]

How many good images emerge from misreading<s of> words!

Stories:
  1. Two young men in swimming pool with water pistol. Boy: "Goodbye croo-el world" (off diving board).
  2. Ex-soldier (artillery: Ft. McPherson) trying to get a summer job as lifeguard at an exclusive place. Psychology and metaphysics of the "interview." "Soldier, Soldier," they shouted (end line). How he has played with the children of the post: scenes from Ft. McPherson: parade and polo grounds, old barracks.

Observe more: you cringe from it. *Think* about (describing and evaluating) *everything* you see.

Biloxi poem:
  "Lord, take them _____ where
  Thy lesser (altar-) gods prepare for war

---

37. "The Anniversary" appeared in the June 1953 issue of *Poetry* and is included in the appendix of Dickey's poems herein.

With this same _____ (ardor),
↑Another line or lines↓
The burnished wagon (and) the polished spear."

The game of tennis as "exhibition and rehearsal," the possibilities of *movement* the game creates all realized, and the ball plied effectively back and forth over the net—it is not a game at all here. Everything is directed toward a *future* realization ("if he really poured it on") except that he never does but only hints at what would happen if he did.

To write (poetry) in ways that are difficult for you and alien to you is one of the major tools of exploration one can have. Cocteau: "Learn what you can do and then don't do it."[38] You can write any kind of poetry in any form. To assume the mask the poem requires.

Notebook: record in small notebook during day things noticed in brief note, then ponder them and write them up at night.

Man and woman injured on motorcycle—remember and write up. Use in novel or short story. I need not be afraid of life, blood, or people now.

"Lord, I near Biloxi. (Girl on girl
Is mine.)"

"Under the increasing weight of the rain." Rain's "gentle urgency."

In story "Sennacherib": names she has learned—Sennacherib, Sargon, Pul.[39]

The poet: his careful choice.

Biloxi poem:
    "↑(and)↓ the grave children, rattled from their play,
    (Under) ↑Beneath↓ the unpropped comber's curling breath
    In <each>(their) sand↑(y)↓ castle↑s↓ hug themselves to death."

The war poems of Shapiro and Jarrell are not quite convincing. It is as though someone, dropping a coin on the table to hear it ring, had let the edge hit first.

---

38. Jean Cocteau (1889–1963), French writer, visual artist, and filmmaker whose versatility caused him to experiment continually in almost every artistic medium.
39. Sargon, king of Assyria (722–705 B.C.), destroyed Samaria and subdued Babylonia. Pul is the biblical name of Tiglath Pileser III (746–728 B.C.), the Assyrian king who invaded Israel. See Notebook I, n. 139, on Sennacherib.

"Biloxi" will take a great deal of work: Jefferson Davis' home.

Reading for analysis:
    Saintsbury: *History of English Prosody.*
    James: *Art of the Novel.*
    Poems: 1. Traditional; 2. Modern.
    Novel:
    Story:
    Philosophy:
    Notebooks: reflections, plans.
Bring the full play of the mind to bear on each task.

Novel and story: fiction.
    1. The *incidental* <background the action is played out against> fore-
ground
    2. The *emotional* background
    3. The "geographical" "
Interplay between #1 and #2 aided, abetted in whatever way, by #3
↑for↓ *tone.* #2 *issues in* #1: *interaction of these.*

"Biloxi" poem: Lemnos (from Milton).[40]

"He had a perpetual, soaked (wet) look."

You get the feeling that D. H. Lawrence never drew a full, easy breath;
he was always panting so.

In future allegorical novel: character: *The Pistol-Shot.*

End of "Biloxi":
    "Resource of that (bright world), ↑[renounced to (keeping)]↓, but
sleeping, sleeping."

The kind of intellectual snob-value that attaches itself to *precedent* in
imagery.

In story "Sennacherib," hint at something which would bear on the
<actual> historical Sennacherib's destruction by his son. "Like his own
blood rising up against him, as he said, with the (terrible) weapon of
pleasure" (something on this order).

"Sennacherib":

40. In *Paradise Lost* Lemnos is the island on which Mulciber lands, having been
thrown from Heaven by God (1.746).

"This kind of talk is hard to get into, you <being> from out at Pine Mountain estates, but (you) being a Pleasure Seeker, like, I guess, the rest of us, makes it where I don't fall <off the peg> plumb off the peg behind the stove and don't say nothing, but just take your money without no telling why.

There must be a <million> thousand women (sitting) like this, where it's raining and the streets looking like they're trying to turn blue (before night), with just no way to say where they're eating or knowing why <they did>."

Work on "Sennacherib" a long time. Get what you want.

Where would I improve on Graham's poetry is in having better particularized *objects*.

Second novel, aftermath of war, to be called *Figure:* essential that the protagonist be passive, a sensitive recorder but with numbed or atrophied (moral) judgment, that he be passive except <with> for a single, blazing (bizarre) act at the end, which is prepared (subtly) for during the narrative but is not anticipated.

Story: "The Grotto": about two (young) recallees (Joe Sokolewicz and myself)[41] living at Doctor Lemly's, drinking beer in that <cold> cool, dark-panelled atmosphere: the rapport established: both awaiting children: one brings in girl: "Would you like to go out for a while?" "Sure. I think I'll go to mass" (end). Music, "pragmatism." Polish boy calls other "Wolfgang Amadeus" as a term of affection. Precedent for talk (one is a petty intellectual, a Nietzscheite or existentialist) in Hemingway's "The Three-Day Blow." Perhaps have Pole "save" other from gas in tub. He talks of Polish history and patriots (attempting to give himself importance to match the other's) (this is destroyed in last act). Dedicate to Joe.

The poem should struggle and battle to reach, justify the last line. The end line of a poem must never be achieved (too) easily, must never be *donated* to the poem.

In fiction, as a rule, *episodes, occasions* are made the vehicles of meaning, whereas in poetry symbols are usually *objects*. This prefigures the *action* necessary to fiction, which is optional in poetry.

---

41. Sokolewicz roomed with Dickey in Waco, Tex., after both had been recalled to service during the Korean conflict. They became close friends partly because both had children born on the same day and partly because Sokolewicz read literature, particularly Robinson Jeffers and Norman Mailer.

In conscious poetry I want something *strong,* fast or ponderous, full of rapid passages and heavy ones like blocks of concrete (pathos of heaviness and anger). Let Cyril's stuff come and be what it will.[42] I suspect some of it will be delicate, full of light thews and unspoken regrets, light syllables and unresolved scorn, mythology and history.

Surely I can write the couplet with more success than Robert Lowell.

I:	12:00 – 6:00	Write
	12:00 – <2:00> 1:30	My poetry (conscious) craft
	1:30 – 1:45	loosen up: "image bank": 2 pages
	1:45 – 2:30	Cyril Swift
	2:30 – 5:00	Novel
	5:00 – 6:00	Stories

II:	6:00 – 6:30 or 6:45	Exercise
	7:00 – 8:00	Eat — Family

III:	8:00 – 9:00	Analyze poems: reconstruct them: notes
	9:00 – 10:00	" novel: notes or stories: notes
	10:00 – 10:30	Read philosophy (any form)
	10:30 – 11:00	<Read criticism or as desired> Outline book on

prosody: notes

	11:00	Bed.

Biloxi: protagonist accepts all of its sensual gratifications so fiercely that it becomes the strongest kind of condemnation of him and it. Keep mythology and Robert Lowell out of the poem. Get your own kind of metrical and imaginative drive.

Second novel: may not the scene in the deserted AF base partake of some of the terrible humour of Buster Keaton's and the girl's search for each other aboard the otherwise deserted ship in *The Navigator?*

"Biloxi": theme: Augustine at Carthage (slight reference).
    (End): ". . . that I (may) burn /
    Tight as ↑an arrowed↓ candle through the ↑fluttering (scattered)↓ corn
    To its calm light-empowered other face
            ↑ " -empowered (space-) place / ↓
    Myself
            its protruding wings /
    Lost

42. Cyril Swift, Dickey's proposed pseudonym.

adj. "Carthaginian"
(Dredging) Pulling the maidens from the shallows
By their fish-scale glittering hair."

Augustine: (1) starts from things without, (2) proceeds to things within, and (3) proceeds upward to God.

Beginning (2): "I wish it all."
   (1) (Avid) description (shark, gamblers, etc.).
   (2) Acceptance: *my* attitude toward "dredging the maidens."
   (3) Transcendence: phrases from Augustine.

Book: *The Responsibility of the Critic* — F. O. Matthiessen — Oxford.

Poetry: there is a sense in which you have to let the words flow up into the thought and blood it in, so that it becomes really possible to you. The words and rhythms coagulate about the idea in expressive or clumsy ways, when you turn the mind loose on <them> it (the idea). The poet's job is to pick up and work out those that are expressive and pick off and eliminate those that are not.

"The ceremony of communication."

A poem must have a center, usually not deliberately concealed.

Poem: "Sonnet in Couplets."

Story about an old professor who is a peeping Tom: "The Attendant": I'm the last who remembers her like that.
   Actually, he has never really been near the girl he remembers, but he imagines to himself *that she would have looked like this.* Write this after you finish novel.

Prosody: if you hear a line out in your head, you can hear the progression move into the next line, and so on throughout the entire poem. That is prosody—the product of the individual ear.

Novel: Julian has created a situation which he controls, which works for his private (most private!) interests, but in which he doesn't have to participate: the ↑(dramatization, ritualization of the)↓ inner success for the outer failure, ↑which↓ overtakes it, is substituted for it, replaces it, and overcomes it.

A poem must sing, itself, *together.* It must *sing* itself together.

People who talk about "adequate aesthetic theory" in regard to writing poetry are mistaken. It is enough to stand naked before experience and render <it as> selectively and passionately what of it you can.

Hart Crane's poetry grinds Winters' machine to pieces.

Auden is not nearly faithful enough to *objects,* as they *are,* in themselves.

Story: "Cyclops" (Boca Raton).[43]
    "Hurrah for Cyclops."

Most poets don't have any *drive.* That's why Robert Lowell looks so good.

My differences with R. P. Blackmur: his emphasis in poetry is in what the words move; mine, on what moves the words, what is realized *through* the words, not the realizing process. (The poetic experience rather than the means of evoking it).

Story: "The Flower-Room": back room of any flower shop: man tying funeral wreaths, etc.

Novel: *The Snows of Brothers:* the keeping apart by misunderstanding and interests people (two men) who should be devoted to each other.

Poetry: when I improvise freely and rapidly *within a form,* I get my best results. The poems look like they have occurred to me because they have.

Big novel: yoke "by violence" together:
    1. Florida: old people.
    2. *The Journey of the Brothers* (shorter: old man).
    3. *The Repossession of Assyria:* taken on by the old man: "to take what (I) know and *invent* from it is the only excuse for an historian. If I can regain Assyria, I can understand everything."
    4. The Pacific war: return: denouement.
Publish in separate volumes: 4 of them.

The Honeycomb: the problem is that of maturity. *How* does one reach maturity and can one ever reach it if he is not *recognized* as being mature?

43. Dickey was stationed at Boca Raton, Fla., in March 1944 for a radar course. While there, he qualified as a radar observer.

Important: the conjunction of metric with *jazz* solo. You get here what I want—the sense of improvisation and form. Everything from the slowest blues to the fastest runs—*this* is what Hart Crane missed. Langston Hughes uses only the blues *words:* high notes—thin vowels: low notes—long vowels: time measures, cutting of notes short and sharp: punctuation.

A poetry of really sincere body-worship. To carry on what Spender only hinted at in "Oh young men, oh young comrades."[44]

Novel with the really conscious use of words in a sentence (i.e. David Jones' *In Parenthesis*) as in poetry.

There should be a kind of poetry capable of being written, "great" without external references.

"Jazz" metrical theory: make some attempt to keep the musical phrase *and* the meter close to the meaning at points, from point to point, without destroying the enveloping rhythmical structure.

Idea for a novel: (mother) tries to raise (son) according to dictates of sensitive, dictatorial father. Makes him read, study music, philosophy, etc. She is quite ordinary, brings someone in from the outside: he seduces her: they have a lot of money. The boy loses himself in the Army. Hint at end that he is "trying to start at the bottom (with pulp magazines) and wind up where you made me begin." Affair with "arty" girl the mother thinks is "intellectual." Father: non-creative, but very intelligent, sentimental, and cruel.

(Long Story) ↑Short novel↓: (about a hundred pages long): about AF recallees: the housing shortage: the house on the lake owned by one of them, Haynes, who looked like a professionally-seedy-looking character actor, and his curiously unfocussed and drifting wife. The house, on the dammed lake, way out. Part of the story dealing with Haynes and his wife, and part with Dahmen and his girl. Dahmen is married, is having an affair with a town girl who is estranged from her husband. Dahmen: an ex-javelin thrower. The girl is mad from grief over losing him. Haynes lends Dahmen his house, and he takes the girl out and beats the hell out of her. Haynes hears her screaming; then D. pushes her out the door into the wind off the lake. Her head back and face uncaringly wild and fixed, they get into the car, and so on. That night she tries to

44. From "#29 [oh young men oh young comrades]," *Poems* (New York: Random House, 1935).

kill herself. Dahmen's fear. Walks out into pasture near railroad track: old horse, etc. His wife's grief: his child. Spring. Haynes kills the coral snake with a .22. Steps outside and sees it in an open gravel-patch, unbelievably bright, corded, pencil-thin. He lies down on a bank above it, telling himself: "Don't miss," though its head was ridiculously small. End with his killing the snake: the image of sticking his tongue between the snake's open jaws. Episodes: the cadet dance; flying, overcast, approach time.

Story about troop train stopping for a few minutes in Missouri and the conversation between some little country boys and the returning soldiers on the train: souvenirs, etc.

Another novel: perhaps *this* one called *The Heraldic Criminals,* perhaps not. This is about a rebellious, rather arrogant and unsure boy who, because of the settlement of his family's property, goes away to another city, where he rents his grandmother's house to a religious sect (like Jehovah's Witnesses). Because of this, he is drawn into their sect (partially, also, because his wildness is ending and he has no values, etc.). After a few years with them, he returns to the city he was raised in and goes around to people he remembers having offended in various ways and tries to make amends to them. They don't remember what he has done in some cases. He has tried to cultivate a sense of guilt, but it is wasted, or impossible, has no context. There could be some really good comic situations here, and the book should be comic to a large extent. It is about the deliberate manufacture of guilt feelings and the luxury of expiation, which process, however, somehow gets infected with enough of the real thing to make it a conclusive experience.

The thing is there! *Any event* I can remember, immediately I begin to think about it, to let my mind form up on it, is packed with usable detail, and somehow also develops a meaning. I could work this mine forever. For instance, there is a novel in my Clemson experience, short as it was. Monty Byer's girl, the high school basketballer, the Clemson campus, the leaves, the power plant, and all. Example: Chip Clark, Emerson, McIlwain, and I at Carol Thomas' house: "he in strong sunlight," etc.[45] I should write one of these episodes a night, thumbing through possibilities, sorting details.

A new novel: about a young couple not certain, really, of their relation to each other except in their devotion to their child. The husband kills

45. Byers, Clark, Emerson, and McIlwain all played football with Dickey at Clemson. Jack Emerson and Tom McIlwain also played at North Fulton High School. Carol Thomas attended North Fulton with Dickey.

the child by accident (whirling him around: sundial or birdbath). They are given a grant (he is an architect?), and they go to Europe. Here the story about the two young men. The wife has her own adventures (Mansfield: he is sick),[46] and at the end they get back together. Make this real harrowing, exacerbated.

Journal of the Novel

14 November: the main difficulty with the book, stylistically, is the impatience with detail. The style gives you the impression that the events are taking place at a great distance from the reader. This might be of advantage in the first part, but it should be progressively eliminated.

{Dickey's final entry occurs in late fall of 1952; thus, Notebook III overlaps parts of the first and second journals.}

---

46. Lester Mansfield was a professor in the French department at Rice Institute and Dickey's best friend while he taught there. Dickey stayed with Mansfield while in Paris traveling on a *Sewanee Review* fellowship, and he dedicated *The Eye-Beaters, Blood, Victory, Madness, Buckhead and Mercy* to him.

Notebook IV

The fourth notebook is a bound ledger consisting of ninety-five handwritten pages. Dickey dated the initial entry September 29, 1952, and other notations are dated the next day. At the top of page 79 of the ledger, Dickey drew a line with the date August 1956 above it. The entries that follow are phrases designed to achieve language that is strongly imaginative rather than merely poetical. Page 81 of his notebook begins a series of translations of the French poets André Frénaud and Jean Lescure, though pages 82, 84, and 92 are blank. Dickey taught at Rice until May 1954, when he won the second *Sewanee Review* fellowship. He had been invited to apply for the award by Monroe Spears, his former professor at Vanderbilt, who had assumed the editorship of that journal and who had recently accepted for publication Dickey's poem "The Ground of Killing." Dickey used the fellowship to spend a year in Europe with his family, primarily in France and Italy, where he wrote many of the poems in *Into the Stone.* Upon his return, he was asked by Andrew Lytle, who had been an advisory editor of *Sewanee Review* and who headed the Creative Writing Program at the University of Florida, to become his assistant. Dickey accepted and taught courses at Florida until 1956. Before the end of the spring semester, he resigned following a reading of his poem "The Father's Body" that offended some of the audience and for which he refused to apologize. He was hired as an advertising copywriter by McCann-Erickson and moved to New York, where he struggled to write commercials during the day and poetry at night.

Entries in the fourth notebook are eclectic. Some reveal continuing concerns, such as poetic analysis and construction as well as Dickey's consideration of what he believes are the two essential types of poems. Other entries describe new ideas for stories, novels, poems, and critical studies. Dickey even begins working on a play. His interest in what are not so much translations of poems in other languages as creative reinterpretations also evidences itself in the fourth notebook. Of major importance, however, are entries that clearly present the framework for the characters and scenes that eventually become *Alnilam,* Dickey's most ambitious work. Its original title is *The Romantic,* and he intends the story's three-day time frame to possess archetypal significance.

Although Dickey in interviews has termed *Alnilam* his "big novel about the air," he certainly did not project a long fiction, one that when published would total 682 pages. Conceived initially as a story and then as a novella, *The Romantic* presents a father, a widowed automobile sales-man now employed as a timekeeper in an aircraft factory, who arrives at a primary training base to interview various individuals about the death of his only son, Joel Mitchell, whom he has neither known very well nor seen for some years. Like Joel Cahill in *Alnilam,* the protagonist in the novella has died in an unobserved plane crash, having inexplicably flown through the turbulence of a fire. Before his death, too, Joel had become obsessed with the poet James Thompson. Although Dickey eventually changes their names, other principal characters in *Alnilam* are also recognizable. For example, the Commanding Officer becomes Colonel Hoccleve in the published novel, and the Commandant of Cadets, Joe Riley, is Colonel Malcolm Shears. Tactical Officer Bean is Lieutenant Spigner. Joel's flight instructor, Willis, becomes McClintock McCaig; his check rider, Broome, is Lieutenant Foy. Dickey does not name the woman with whom Joel Mitchell was having an affair; she be-comes Hannah Pelham in *Alnilam.* However, he bases her on Matilda Weller, the girl with whom James Thompson was obsessed and whose death at an early age aggravated his tendency toward melancholia and contributed to his imaginative visions. The narrative centers not so much on the use or abuse of power (the entries, for example, do not mention a plot to disrupt the military) as on the archetypal search of a father for his son and on that son's efforts to achieve individuality in the midst of training for war. That Dickey became caught up in the idea of men fight-ing a world war is also indicated by his beginning a play whose characters he partly derives from his own experiences in the Pacific.

Other novels detailed in the fourth notebook include *The Entrance to the Honeycomb* and *Done in the Thorn Tree.* Notations for the former indicate that Dickey intends the protagonist's search for "some final and ultimate act of degradation" to be allegorical and that one scene involves a deserted air base. Like Julian Glass in *The Casting,* the main character labors to create a situation that satisfies private interests and that involves his sense of aesthetic possibilities. Although Lee Barker, the editor from Doubleday, declined the manuscript in 1953, Dickey later used at least one aspect of it. The wooden labyrinth that Frank Cahill builds as part of his Atlanta amusement park in *Alnilam* is called The Honeycomb. *Done in the Thorn Tree* concerns the problem of communication among family members—the failure of Sidney Etter IV, a good and well-intentioned but unorthodox and perhaps partly insane central figure, to re-create his family by bringing it to a greater understanding of itself through imaginative language.

Entries detailing ideas for short stories far outnumber those that develop poems; almost a dozen stories are identified by title. Those in which Dickey presents a narrative outline suggest that the principal theme is the use of illusion to sustain an individual, particularly with regard to human relationships. In "The Prince's Mask," for example, a private in New Guinea, suffering from huge lumps in his face caused by tropical worms, silently idealizes the nurse whose hands routinely administer to the scabbed patches. Despite her indifference, he becomes filled with "quiet rejoicing." The protagonist's reaction anticipates the idealization of women in Dickey's later work, including *Deliverance* on the one hand and poems such as "The Leap," "The Scarred Girl," "Falling," and *Puella* on the other. The central character in "The Integral" (Dickey also considered "The Integration" as a title), having been rejected for military service, uses illusion to re-create the war for himself so that he imaginatively participates in it. Securing the position of town archivist, he utilizes war photographs and letters to transfer himself into the conditions and actions of combat, a situation not unlike that which Dickey intended for another novel, *The Repossession of Assyria*.

In other stories, however, such as "The Leaf Hazard" and "The Bitter Box," illusion fails. The first story depicts an aging athlete (Dickey's model is Jim Thorpe) whose physical deterioration evidences itself when he is invited to run a homemade track course. The story is told by the father whose children have made the outdoor course, and while Dickey intends to reveal both the innocent diabolism of children and the pride of athletes, the first-person perspective precludes any sense that the effects of aging are mitigated by individual imagination. "The Bitter Box" is a psychological study of a young bank employee whose attitudes regarding his mother yield to illusions about a young waitress. Dickey seems to have intended the story to interweave ideas about matriarchal societies, technology, religion, and sexuality. In the end, the young woman's husband laughs when he discovers the protagonist staring at a naked, dismantled mannequin in a shop window.

Dickey continues to distinguish between poems he terms "rational," those consciously constructed or built by the poet who endeavors to sustain the imagery and ensure that the poem's conclusion is implicit in its beginning, and those he labels "immediate." The latter, which spontaneously develop from or out of the unconscious, most interest him. Dickey also attempts to broaden the thematic concerns of his poems, listing subjects that seem to him to monopolize his poetry and then cataloging other interests that he hopes will inform future poetic efforts. Among these new subjects are power, the meaning of individual existence, the hero, and preparations and departures, all subjects that characterize the fiction and poetry he later published. Indeed, Dickey often works out a scene or subject poetically after first outlining it for his fiction, allowing the two genres to cross-fertilize. Although he works only sparingly on his poetry in the fourth notebook, he does project a volume titled *Wells, and Other Poems.* Its title poem, which he anticipates to be approximately 100 pages long, reflects the same interest in lengthy poetic works revealed in the second ledger. As in his fiction, "Wells" depicts an individual interacting within his society or culture to mold his own identity. Dickey realizes that perspective is "the secret of poetry," and he plans a critical essay that examines not only what he terms a poem's overall perspective but also its local or "vehicular perspective," a distinction that later characterizes such long poems as "The Firebombing" and "Slave Quarters."

Dickey's list of eighty-three principles or imperatives constitutes an effort to systematize his use of the notebooks and not an attempt to establish new critical insights, for these entries are similar to those elsewhere in his notebooks. Indeed, he occasionally admonishes himself for not better using the journals, since he departs widely from his original intent to provide each notebook with a specific purpose. Even the listing itself, however, is interspersed with other entries. The list ranges from almost strident injunctions about his poetic efforts ("The mind must be forever in poetic gear, deeper and deeper"), to brief statements cautioning himself about method ("Pack more than one reference, one image, into a line"), to verbal experimentation that seeks to extend what might be termed the agency of language—metaphors or images in which an agent now acts rather than be acted upon as in its usual verbal context. If the list exhibits one constant, it is that the statements, written almost four years after the initial notebook entry, now center almost exclusively on poetry rather than fiction. This shift constitutes a significant change in Dickey's creative efforts, evidenced by the subsequent translated drafts of poems by André Frénaud and Jean Lescure. While an undergraduate at Vanderbilt University, Dickey took Elementary and Intermediate Spanish, courses for which he earned an A and a B, respectively. Despite his statements in *Self-Interviews* that he also studied French and German, his university transcript reveals no such enrollment. That he was now endeavoring to re-create poems written in a language for which he had no formal training suggests that he was engaged in rediscovering the world through an imaginatively informed, verbal cross-fertilization, what he labels "Free-Flight Improvisations from the unEnglish" in *The Strength of Fields* and "Double-tongue" in *The Eagle's Mile.*

{The initial entries, dated during September 1952 when he had just returned to teaching duties at Rice, indicate Dickey's use of Notebook IV while simultaneously involved with the bound ledgers numbered here as I, II, and III.}

Prosody   29 Sept 1952

Auden and Pearson:[1]

1. Nearly all poetry in the West has been written in *verse:* lines constructed out of a regular pattern of metrical units.

2. Each metrical unit, or foot, consists of an emphatic nuclear syllable and one or more unemphatic satellite syllables.

3. The criterion of emphasis can be (a) the length of the syllable (b) the degree of vocal accentuation or (c) a mixture of both.
[What is meant here by a *long* syllable?]

(a) In classical Greek and Latin poetry, the nucleus is a long syllable, which contains either a long vowel or a short vowel followed by more than one consonant, and the satellites are short syllables.

Āll cōm | pōsed ĭn ă | mētrĕ | ōf Că | tūllŭs

Such verse is called quantitative.

(b) In most English verse, the nucleus is an accented syllable and the satellites are unaccented syllables. Such verse is called qualitative.

(c) In Anglo-Saxon verse the emphatic element or lift is either a long accented syllable or a short accented syllable plus a short unaccented one.

4. There are two opposite metrical extremes possible in English:

(a) To count only the accents in the line and to ignore the number of unaccented syllables (Hopkins).

(b) To count only the number of syllables in the line and to ignore their accented or unaccented quality (syllabic verse).

The bulk of English verse is written in a way that lies between these extremes, i.e., equivalent lines contain the same number of syllables and the same underlying regular pattern of metrical feet scanned qualitatively. But the musical art of the poet depends on his capacity to vary from this pattern without the sense of the pattern being lost.

---

1. See "Introduction to Volume I," *Poets of the English Language: Medieval and Renaissance Poets* (New York: Viking, 1950), esp. xviii–xx. Section 4 in the entry is mislabeled and represents section 5 in Auden and Pearson's anthology.

Analysis: Brewster Ghiselin: "Formation of the Soul."[2]

Rule: the longer a hard (strongly stressed) syllable is avoided, the harder its stress when it comes. It is not possible to forestall some kind of accent for more than four syllables, and these have to be very short.

"Formation of the Soul": metrics: a good many variations on iambic meter: substitutions, inversions, dactyls, anapests. Frequently two hard accents come together. Why?

1. First line: he wants "stumbling," "dark," and "CELlar" emphasized, so he places "stumbling" first. With its 2nd syllable unaccented and "frŏm thĕ" following, considerable weight is thrown on "dark." Rule: of any word of more than one syllable, one syllable at least must to a degree be accented. Unaccented syllables are unaccented syllables in words of more than one syllable and words of one syllable. The end word of a line, or the accented syllable of such a word, is invariably a heavy stress (the last stress in the line).

2. Second line almost identical with first: "sweet," "tired," "PLAY-mate," "frock."

3. Carries forward the unit of description: what the light "was sweeter than," a relatively smooth descriptive flow, accented strategically. The point is to get the kind of movement which will best suit your subject, or that portion of it, to accent the important words or syllables of important words, all within the <normal> normative laws of versification. Caesura: partly a matter of accent, partly of punctuation, partly of intonation. Meter should build on the natural rise and fall of the voice in speaking the syllables.

Auden and Pearson: 30 Sept.:

What variations are possible depends on the poet's ear. The only rule seems to be an empirical and negative one, namely, that two successive accents cannot be suppressed or displaced without destroying the underlying pattern.[3]

Also, I don't believe it possible to get more than four consecutive, unaccented syllables no matter what conditions obtain.

Since the poet cannot write entirely in monosyllables, and given that any word over one syllable demands an accent, the problem is to manipulate the monosyllables and given (or *demanding*) stresses throughout the line in a movement that best allows your poem ↑poetic line↓ to say itself. From line to line there should be a developing <rhymical>

2. Ghiselin's poem was published in the June 1952 issue of *Poetry* and included in *The Nets* (New York: E. P. Dutton, 1955).

3. From *Poets of the English Language: Medieval and Renaissance Poets,* xxi.

rhythmical structure. The lines do not stand alone but flow out of each other, the latter from the former—this should be observed. There are certain problems local to the line, certain to the developing metrical progression. No line is autonomous, but each must be paced in its own right and <in the> from the aspect of the entire poem (or, if a long poem, its section).

In scansion it is fairly easy to tell where the heaviest accents lie simply by hearing the line in the mind in a "normal tone of mind." (Curiously, this does better than reading the <poem> line aloud, for there you get to playing around with your voice and it's easy to get confused that way). It follows that you have most difficulty in recognizing secondary accents, whether the syllable is unaccented or carries a secondary accent. Reasons for metrical pattern:

    1. As an organizing factor as to rhythm.
    2. Emphasis: meaning.
    3. Relation of #1 to #2, which we might call movement.

Variation of normative, rhythmic pattern, <coupled with> implementing the meaning, ↑(however this is done)↓ ↑giving↓ the emphasis needed, is the purpose of metric.

Interpolation: photography can never include the gesture that <let> *led up to the scene* (*a child laying its head* on its mother's shoulder). Painting must.

Inter: I have always believed that if one did a thing long enough, one would do it well, and this is in certain ways true, but it was not practice that made Jack Herlong smash head-on into his tacklers. It was will, abandon, but more the latter. This says something about the composition of poetry.

Inter: the point in philosophy is not to be consistent but to tell what truths you think come to you.

Inter: story about mild boy who walks through unknown suburbs at night before going overseas.

Inter: war novel: survival: has created in the protagonist a sense of the *ordinariness* of his environment: "there should be a ruined orchard here, or a broken ration-box."

Future work: to create a hero: write an heroic work.

I believe at times that it is no philosopher's or scientist's prerogative to intervene doctrine between the poet and the naked human act. The poet himself is plagued with ↑a necessity for↓ assigning meanings to ↑these↓ incidents which so desperately ache to mean, but essentially all he can do is record and feel.

Poem: "Cyclops": after Redon's painting rather than Homer.[4]

Story: about a pfc in New Guinea with immense lumps in his face caused by tropical worms (look up): at hospital. Story turns about the nurse's fingers on the scabbed patches of his face. She talks to someone else all the time (doctor), but he comes away full of quiet rejoicing: the clumsy mask of his face, his eyes "murderous": title: "The Prince's Mask" (King's).

My prose deals with the unknown (inadvertent, accidental) and important things that happen between people or to people.

Granted that we live among illusions, that science can explain in its own terms, which are unknown to us, the phenomena we live among. Yet these phenomena, illusions are what we live and die among. It is the kind of reality that art deals with.

Poetry: language creating its own objects.

A swift line should have at least 3 feet to establish itself as swift. Over 5 or at most 6 feet merely a virtuoso performance. 4 feet best: parts of "L'Allegro."

"The Bitter Box":
"So his adventure began" (rather a childish device). Crosses against lights ↑"innocence"↓: goes home: child watches him: first time he has noticed: musty air in hall.

Returns at same hour as always: thinks momentarily of excuses: room looks strange: pills, mother's picture—Mother's forbidding picture. Connection here between matriarchal society and the "Temples" it produces. He realizes this dimly now. He has a little of her will (nose).

Dislikes other picture—fishing girls.

Distracted by sounds: old man, religious and housecleaning fanatic. Gives Temple a tract: the "dormant skill" of Mr. Temple's hand: T's mouth twitches. Takes tract. "Give freely," etc. T goes out.

His first time in city at night. How he has been made secure by the paraphernalia (mechanical) of the bank.

---

4. Odilon Redon (1840–1916), French painter and lithographer. Often depicting a dream world, his symbolic works are related to those of writers such as Poe, Baudelaire, and Mallarmé. "The Cyclops," measuring 25¼ inches by 20⅛ inches and painted circa 1898, depicts the mythological creature looking over a rocky crag at a naked woman sleeping below him in a colorful landscape.

Feels branch of tree, whistles, etc.

Goes into restaurant, one of those mechanical kind. Recalls girl who came in bank from there: the *machine* ringing the "possibilities" of ↑"man's↓ choice." The waitresses and the electric-eye doors: their faith in the photoelectric beam.

The young girl he remembers is a waitress: remembers name (Hilda Brand) from his banking. He likes her: his first human contact: she <has> shares somehow his "emancipation." Her husband: talks to un-pleasant-looking man, who has T's first name, scarred face.

He goes out: follows airplane: shop window: naked mannikin dis-mantled: Mr. Brand comes by, begins to laugh at spectacle.

Inter: an odd feeling when the meter of a poem corresponds exactly with the beating of the heart.

On the associative power of the mind: absolutely free, the mind must churn for hours in order to turn up something valuable. Association works better when the associations are *grouped* about a *subject* or topic, which both binds, leashes them, and provides the mind with a context to operate in, wherein the associations will in some sense bear upon each other.

I would like a poetry of *immediacy* and *strangeness,* full of the odd ex-citement one feels at crucial times, and expressed in jagged, perhaps clumsy, metrical and syntactical forms. *As one would* talk if he were imag-inative and <had> quickly put down the unformulated speech of his affliction. "The Anniversary" should do this, but there is not much in it yet that <suggests> exemplifies what I say here. I will at some time break through. To speak out of the complex and blood- and image-filled throat. Lorca is very near what I want: "image filled with the throats of blood." There is a lot of dead wood in "The Anniversary" as it now stands.[5]

Complication, development is the difficult portion of any poem. Perhaps it is a good idea to write the end of the poem first; that way you can have something on which to build. You can develop the poem toward your conclusion.

Rational poem:
    1. Write out poem in prose: ideas, possible images.
    2. Write end: in form.
    3. Write beginning: implanting threads to be resolved.⎫ stick to form
    4. Complication and development; sustaining images.⎭

5. See Notebook III, n. 37.

5. Transition to conclusion.

6. Change end if need be, if poem has taken another direction. Tighten up all screws.

Immediate poem:

1. Let it develop as it will.

2. Go back and strengthen what coherency it displays. If not unified, take its most significant track, junk the rest, and follow that.

3. This process (#2) may have to be repeated many times.

4. Let sound and rhythm dictate themselves.

5. Afterward go back and implement these as the need arises.[6]

Get other subjects besides

1. Lust
2. Sea
3. Body
4. Christ
5. Love
6. Places
7. Woods, hunters
8. Animals
9. Battles, castles, armor, history
10. Dancing
11. Mythology
12. War.

Try

1. Individual existence: meaning (Sewell).[7]
2. The meaning of the past $\begin{cases} \text{history} \\ \text{individual.} \end{cases}$
3. The expressions of men: cities, factories, dams, amusements (symbols of men).
4. The will (entanglements, justifications).
5. Power (chance here for a *big* poetry).

6. Dickey details the building of the "rational" poem in Notebook III. The "immediate" poem is elsewhere also termed "unconscious" or "word-led." These entries establish Dickey's belief in the duality of poetic types and anticipate the distinction he makes in *The Suspect in Poetry* regarding poets and poetry.

7. See Elizabeth Sewell's *The Structure of Poetry* (London: Routledge and Kegan Paul, 1951), esp. chaps. 4–5, "Words as Individuals" and "Words as Individuals in Ordinary Life and in Poetry," respectively. Sewell argues that language assists the mind's effort to order life, bringing unity to diversity. Because experience can be ordered and simplified into units, we assume language can also. However, while a word exists individually in everyday life, it does not in poetry, where language is bound up in a system of relationships.

6. Ancestors (the racetrack of my grandfather or on a picture of his or of grandfather on Swift side).[8]

7. Rituals of savages (Ajanta)(research).[9]

8. Miracles of Old Testament.

9. Any dramatic (spoken) subject, preferably by someone who has a tradition (broken or whole) behind him.

10. Descent, return.

11. Preparations and departures, metaphysical or otherwise.

12. The beliefs of people when they are broken or sustained, or broken or sustained wrongly.

(Augment list every night). In rational poems, try to get real things, people immediacy, into a formal pattern with concepts, expressed or not. In immediate poem try to get archetypes, (irrational) emotional equivalents for states of feeling, being.

13. Begin to try to make a hero. Speculate on what he must do, be, be in, etc.: an American hero (Bill Williams): series of poems about him.[10]

Robert Lowell has sacrificed the epigrammatic quality of the couplet; Pope or Dryden would not have understood him. Lowell has more run-ons than end-stops.

Stories:

"The Minotaur('s Breast)": parallel of myth.

"The Easter-Egg Hunt": man does something because of his childhood.

"(The) Genocide Pact": pseudo-mythical, racial.

"The Stock Car Race" ("The Racers").

"The Spur."

Story: about father and his father:

1. The father: a tall, straight, soft-spoken man with a heavy, strongly-sculpted forehead and a heavy, yellow moustache: worked for railroad, now laid off: wears shoes too little for him: trotting horses.

2. Mother: painting her landscapes from memory.

3. The boy: with his baseball ambitions and gamecocks: spur through hand.

4. Reddy Long: the rock-throwing, the gamecocks, the episode with the niggers.

8. Dickey's paternal grandfather, James Lafayette Dickey, owned trotting horses and a racing track at the present site of the Atlanta federal prison.

9. A village in India near which are located the Ajanta caves, temples carved into the mountains from the first to the seventh century A.D. that are the site of religious fresco paintings now ranked as masterpieces in world art.

10. The hero of Phelps Putnam's projected epic about an American searching for experience. See Notebook V, n. 6.

Child and father unable to come together. Child identifies father with Reddy and then with rooster. When rooster loses to Reddy's, he picks him up, weeping, and carries him off with gaffs (stolen from Reddy's father's gaff box), talks to him; cock puts gaff through hand. Kills cock with stone. End: "And you love me, you love me," he cried, striking again and again, "you *love* me."

Earlier scene with father when father brings him a doll. They try to play, but it is no good for either of them.

Boy later tears eye out of doll to use for marble (disappointed it is only half-marble).

Novel: fantasy: last two pages of *Prothalamium*.[11]

Story: "The Leaf Hazard":

1. Old athlete (roughly like Jim Thorpe),[12] told about by father of family (at one time a minor athlete: same event).

2. Father <takes> meets him at Sportsman Club meeting.

3. Brings him home to meet little boys (they are "interested in track"): have a track behind a neighbor's house (another little boy's): have stopwatch father gave them.

4. The boys take him out to it.

5. Mother and father talk awhile. Athlete is pretty much down and out: "He got fifty dollars for speaking yesterday."

6. Go out behind cultivated back yard. A long <path> narrow path, sprinkled with cinders from the furnace, stretches near a vine-covered fence.

7. The old athlete is <running up> to run up this. He is now at the start. The leaf hazard is explained; it is near the finish—an overhang of heavy leaves from a low branch swept across the path. One must stoop. <"Look> Waves handkerchief. "Look, he's started." Stopwatch: "The Record."

8. As he approaches them, he is dead white. His eyes are bulging: obscene waddle, tie flying, bearing slowly upon the leaves, until he disappeared as he prepared to stoop under it, under the innocent leaves. (End) bearing down slowly upon the leaf hazard.

Try to get here some of the innocent, well-meaning diabolism of children ("The Innocent Voyage"), the pride of the old athlete.

---

11. By Philip Toynbee; see Notebook I, n. 171. The narrator in the final two pages of the novel relates a fantastic marriage uniting Life and Death, the animal and human, and the physical and spiritual.

12. Called the greatest all-round male athlete the United States has ever produced, Jim Thorpe (1888–1953) played college and professional football and won gold medals in the pentathlon and decathlon in the 1912 Olympics at Stockholm, Sweden.

Speculations of the Forms of the imagination.

Absolutely free association, if there is such a thing, <is> results in a great deal of wheel-spinning: the <trick> thing is to have a skeleton, an *associational medium* (or media), a distinct frame of reference for the associational clusters to group themselves round, like the ↑salt–↓ crystals round Stendhal's branch.[13]

The *response* toward a work of art is exactly what you don't <get in> have toward scientific documents. This is because it is human to respond to the situations of other human beings and to respond to the *connotations* of words, the effect of colors or musical tones on our eyes and ears. It is this *response,* this communication *out of* a human situation, that gives us ↑a kind of↓ knowledge, even, that scientific knowledge cannot give.

Call Margaret Young, 700 Chelsea, 1 Jan. about novel.[14]

<"The Watch"> "The Guardians": story about guard duty:
    1. The young lieutenant.
    2. The AWOL major with the "highest I.Q. in the Air Force."
    3. Connolly guard house.
    4. Kafkaesque sending the Major out at midnight on the bus: sealed orders: "But you (the O.D.) have to <be> certify it, Sir."
    5. Guard mount (Provost Marshall's Office).

Books: Louis MacNeice — *Modern Poetry: A Personal Essay.*
    Robert Graves — *Poetic Unreason*
                            The Common Asphodel.

Perspective, or ↑the↓ *attitude toward the subject* expressed in conceptual, rhythmic, and imaged forms, is the whole secret of poetry. It must needs <the> be the attitude, etc., proper to *that portion* of the poem with the eye on the whole structure. There is thus an *over-all* (perhaps a developing) perspective and a local perspective, or <perspectival vehicle> "vehicular perspective." *The attitude must find its means* (image, meter, stanzaic <construction> structure, etc.).

Article: "On Perspective in Poetry."

13. The image comes from book 1, chap. 2, of Stendhal's *De l'Amour,* published in 1822. Stendhal compares the beginning of love to a leafless branch left in a salt mine and later discovered to be so covered with crystals that the branch is no longer recognizable. Similarly, love is a mental process, or crystallization, that draws from everything new proofs of the loved one's perfection.
14. Perhaps Marguerite Young, book editor for the *Houston Post* while Dickey was teaching at Rice.

Through all this there must be found a way to speak to and for the naked human creature.

In the poem, the beast of the experience should still tremble the cords of the net, almost held.[15]

If the mind is set to dig in, engage its teeth in the cog of the problem of aesthetic recovery (reading, analysis) or into <its> creation (of the poem, or fiction), not only will the secondary (elaboration, fitting-in and together of detail) but the primary (new thought, the flash of insight, analogy, and perspective on and from which a new work "opens up") problems of composition begin to be solved.

Every poem is the creation of a new mind.

Poetic form seems to be thought of now as a kind of coincidence of *cleverness* of expression with what is expressed, a kind of pseudo- or ersatz insight very easily manufactured for the trade.

Novel: in the scene with the Doctor at the end, have Julian's structure of rationalization begin to fall apart (but not quite collapse). None of this was intended against him—or perhaps it was (show this: Julian is wild with confidence and defiance: the Doctor is tired and old and, really, kindly): Julian's staring into lamp: the blood opens up again: epic nosebleed: describe fully. Leave ambiguity open: has he triumphed by his method and is as he always was, or has he been released from it and therefore able to enjoy a fuller existence? Don't tell.

"The genteel outrageousness of Firbank."[16]

Human life is a search for the images, *personal,* experienced or imagined, that will redeem it by ecstasy from <death and> sloth, ennui, and death.

<next> *Rational Poem: "Letter to Richard Gray."*[17]

"The snare of the athlete."

I need every day to go into "the quarry," the bank of memory and association peculiar to me, to find details, configurations, and meanings.

15. Compare Dickey's entry early in Notebook III dated February 11.

16. Ronald Firbank (1886–1926). Delicate and eccentric, Firbank lived his life as a leisured aesthete. His novels, characterized by a highly personal, satiric style, are disciplined journeys into a world populated by bizarre characters. See Dickey's comments on Firbank in *Self-Interviews,* 60–61.

17. Dick Gray was a star football player at North Fulton High School before getting polio his senior year. He recovered and later played at Georgia Tech.

Go through the dictionary 15 or 20 pages a day. You need to build up your vocabulary.

Getting down beforehand, or when the poem begins to come clear, the overall progression of the poem and the point-by-point means of expressing, fulfilling, and achieving this progression [what the poem *is* (or *says*), totally, and what it needs at each point to *be*]—this is one of the most valuable things about writing it that I have learned.

Story: old woman and her inability to (and helplessness before) do anything about young, disorganized and essential and destructive love which here involves her granddaughter (Mrs. Webster).[18]

How many insights you can get hold of, if you just apply your mind to the problem, sometimes rather loosely, without the urgency of real effort, but keeping firmly "somewhere around" the subject or its tangential suggestions!

"Where is the cry to be found?"

A story about "passion" (chance acquaintances?) where there is plenty of passion, all right, but "it isn't doing them any good."

The belief in an informing, conserving, personal image one of my emergent symbols: delusional and illuminating, like those of poetry.

Words' meanings are extendedly complex. The purpose of poetry is to manipulate <the> this complexity and in a sense to "alleviate" words from the intolerable milking-about of connotation by providing these with a motivating center, a (loose) penumbra of significant association.

To write a poem of exultation rather than analysis! To restore exultation to poetry! Raptness, even.

Poetry: vision, intensity, and technique. The first two by far the most important. If you can get vision and intensity into your poem without consciously applied technique, if it just comes or was always in, so much the better. Real depth, intensity of feeling, not easy. Most poetry now is "polite commentary," "little observation" poetry. Little is really felt, moving, tragic, exalted.

"Now could I from the cutting air
Loose out a heart."

18. Maxine Webster, the mother of Maxine Webster Syerson, Dickey's first wife.

I came to poetry when I saw that I could put the words where I wanted them, and that they would stay there, and that I could change them.

The one word that will break the poem open to possibility like a half-back through the line.

Let my poetry be that of an uprooted, untraditional, and therefore unsymbolical people trying to create a personal, integrative order out of the materials of (their) personal experience, aspirations, and fears.

Keep a notebook in which you analyze scenes, people, etc., out of <the> your past, and attempt to re-render them. "Limey" the trumpet player ("*loudest* damn trumpet player when he gets wound up").[19] The saxophone player fixing his instrument ↑(the stop)↓ with the table-knife blade.

It strikes me that no one has ever really caught and rendered the upper-middle class, adolescent period.

One kind of poetic structure: to turn the poem toward revelation, so that when the moment of illumination comes, the reader has the sense of discovering something of tremendous import that has been with him all the time he has been reading, yet is unpredictable until the "turn." This hits him with the force of a revelation, a discovery, and an awakening.

To make the poem a real *voice,* not (simply) a synthetic, learned clatter.

To paraphrase Marx: it is not enough to interpret the world; the poet must *create* one. Make your own landscape and typical figures: Eugene Berman and Max Beckmann.[20]

The theory of the brother: he is born consubstantial with us (symbol).

19. One of the members of an Atlanta band called The Emory Aces that played at area high school dances.

20. Eugene Berman (1899–1972), neo-romantic Russian American painter and stage designer best known for paintings of melancholy, deserted streets and courtyards of baroque buildings that possess a dreamlike, lyrical quality and against which isolated, hooded figures stand like apparitions. Max Beckmann (1884–1950), German painter who developed in the twenties a rich, personal, and symbolic art. Early in his career, he painted religious and classical machines and versions of contemporary disasters such as the sinking of the *Titanic.* Later, responding to the cruelties of the Great War, he painted dramas of torture and brutality whose pale figures were twisted and distorted within a compressed space. Throughout the 1930s and 1940s, his paintings exhibit a coloristic richness, monumentality, and complexity of subject, including his triptych *Departure,* which depicts the triumph of the spirit through and beyond the agony of the modern world.

Important: the notion of rifling other poems for rhythms, types of figures, movements, images that we can pervert and use.

Theory of the cry: it is the purest form of voice: it is pure being or reaching or expression.[21]

Story: "The Silk": silk shirt: to idiot country boy (Walter White) drumming on lard-can: puts on shirt and stands at torn brow of field in wind, feeling fine (Wright Morris).[22]

Story: "Non Omnis Moriar":[23] old man: operation: drinking: sitting in ambulance among flowers, "smiling like a child."

Poem: "The Theory of the Cry."

Poems: 1. "The Child in Armor."[24]
        2. "Rainbow and Unicorn" (on "illusion": neither is real, both are).

"For that is the true way, and no redemption."

"In the Loft": Ira: "he <could> let the scene spread and thicken before him; somehow the slowly(-) rising dust was the terrible thing."

For "In the Loft," read "When Every Candle Faileth."

Novel or story: *The Entrance to the Honeycomb.*

{The above entries citing "The Child in Armor," published in June 1953, and Dickey's novel, *The Entrance to the Honeycomb,* declined by Doubleday that year, indicate that it is late 1952 or early 1953.}

21. An almost primal cry frequently appears in Dickey's fiction, including Bobby Trippe's scream during the homosexual rape in *Deliverance,* McLendon's "varmint call" in *Alnilam,* and the scream issued by the captured airman whom Muldrow sees beheaded in *To the White Sea.*
    22. Walter White was the mentally retarded son of Mary White, who kept the gamecocks of Dickey's father. Before Eugene Dickey bought the grown man a banjo, he beat out musical tunes on a lard can. White is the prototype of the albino boy, Lonnie, in *Deliverance.* Wright Morris is a Nebraska-born author whose works are set in the Midwest. His novels present acute observations of characters who establish relations with or undergo separations from other people. Morris's brief but pungent 1951 novel, *Man and Boy,* depicts the search for a meaningful life.
    23. Literally, "I shall not entirely die." The line is from Horace, book 3, "Ode XXX," titled "A Poet's Immortality."
    24. The poem was published in the June 1953 issue of *Poetry.*

Theme of vicarious achievement a powerful one for fiction.

Story about unsuccessful but promising basketball player and professor (Stan Fulfer).[25]

Poem: "Gilgamesh."[26]

Third novel: *Done in the Thorn Tree:* ↑Graham Sutherland's painting on cover↓:[27] the problem of communication involved in it. Various failures, ironies, paradoxes: comic, turned thoroughly inside tragedy at the end: drawing rooms, sudden seriousnesses, farce, the "queer" member of the family some like, some hate, one loves, the others mistrust or are made uneasy by. "No one could understand anything unless he could talk to them": perhaps partially insane: curious actions: sending them bits of verse, fables, etc., which they read at parties, card games, around swimming pools, etc. One, not addressed to (him) her, profoundly affects one of the characters, a clear, healthy girl, so that she gets into a situation of some kind she is hurt by: a tennis pro (vulgar) or bird-seed salesman (grotesque love-scene among pictures of parrots or real ones). She tries to apply what she thinks the communication means. At end, central character goes into exile, permanently cracked: "The effort to understand is what confuses you." Gets to be sort of a Sidney Hirsch.[28] End: ", or when (if) you go there, may want to see you." The type ending of *The Way of All Flesh.*[29]

Try weaving the characters in and out a little more than you did in *The Casting.* Told in the third person. Main character: <Simon Etter or>

25. In the margin Dickey brackets this entry with the one preceding. Stan Fulfer was a basketball player at Rice while Dickey taught there.

26. The Gilgamesh epic, a work of approximately three thousand lines, depicts the adventures of the warlike and imperious Gilgamesh, who, when his friend Enkidu falls ill and dies, becomes obsessed with the fear of death. After he obtains and then loses a plant that gives him eternal life, Gilgamesh turns to the ghost of Enkidu for consoling knowledge of the afterlife, only to be informed that a gloomy future awaits the dead.

27. English painter, born in 1903, well known for a series of works entitled *Thorns,* which are realistically painted in sharp, cruel forms and depict the Passion. Named to the position of War Artist in 1940, Sutherland painted works centering on man, nature, and machinery.

28. Sidney Mttron Hirsch was a member of the Nashville Fugitives, which included Robert Penn Warren, Allen Tate, and John Crowe Ransom. His subjective, mystical approach to poetry included a belief that the great poet must express nonbeing passing into being through the use of appropriate rhythms, meter, and lofty language.

29. By Samuel Butler. The novel, published in 1903, attacks the Victorian will to power and its emphasis on spiritual and material power, which denies life and vitality. A case history of the Pontifexes, a family Butler presents as a lingering malady, the novel ends with the narrator directly addressing the reader and relating what has happened to the characters in the fifteen years since he finished the preceding chapter.

Sidney Etter: "Jordenia"—sleeping with Kotex on ("She *will* be undisturbed, you see.").

Intended recital by Sidney Leicester Etter, IV: monologue or account of something by Sidney Etter in the middle of book, showing the kind of family, self-understanding, traditional, he would like to mould. "↑It is the only family I have.↓ And I thought I spoke to them all, though one by one they left, all except Hermia, who sat, wringing her hands, as I lugged out all the metaphors about the sun I had ever concocted and turned them loose; <and> then she left too, and the moon came and fell directly onto the stringless piano, and stood, very priceless, exactly ↑and perfectly↓ in its polish."

Sidney Etter: a man like the photographs of E. E. Cummings: ↑About 45 to 55, almost bald↓: wry, full of love, rascality and sanctity: a clown (a pathetic one) and a genius with no formal mode of expression. "But I could never master the formal part."
   Gully Jimson in *The Horse's Mouth:*[30] make delicate, concrete, and fanciful, a man whose hurts and hopes take curious, active forms. Who may help:
John Hawkes
Firbank
Waugh
Ehrlich (Robert Macpherson)[31]
Projected story on old poet (Cummings)[32]
   "   "   on swimming pool: two young queers and water pistol: firing of soldier: Sidney's and soldier's conversations[33]
Huxley
Henry Green
Angus Wilson
He is wealthy: something of a ne'er-do-well. He lounges around in the comforts of his class but wants something better for it. *A good character.*

The Entrance to the Honeycomb: turns about some final and ultimate act of degradation, probably having nothing to do with war, "but here given its proper scope and setting" (its "ultimate terms") from which many may or must build "The Honeycomb."
   "I wished to find the worst, among things which are only worsts, and I am looking for a friend of my father." "I wished only to find the

---

30. The protagonist in Joyce Cary's 1944 novel, Gully Jimson is a completely mad painter who lives like a bum but whose talent is as brilliant as it is unorthodox.
   31. Macpherson is a half-mad composer in Leonard Ehrlich's projected novel "The Free and the Lonely." See Notebook I, n. 112.
   32. See entry in Notebook III, p. 124.
   33. See entry in Notebook III, p. 128.

worst." Concrete descriptions of fanciful (symbolical) scenes. "And even if I were the last one, I would try. I came to this decision early, while crossing a deserted field in the absolute silence (of desecration). It occurred to me that I was a bit of an aesthete, and so I was." In this landscape, though, one can indulge any whim or attitude or sensation, and all are comic.

"Making love to abandoned cattle": good comic scene here. Subsistence not hard to find. That is not the problem. "And I have always enjoyed hiking."
On the Marble Cliffs [34]
early Sansom [35]
Kafka

His humour is, or has to do with, the final degradation. The attitudes implied and possible therein.

A scene which made it impossible for me ever to laugh again. (Good).

<I had> Deserted air base: "Though it <was> had once been ours, I was glad to see it standing <where> deserted, for I had always hated military life, with the really profound hatred of uninterrupted irritation and interference, though I had ↑had↓ nothing better, or other, to do."

Epigram from Ern Malley for *Thorn Tree:*
"now have I found you,
My Anopheles."
                Ern Malley
Or, better,
"Sting them, sting them, my Anopheles."
                Ern Malley [36]

Story or short novel about a (timid) man, rejected from military service, who gets himself a job, on purpose, as archivist of the war photographs and letters a "civic-minded town" (High Point) [37] has kept in order "to

34. By Ernst Jünger. The 1939 novel, whose German title is *Auf Den Marmorklippen,* is an anti-Nazi allegory.

35. William Sansom (1912–1976), whose early story collections, including *Fireman Flower* (1944), *Three* (1946), *The Equalibriad* (1948), and *Something Terrible, Something Lovely* (1948), present experiences that are allegories of man's search for harmony. The endings focus on man's inability to alter unhappy or "terrible" aspects of life into aspects that are beneficial or "lovely."

36. See Notebook III, n. 6. As part of their hoax, Donald Stuart and James Macauley concocted the whole of Malley's work from a random collection of books on their desk, a rhyming dictionary, and certain technical journals. This line from one of Malley's poems, "Culture as Exhibit," derives from a scientific journal on the breeding of mosquitoes.

37. Dickey, having enlisted in the Army Air Force after a semester at Clemson, was stationed in High Point, N.C., from April through early June 1943 for training as an aviation cadet.

feel himself into" the situations depicted in the letters, photographs ("I was sure it was the same hill"). His notions pass from a superficial knowledge of the subject to a more thorough understanding than the lawyer's son, the Junior Chamber of Commerce, Silver-Starred overseer of the records, who takes the credit.

Also, the relationship to and with his son "to whom I could say, at last, that, yes, I had been there."

"Though there were some things I would never know, I knew much."

"There are those things which are too terrible to believe, but one must try to believe them. Somewhere in that effort understanding lies."

An effort to understand warfare: letters from one homosexual soldier to his buddy: the one at home Graham gets to know, a desolate drug-store worker: then is able to understand some of the references in the letters: had been simply lost: a Bronze Star winner.

Graham's wife: cannot understand his problem but is sympathetic. Letters and pictures for a photograph-happy (standing with a purchased flag), souvenir-hunting colonel. This homo (one killed) knows and hates: <who endowed> whose widow endowed the museum. His uniform, with medals, in glass case. Colonel's nurse: Helen Webster.

Love affairs take place by proxy: seriously applies his "inscape," "think-ing-into" to these, also, "for these are as important as the battles," etc.

Aerial photographs—something about flying.

Arranging the articles in "sequences," trying to arrive at correlation, evaluation, understanding, "but more than anything, participation."

The homosexuals: the one killed has been "taught to see," etc., "awakened" and then killed.

The remaining one has lost all faith in that kind of thing. Timid, thin-ning red hair, very clean hands.[38]

Notes: "The Integral."

He comes upon a girl through some one of his researches. As he lies with her ("it took him some time to work through the stolid resigna-tion of the embrace with which he held his wife"), he makes her tell him stories ("I have just come in from the lines") about himself and the war.

Against this, play off some real injury he does her, perhaps acciden-tally, but impossible without him. "It was as though he were going away."

At the end, he goes back to his family, having something of what he wanted to find out.

"The Theory of the Cry": "the only *translatable* utterance."[39]

---

38. Following this entry on the bottom of p. 41 of his notebook, Dickey parenthet-ically wrote "see 43." His discussion of this story, which he had titled "The Integral" or "Interpretation," continues there, and the format of this entry follows his intent.

39. This notebook entry as well as the several after it originally follows directly after the notation above that ends "very clean hands."

Possible title: "Interpretation."
   "The Integral."

Aids: Melville's "Bartleby."
   Pictures and accounts of the war, esp. Ernie Pyle.[40]
   Kafka's "heroes."
   The correspondent he comes to love (Ernie Pyle) and who was killed
in some incongruous way.
   Rilke's *Letters.*
   Poetry, introspection, analysis, and work.
   Allan Seager: for the way things look, their cost, etc.[41]

Poem or story about the (gradual) loss of the poetic imagination.

W. S. Graham is important to me because he opened up to me my
present *method* of poetical composition, helped me loosen up my mind
to the images and combinations and releases of words, and showed me
a good deal about syntax, especially prepositions, and, to a lesser degree,
adverbs. The two important influences now are Graham and Rilke, and,
increasingly, myself: Graham—method, diction; myself—situations,
"drive," interests.[42]

Poetry: the new theory of the line-ending.

The Theory of the Long Poem: America the projection of one monstrous
ego: foreshadowed by one or two sleights from history. A poem in which
crime, the criminal, will enter prominently ("Wells"), the sentimentalist,
and under this somehow the real concealed love "that will make him
blind." 100 pages. A device: perfect lines running off into prose, and
prose into, say, couplets. The crime turns into a crime in a magazine (the
magazine stand as cultural symbol), athletics. Athletics, <and> earning,
and sex other important themes: machinery, the will breaking through
everything to stand empty (then look round to fill its rooms).
   (*Wells, and Other Poems*).

Criminal: Genêt, etc. Have the real people real ones, and the apocalyptic
scenes really apocalyptic. "In all this violence, to find a way to mean."
No panacea: only the dilemma presented and explored.

40. American journalist and war correspondent in North Africa, Europe, and the
Pacific. His informal writing about American soldiers in World War II was extremely
popular, and his death from a Japanese machine-gun bullet on Iwo Jima in 1945 made
him a national hero.
   41. American novelist and short-story writer (1906–1968) whose works, such as
Equinox (1943) and *The Inheritance* (1948), often present characters involved in violence.
   42. This entry originally preceded that notation above that reads "Notes: 'The
Integral.'"

A convenient parallel: artist's and criminal's impulses akin: that is why we have so many criminal-poets: Crane, Poe, etc. Reject this. No allusions. Plenty: montage, "imagal" speculation, "reality," events, etc., scenes, etc. Also, the unwanted military experience: two short episodes: infantry (beachhead) and flying: at night <"groping> "the parable of groping by instruments" stands for national dilemma: violence, business, no repose, etc. Sex: "the wandering jet."

We despise those who make it difficult for us to fool ourselves.

End of story (perhaps about a child): "he managed to (tap) him with his foot (a finger)(as he passed), feeling that to touch him once before he went out ↑left↓ was enough."

We are our own inventions of each other.

One of the important themes of my poetry is the maintenance of that precarious inner landscape which we all depend on for life: its scenes, characters, and what they represent in us, the similarities, differences, and balances between this (these) and the lives (outer) that we <must> have to live. Not dream, especially, but more important—fantasy, daydream, re-creation of the world ↑deliberately and/or compulsively↓ on *our* terms.

The Clown as Death: figure in a fantastical novel.

<Story:> (*The Romantic*):[43] novella: story about a father's coming to a primary training base (Camden)[44] during the war and interviewing various persons about his son's death: Commandant of Cadets—Joe Riley. Tac-officer—Bean. Commanding Officer—Colonel and his girl. Instructor—Willis (and his check-rider—Broome) ↑his buddies↓. Also the librarian.

The boy's obsession with B.V. (James Thomson).[45] "Who is it? A town girl?" He has dived into the ground. The boy's character comes through,

---

43. The projection for a novella is the first sustained description of what will become *Alnilam*.

44. Dickey was stationed in Camden, S.C., from October through December 1943 for primary flight training.

45. Scottish poet (1834–1882) best remembered for his darkly pessimistic poem *The City of Dreadful Night*. The initials *B.V.* represent the pen name used by Thomson and stand for Bysshe Vanolis, the former being Percy Shelley's middle name and the latter an anagram for Novalis, the pseudonym for the German poet Friederich von Hardenberg. At the age of seventeen, Thomson became obsessed with a beautiful Irish girl, Matilda Weller, whom he had met and with whom he fell in love while studying in Ballincollig, Ireland. Weller, who was only fourteen years old, became engaged to Thomson but died shortly thereafter. Her death, if not fostering Thomson's predisposition to melancholy and insomnia, at least aggravated it.

but some mystery left. Father: an ordinary man. Snack bar: swimming pool. The boy's name is Joel. The auxiliary field where he took off: taken there by instructor: CAA man:[46] go in bus. Father is a widower: only son. CO: "Here are his flying things. We can't use them. You can have them if you like." Initials B.V. on strap of goggles.

His girl is dying: "Matilda Weller": picture hat: base set among trees: PT files: at the flight line: chow hall: aircraft right up against it: dormitory (or barracks) shown by Tac Officer.

His buddies ↑at PT. He walks suddenly among them↓:
    Mitchell: Did any of you know Joel Mitchell?
    One says: Yes (doesn't know relation, but guesses).
    M: What did you think of him?
    One: He was a good basketball player. (Looks at others). He sure could hit from out, with that jump shot.
    Another, quickly: He hardly ever missed.

There is a suspicion that Joel has had something to do with the CO's girl, who works in the equipment pool. She is heavy, soft, and white.

End:
    M: I hope you win your war.
    CO: If I could. . . .
    M: You little son of a bitch, etc.
    M: Any suspicion. You had better allow me to abuse you, or I'll kill you, whether you had anything to do with Joel or not. You have to make allowances for a man in my condition.

(Joel's walking excessive tours): Commandant of Cadets: CO has fixed this up some way. M. gets it out of him.

CO's playing ping-pong: long black hair: very young.

With the CO's girl: "If I have to, I'll slap it out of you, honey. I don't give a damn. I'd just as soon."

M. is an automobile salesman: has never been satisfied. Now working as time-keeper at the aircraft factory.

The archetypal, melodramatic figure of the three days he spends there.

---

46. Civil Aeronautics Administration. Created by Congress in 1938, the CAA was charged with encouraging the development of civilian aviation and the formulation of economic and safety regulations in air traffic.

(*Trouble Deaf Heaven*). Ask Mansfield.[47]

The dying girl has a certain tipsy gaiety: terribly thin.

This is also Mitchell's chance to be someone, to dramatize himself, and to vent some of his frustration on others.

Through the action he comes to love Joel (and) a great deal more than he ever had in life.

At the end he does something for the dying girl. They both begin to cry.

Section: from viewpoint, or about, the dying girl: leukemia: her association with Joel: playroom, seduction: her "most wonderful weakness": "as though his eyes opened into his throat."

The CO's girl: her passion for Joel Mitchell: his hair, not blond, but deeper gold: his clear skin and red lips. He was always worried, etc., never satisfied: he hated everything. "He wanted to be an intellectual and didn't know how to be one. His eyes came right out of the crowd."

Broome: washed out at RTU[48] for cracking up three P–40's. Broome's telling someone at the club about how much liquor to bring, after he has washed out this cadet (Cook). "Chug-a-lug," he said delightedly. He has been afraid of Joel.

Joel may have been mad, may have killed himself. Scene of crash: no one saw it: <at> in the wood at the edge of a field: *or flying through fire,* turbulence, etc.

Joel has been off at school (Darlington) ever since his thirteenth year.[49]

End: as he looks at girl, dying, with her countrified hat on, "he saw that Truth, or its (likely) shadow, stood beside him ↑(her)(between them)↓, and that it was trembling."[50]

Joel: good-looking: his upper lip curled a little ("peeled") away from his gums. This at times gives him a look of smiling (mechanically) when he

47. See Notebook III, n. 46.
48. Replacement Training Unit.
49. After graduation in 1941 from North Fulton High School in Atlanta, Dickey spent a year in the Darlington School in Rome, Ga.
50. Dickey in the notebook margin connected this entry with those following here. I have arranged the entries to convey his intent.

is not (even when he is angry) and creates a strange disparity between the upper and lower halves of his face.

The Cadet Club: speech of townswoman on town girls.

Fight: cowing of Hleske by drunken cadet Cutting.

Joel's one book: a textbook: words underlined heavily: "savage melancholy": "lost love" (Matilda Weller).

The dying girl: when she knew Joel, she had just come from the Mayo's. She met him beside the fire at the Cadet Club: drinking beer: "We were just making conversation until I told him . . . I had leukemia."

I want a poetry ↑that is↓ lean, athletic, driving, and imaginative: Skelton and Lorca.[51]

Does Yvor Winters believe that the quatrain, the sonnet, and the couplet completely exhaust the possibilities of poetic form?

Does the road or path know where it is going? Or whom it carries?[52]

A play: three acts.

Setting: Air Force tent in the Pacific. Equipment: helmets, goggles, parachute under tent awning. Concern: disintegration of one, unchangingness of others, metamorphosis of another. CO: full of drink and duty. Easy: working on rings. Nettles: pilot: becomes killer: desperate, etc. Scene of CO and Nettles: flashlight shining across stage, conversation. Beheading of one of the characters. Pilot who cannot fly. Drinking. Easy hammering rings. Replacements. Sounds of aircraft. The "Jug." Celebrations. "Dennis." The one who can tell good fuck stories: "I'm a kind of poet. God has seen fit to supply you with me." Someone's relation with his wife corrupted by this: the picture drawn in Manila.

A: It's like she don't trust me anymore. She won't look at me straight.

B: You've only sweated it up by <looking at> holding it and looking at it so much. You need to. . . .

A: No, by God, etc.

The point is that his faith in himself has been destroyed. He is obsessed with this and finally, at the end, tears it up and stands in the center of the floor, making sudden movements, none of which he completes.

"Shit. . . . Shit, shit, shit." He breaks into <sobs> wild, uncontrollable, hopeless sobs.

(Blackout, or curtain).

---

51. This entry on p. 50 of Dickey's notebook as well as the two after it originally followed the entry ending "it was trembling."

52. This entry originally preceded the one above that begins "Joel: good-looking."

Earlier.
　　A: You know, probably I shouldn't talk about my wife this way but. . . .
　　B: —
　　A: Well, I first noticed her in this swimming pool, etc., the pink bathing suit.
　　C: You're better than <Holley> Toby.

The planes going over. The murder of the children by Nettles.
　　C: Jordan's just an excuse. He never cared for Jordan. He's a murderer. CO <talks> deliberately talks Nettles into this frame of mind in the flashlight scene by playing on the "God-like" frame of mind. He is finally himself killed by this.
　　CO: There's not any of them I don't know how to get the best out of. Some you got to help, some you got to knock back.

Tent flap is toward the rear of the stage. Cots and "air-sacks." Someone explains to Nettles and the other replacements (question and answer) what the outfit does. White is a harmless braggart: tries to get along with others, be one of the boys. "Old boys," "new boys." Toby. Shorts, cut-off GI shoes, pants, shirts without sleeves, flying suits. All kinds of hats: flying caps, baseball caps, one Australian bush hat, fatigue hats, tropical topees, etc. CO playing harmonica: drinking.
　　At end, CO replaces White with a young, eager recruit, then last scene.

Uncle Toby's bedtime story. CO breaks in at crucial point: he wears GI shirt and trousers: has a small paunch: he looks too old to fly.

Nettles' or White's description of first mission over burning Manila. "You know, it was like. . . ." Talk excitedly, like boys, etc.

White volunteers almost immediately on first mission, doesn't on later. Another replacement crew that came in with this one is killed.

Sounds of aircraft going over.
　　"　　　" buzzing, then whoever it was comes in, dressed fantastically. .45's.[53]

Telling the story:
　　A: You're getting to the point too fast. (Agonizingly).

53. The semi-automatic pistol, .45 caliber, was standard, small-arms issue for all Army Air Force crews during World War II.

White: (partly really enthusiastic, partly to curry favor and say the right thing): Not fast enough, not fast enough!
(They all stop and look at him).
    C: (to the others): He'll learn. (To White) Just listen, OK?
(Toby continues after a long look at White).

My poetry: the image or fantasy-life against and in conjunction with "real" life events and things. The need to reconstruct, or arrive at, in the mind a tapestry of events in which the self can move in harmony with what it contemplates and so gain (transcend) the outer world.

The jazz metrical system will work for prose as well as verse. Rewrite "In the Loft" using this.[54] "Their eyes clinging past." Without dialogue: precedent: David Jones' *In Parenthesis*.

Example: $/ \breve{}, \breve{}/\breve{}/\breve{} \, \breve{}/\breve{}/\breve{} \, \breve{}/\breve{}/\breve{}, /. \, //\breve{}, ///\breve{} \, \breve{} \, \breve{} \, \breve{}//\breve{}, \, \breve{}//\breve{} \, \breve{}/, \breve{}//\breve{} \, \breve{}/\breve{}/.$ Young man, <with> among others, out of the sun with tongs and decorous hammers, moved. Leather-coated, he turned, <paused> looked slowingly at: the square windows, the close-bracketed awnings tremble, then strode, quickening pace to pace.

Play:
    CO: The whole secret is getting two things together in their minds. Some're easier than others. If you got the knack, they'll do anything. It's like a kind of game where you match things.

Opening: Whitney lying on cot, Easy tapping coin with small hammer. Tap. Tap. Tap. Turns ring.[55]
    Whitney: Get me a drink of water, will you, Mush?
    E: (looks at him a while): OK. (Goes to GI can. Pours drink into canteen ↑cup↓ taken from end of Whit's bunk. Gives it to Whit. Stands over him).
    W: (raises his head painfully to drink, then hands cup back abstractedly to E., already concentrating again on his pain): God, that's foul. Why don't you scrub that thing out with sand, Mush?
    E: It's your cup.
    W: Oh.

54. See Notebook III, n. 30.
55. Whitney is partly based on Harold Whittern; Easy, on Gilbert Eissman. Both were pilots and original members of the 418th Night Fighter Squadron (NFS), which sailed from Hampton Roads, Va., on October 6, 1943. Whittern is the subject of Dickey's poem "Whittern and the Kite," published in the summer 1949 issue of Vanderbilt's literary magazine, *Gadfly*. The practice of tapping rings out of coins is mentioned in another poem, "The Wedding," which is collected in *The Whole Motion*.

E: You better let Doc look you over again. You look terrible, Whit.

W: I just got back from the hospital yesterday.

E: You ought to go back.

W: <Nah.> No. I'll be all right. (He sits up on the bunk). Why doesn't fever make you have pretty dreams? All I can think about is the house where I used to live that burned down and my kid brother that died of meningitis? (Stands up painfully. He is thin and yellowish, with a strong lean face.) How're you coming?[56]

E: (holds up coin): OK. This ought to be the best one yet.

W: (W. takes down an Australian ↑(captain's bars on hat)↓ bush hat from the tent-support and puts it on at a rakish angle. Its three great feathers, blue, red, and yellow, nod strangely over his painful face): Your little girl ought to have plenty of rings, time you get home. How many you made?

E: Ten. One a month.

W: Won't be long, man.

E: (smiling slowly, full of love and regard): Hello, Bearcat.

W: Hello, Easy Man, Mush-rat. (grinning). How many ↑Nippon craft↓ we got, chum?

E: Seven. Two in one night, (with Aussie accent) myte?

W: Must of run together in the searchlights.

E: Or it might have been something else.

W: Like a little expert tracking?

E: Or like firing the guns, eh?

W: Can't tell, you know. (He sits down, suddenly haggard, trying to be comical.) I sye, myte, I'm blowed. I cyn't go up no more to the bloody war. (He puts his head in his hands.)

E: (E. gets down beside him): Man, we're through with 'em. We got all our time in. We're going Stateside. We got no more worries, Tiger. They'll give <ya> you a parade in Eureka. And I don't have to make no more rings.

Whit is going home. He wears ↑a↓ tropical uniform, full of medals, and a polished leather jacket with the insignia of the outfit on it.

Whit.: I hear you got yourself a new killer, Boss.

Songs: about Sydney, and so on.

Flashlight scene:

CO: (begins to talk excitedly. The roar of aircraft engines becomes louder, drowning out to CO's talking. Then, mixed faintly with this, there is the sound of a woman's voice screaming.): "No, don't, please,

---

56. Eugene, Dickey's older brother, died of meningitis, then called "brain fever," at the age of six.

you'll kill me. No. No. No. (I'll do it, I'll do it) No." (These blend over-whelmingly.) Nettles: Yes! then stop abruptly. ↑(Long pause)↓

CO: Take-off at 0300 hours tomorrow.

N: (no answer)

CO: Zero three hundred hours.

Snaps off flashlight. (End scene).

Someone ↑picking up paperback, French book↓: The Mar-quis de Sade? (American pronunciation). Who's that?

When writing a scene: visualize strongly, remembering

1. Overall impression of scene or description, expressed in details.

2. The actual memories, or the inventions, that will contribute to this.

3. How this is to link up with the rest of the story, both with other parts and in the developing structure of the whole thing.

Play: one scene where the CO indicates that he does not want Nettles to see the Flight Surgeon at the hospital. He browbeats the weak and drunken and volleyball-playing Doc.

Another scene: the outfit is "in" for a Presidential Citation.[57]

"Poetical" and somewhat pretentious account of the burning Manila by Nettles, then a contradiction by one of the others.

X: Why do all that talking about it, anyway? Look, <there go> you go up there, (and so on), and there's a fire there (points), and there (points), and over there, and then you get to—see, what's the use of all this? The thing's there. You see what you see, and so what?

Big novel: someone is killed on or near an esplanade and dies clutching the "tough hair of palmetto bark"—"the reallest thing in the world"—"the tough, grainy ↑coarse↓ hide of the world."

When Julian falls, he feels that "If I wished, I could spread my green wings into the farthest corners of the night air and stand or hover for-ever where I wished, built out of leaves and arrogance and skill, moving slightly from my roots into the comic divagations of the air, overlook-ing trivial conversations in the garden" (, and so on,) as the thing created is the equal of the creator and in a sense determines him—now harm-less, but awesome, terrible yet, standing out of the (night) garden on broad wings.

"When I struck," etc.

---

57. The 418th NFS was recommended for a presidential citation in May 1945.

Of a good poem: the page seems barely able to hold it.

Poems:
  "Spell to Be Said Coming in from Rain"
  "Spell for Lester Mansfield's Summer"
  "Unicorn and Bull"
  "Shipwrecked Horseman."

Empathy: begin by saying "To be," and feel the situation, feeling and looking out of the thing, and let this come down to words.

Don't just improvise a poem once. Do it five times, a dozen, a hundred if necessary. Take good details, the *best* of the directions the poem wants to go in, apply the metrical technique, and there you have it, all working carefully and spontaneously.

What I want in my poetry is *fire, headlongness,* and *involvement,* not meditation, reflection, analysis, and generalization.

In third novel: passage about the trumpet *player:* empathetic: *jazz from the inside.*

Don't be afraid of *violence* and *assurance* in your poetry.

Poetry: methods of focus:
  1. Concentrated
    a. Close focus.
    b. Attention to detail.
    c. Logically related figures.
    "Close, moving slowly, inch by inch,
      He . . . ," etc. (Jarrell).
  2. Diffuse[58]
    a. Close focus not often used.
    b. Details passed, discarded for others, just "dropped into the pot."
    c. A general feeling built up out of disparate parts. Neruda, Eluard, Thomas, Lorca (to some extent).
    d. Figures emotionally rather than logically related.
  3. Method using both.

In the second novel, really work the prose hard (David Jones, Virginia Woolf). Compose slowly, at times semi-impressionistic.

---

58. Following this in the notebook entry is a circle containing five symmetrical arrows all pointing toward the center from the circumference.

Novel: about a religious sect (Jehovah's Witnesses) renting a house from an old family. The family. Genteel but <in> getting poorer. Trying to hang onto status. Girl: avidly religious (of the family). One really holy man who really *works* at and for the sect. Family feels that they *must* joke about it. The crackpots of the sect. Lack of clear motive. Tent meeting scene (not of sect). Family: comfort and preferment-loving.

Novel: about an hysterical young man ↑an American↓ in Europe who kills a Frenchman (Italian) over some ridiculously trivial thing and is caught up in the European system of jurisprudence as they try to discover a motive. He feels, someone says, that killing a Frenchman is no worse than killing a dog. He ought to be able to go on with his vacation.

The young man's wife (the young man is sometimes quite decent).

A poet, or composer, or philosopher, or literary critic, well-known and well-regarded (Auden), a homosexual, whom the young man lives with, though he himself is not homosexual, to have contact with his talent. He kills off the poet's talent, abuses him terribly (scene where he holds him by the hair and slaps him). The poet knows about the murder but cannot bring himself to tell. He does at the end; the poet comes out of his terrible, intellectual vacuum into humanity and offers to marry the young man's wife. The young man either is killed or he is to be tried. His own suffering: "I killed him out of my own pain."

The boy's parents come over.

The police inspector, etc.

(1) The fantasy and dream chapter:
1. Mitchell and Lawlor (briefly).
2. Lawlor and Elsdorf.

Late that night the fantasy, the dream, etc.: about four pages.

Mitchell had had his eyes closed for a long time, lying clean and solid on the warm sheets, under the slightly oppressive but comforting weight of the covers, but he did not feel, yet, at all sleepy. Though his window was <cracked> opened a little <, and>, he had run his hand along the <opening> crack like the blade of a knife before entering ↑the↓ bed. The night was completely soundless, or had only the sound of an intense and killing something, a long way off. He was thinking <down> himself down into fantasy, toward the <response> intersection of terrible response and impossible gratification. He imagined the summer dancing unaugmented and immense with heated graciousness, and the compact bodies of young men and women lounging, none of them ever truly still, about the concrete shell of his pool, where the compartments of water dazzled over everything, and the ↑thick↓ sound of <plunging> falling flesh <shocked> plunged again and again, and excessive light was everywhere. He also liked to believe, in the heat and openness of motive, of the dark coming, and the last swimmers climbing from the pools, the cars starting, and in the interval around supper-time, ↑of↓ the slacking-off of business, when he talked to his cashier, Mrs. <Eibel> Ivey, or one of the concessionaires still standing blockily in his bathing-<suit, which was> trunks, which were every year a little more out of fashion (they had once possessed a top). The night crowd was different, more subdued, and there was less diving. The pools stood deeply like jewels, and the couples lay huddled together on the sloping bank, though the summer nights were <seldom> not cold.

Once he had tried having a show once a week, at night, at the pool. <This had not> There had been a small orchestra, ↑singers, amateur craze↓ <what> which naturally had meant the expense of a bandstand, and for a few weeks there had been music blaring out across the neat yards of water into the trees of the small valley. Mitchell had never really liked this, however, and he ↑secretly↓ had been glad that there was not enough increase in the size of the crowd to meet the expenses; he had torn down the bandstand and begun to think about putting up a closed dance pavilion. His had been one of the first establishments in Atlanta to <contain> have an automatic record-player ↑juke-box↓. During the interval of the band, however, an incident had <occurred> taken place which recurred frequently to him, and which seemed to crowd into focus a good many of the unrealized ——s of his life.[59]

Critical article: "Hart Crane and the Dictionary."

"Two Notes on Hart Crane":
   1. "Crane and Jazz."
   2. "Crane and the Dictionary."

1. "Keeps on" (doing such and such).
2. How to reconcile the wretched syntax and the rough, casual, intense, ordinarily-oriented-with-a-catalytic-difference approach? And with the high depth of imagination? This, and spontaneity and participation, is the goal.
3. Spirit, mystery, and imagination.
4. Everything, anything, is grist to the mill and should be noted. The mind must be forever in poetic gear, deeper and deeper.

---

59. Dickey kept a periodic word count of this scene in the notebook margin. The scene, the first extended treatment of the narrative for *The Romantic,* reveals that Mitchell, like Cahill in *Alnilam,* owns a swimming pool in Atlanta and that, though not blind, is business-oriented while disposed to imagination. The inclination to fantasize also suggests a connection with Julian, the protagonist of *The Casting.*

5. The *kinds* of metaphorical relation should be amplified, variegated, extended, and correlated.

6. Given a scene, a subject, part of an outlook, and it is much easier to improvise. And the quality of this is much better, also.

7. Keep the rhythm very varied, fluid, moving, yet within sight of the norm.

8. Be more alive to possible subjects.

9. Keep bringing in new words, in new combinations. When you improvise, don't use any of the old figures ("woods," "sun," and so on), unless one absolutely marvellous one occurs to you. Work with the new words, constantly catching at the world in different ways with them.

10.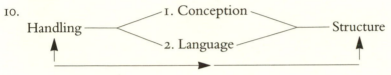

11. Don't always see things connected as similes or metaphors. Seek for new connections, new relations, that will lay bare the hidden anatomy.

12. To get into the deep stream of the subject; to be carried freely along by it.

13. One of the most important things is not to restrict the field; the mind looks after its own limits. A good part of the time these should be foregone, and a recklessness of association encouraged.

14. Always keep the improvisation with at least one leg in fantasy, or, if necessary, more. This gives the rare, true, deep thing a chance to be born.

15. I pass over so much. There are thousands of living images in everything you see, read, hear, think about, imagine, and have forgotten or half-forgotten. The mind must be more alert, must walk about letting these figures quicken their associations.

16. Supplementary method for figures. Take any two figures of a possible comparison, for example, "the moon" and "sickness," and explore the possible ways of combining them with one or the other acting as agent.

    ex. "the moon overwhelmed by sickness"

    invaded by
    apportioned by
    passed by   the moonlight of nausea
    imagined by

    or reverse this: "sickness overwhelmed by the moon," etc.

17. See, deliberately, how complicated and dense you can make a figure.
    "the wounded phenix"
    the phenix wounded at the window

each wound is a phenix

∴ each wound puts at its window the eyes of an awakened phenix.

ex. "straw and flowers"

the flowering straw

the straw of flowers } this is the usual point beyond which it is necessary to go

with the straw in flower (like) the edge of the sky

∴ with the straw in flower at the edge of the sky crying your name.

ex. "the summer water"

the water in summer

the water which touches the summer

the water which pierces the summer

∴ here is the (sacred) water which always penetrates very ↑most↓ narrowly the heart of summer.[60]

18. In events in poetry: *to preserve the fluid context*. Preserve and augment the rich violence.

19. Look everywhere for the rhythm that will be characteristic, not simply adequate; that will be supple, muscular, quick, and inimitable.

20. Two strong principles:
    1. To endow things (objects, situations, actions) with the qualities and attributes of other things (without metaphorical or similical comparison).
    2. To endow things [objects, situations, (actions)] with human qualities: "the migraine of the wind."

21. To perform #16, #17, and in certain cases #20 with everyday expressions is the secret of a certain kind of poetry, entire. But it is too restrictive.

22. To get muscular tension, interplay, resolution, and relaxation into the *rhythm* (and figures) of the poem.

23. The road to originality in poetry leads through the fantastic, the outlandish, and sometimes the absurd, though the result be couched in simple terms.

24. Keep the fluid wildness in the final draft, the poem. Your final drafts tend to be constipated, stiff, and dry.

25. Pack more than one reference, one image, into a line. Instead of "a rose like a smiling saint," this: added: "*Your sister,* the *great* rose where a saint smiles." "Sleep like cables" to

   The *cables* of our *sleep,* so *swiftly filed,* already hang,
   shred ends from *remembered stars.*

60. Dickey wrote in the notebook margin: "Act, Scene, Agent, Agency, Purpose."

26. To get a consistent point of view for looking at things, the world, from, with which to "convert a whole body of material": like Perse (the "Prince,"), Mallarmé, Thomas, or Lowell. This is important. I have athletics and "mystery." (The universe must be live, in continual metamorphosis. Athletics is a kind of crystallization of this, etc.).

27. Try to get a little away from the "situational," or find another angle of attack than the simple present tense.

Terms for #10: permutations and combinations:
1. Nouns and nouns
   A. thing and thing: ex. dog and heart.
   B. thing and quality ↑(quality and thing)↓: ex. tree and spaciousness.
   C. abstract thing and thing: ex. night and heart.
   D. thing and abstract thing: ex. dog and morning; dog and time.
   E. thing and attribute: ex. dog and clemency.
   F. attribute and thing.
2. Nouns and verbs
   A. thing and act: ex. dog and raining. ⎫ Active voice
   B. act and thing: ex. raining and dogs. ⎭

Same: passive voice. Quality: physical. Attribute: <act> name of act. Explore and augment.

28. Stay very far from the pat ending, the pat resolution.

29. Reject always the familiar, pedestrian cadence for the intense, the athletic, the quick, the imaginative. Keep out *reflectiveness* and encourage immediacy, spontaneity.

30. Never settle for the "adequate," the "good-enough," even if it takes you forever to come on the quick, the imaginative.

31. It may be possible to work from simple propositions or situations, *through extreme* complication, to a simplicity that will have the *weight* of the complication behind it or underneath it, and yet will be dazzlingly clear: (like the water when you are swimming in it, in the distance making a blue, impenetrable infinity of all that clearness).
    B. If the poem is better in the state of complication, you must know to leave it that way.

32. Spend some time putting together words and terms (#16) which seem to hold promise of being live metaphors and figures. These should at first be two terms only, but later they may be three, four, five, or even six.
    1. dress   lighthouse
    2. sea   crescent   tyranny
    3. wall   fountain   Martha
    4. wall   fountain   mirror   monarchy   Martha

33. In reference to #31, I think now what I want is a stripping of rich-ness to the *seed,* the *direction of growth,* the *velocity* of richness, so that the richness is implicit and the poem bare and linear, geometrical, spare. Ex. "burned up with rain."

34. Ordinarily, my poetic thinking tends to collect quickly, to drop automatically into three or four stock situations, around three or four habitual figures. Every effort must be made to avoid these traps.

35. The poem should change direction with every line, with every word, even, and add up to an overwhelming vector.

36. Work more toward the implicit metaphor rather than the stated correspondence.

37. Work out another means of progression than that dry, rather prosy, narrative movement. Use a good many short, declarative statements, and work out other kinds of progression. Get away from that tire-some, pedestrian line. Example: several short sentences, then a long one, full of spondees ["ordinary" ("chunk") words], full of action: banging, clanging, etc.

38. Work more *consciously* with the rhythm, deciding what effects you want from it, and then arranging those. You settle too much for just the adequate rhythm.

39. The spoken style, if it were imaginative and held within bounds.

40. Crush the "poetic" to get at the real.

41. The "vision," point of view: in creation, in being, everything is linked—in mystery, in cruelty and evil. However, just as indissolubly linked are love and the passions that produce what we honor: love, courage. These are defeated because the linkup is profoundly on the other side. But the defeated things define us and give us what little is possible against the "ground."

42. Experiment with turning verbs into nouns, and nouns into verbs, participles, gerunds, infinitives, etc. Ex. antenna: antenna'd.

43. There is a sense in which you can *build* intensity, impetuosity, spon-taneity *into* the poem, rather than culling them from it. The poem does not have to be *written* headlong to emerge that way.

44.   the world: experience

term   term

The essentials of metaphor

45. (See #41) Metamorphosis: the *principle* of change: why things be-come some things and not other things. Metamorphosis sometimes continual, sometimes rapid. Show rapid metamorphosis *as* rapid. The mystery of this—the laws beneath the laws: alchemy.

46. It is of the essence, most of the time, to work at a poem over a fairly

long period of time, to try out many spontaneities, until the mystery begins and finishes shining through the many overlays.

47. A poem needs to accrue, and accrue, and accrue. Always have at least two in the mill.

48. Always write violently, with many kinesthetic-sensuous verbs and terms, for even if the passage is to be or turns out quietly, this will give it the glow and characteristic tension you seek.

49. Keep as much as you can to the hard world of *claw*-hammers, bolts, axle-grease, cams, elderberries, and cut out the vagueness of "summer," "the absolute," "water," "sunlight," and so on. *Specify,* and keep on specifying. Specification and violence are two of the keys.

50. Energy, energy; compression, compression.

51. Work much on *tone*. This is a subject which should yield a great deal.

Novel about a young man who has been raised by mediocre people who hated his father (who is dead). They have some hopes for the boy, but in rebellion against *them,* he decides <to> (rather magnificently) to follow his father's path, who was a writer or some kind of talented and unsound fellow. He discovers that he has no talent after years of trying. It ends either in utter defeat or in his turning to something else.

52. Rhythm: feel the rhythm out over the line, over two, over the whole poem, and mark it down in symbols. Feel it for the tone you want, fast or slow. *This* is the rhythmic problem, solved. It only needs perfecting.

53. Do the same thing with rhythms that you do with images and events. Keep trying out new combinations, one after the other. Mix, combine until you get the best possible. Always hear the *developing* rhythm.

54. You must *build up* the inner urgency.

It may be that the (a) long poem will be about the South. It will have to be very good and not dwell much on the much written-about aspects of it. There has not been a major long poem of our time that deals with a military campaign, except perhaps parts of the *Cantos.*

55. It is necessary to have or develop a consistent center or viewpoint [perhaps a concentric center made of several (perhaps) allied points of view] from which the poems shall be *projected.*

56. Think more about a discursive poetry, one whose many *dissimilar* parts will add into a single effect of depth, rather than (rather mechanically) hanging everything to a single, metaphorical peg.

57. And we want a *stranger* poetry—stranger and more real—with a delirious and impelling drive, and mysterious and compelling energy.

58. My poetry is not packed, committed (to the poem), dark, or swirling enough. I am not enough in the verbal element:
    "*dark* with *contagion,*
    Like an *approaching wave* I *sprawl* to *ruin.*"

59. You have not even touched what can be done with meter, with the sound of words and syllables, and all the audible dynamics of poetry.

60. It is in *prosody,* the developing surging-out-and-down of the thousand lines into one inevitable one, that the true line of the poem shall be drawn, individual and susceptible to nothing but itself.

61. In improvising, try to get and keep that high energy <and> of receptiveness and flowing quickness in catching at and linking ideas ↑and images↓. That, I guess, is inspiration—to go fast, with or without a decided-on subject. If with, then surrounding the subject with other subjects, near-allied and far-off or not allied, letting the quick and depth of the mind make the exchanges.

62. Give as much time to concocting metaphors (#16) as to improvising.

63. Take down everything you see, feel, read, or remember: lambs, whirlwinds, ants, daisies, everything. Connect everything with everything. Take down everything you see *in its particulars.*

64. Always override the literal; never ignore it.

65. And write down words—not just the ones from the dictionary, not just striking ones. Make whole lists, long lists of words, thousands of them.

66. Take two or three lines from whatever poem you are working on and take them through ten or twenty transmutations. This should be part of the work of the poem in "taking it up very high."

67. Don't try to "take the poem" up too high ↑at first.↓ It must ↑should↓ be made through many successive drafts.

68. And there is the question of total commitment to the poem, so that manipulation doesn't matter, or matters only to enhance this. This also gives intensity. Also true of fiction.

69. Go hell-bent for the *imaginative,* the strong, the violent at every turn. Leave off so much "art," "form," "detachment," and so on.

70. The point is not to get poems published but to design (or designate) and explore a kingdom. To find the unsuspected and fundamental magics.

71. I want the freedom of the painters—to *discover.*

The hope of the poet: that he may learn to tell lies like those told by dreams.

72. Make lists of different central metaphors of your poetry—the game, the pyre, the hallucination, the hospital, etc.—and work up metaphors from these: "The round flames (of wounds)."
73. Push the poem toward ecstasy, *true* high statement, and yourself toward the poem, closer commitment, ecstasy. Kill the hang-dog. Deepness, sonorousness, all-carrying.
74. The main thing is to have a *subject,* one that can be developed through many poems, from one or many points of view, which will engage the deepest interests and knowledges and feelings.
75. Go always toward the anti-poetic, all the way to the crude. Don't *poetize* things: see them, get at them verbally.

Novel: Joel's vision of the kingdom of cruelty and necessity: a day there: armor, etc. The athlete: clean rites: romantic link with Hitler: wild, hallucinated section culminating in the father-son business: P. Toynbee, *Prothalamium:* breaks off with pathetic plea: construction destroyed: "B.V." a minor part.

76. Keep always after the not-stiff, not-academic rhythms.
77. The willingness to wait *long* enough for the *essential* idea of the poem to appear and not be content with the *adequate* idea.
78. The human situation in the round, held by the imagination. The human moment.
79. A world of actions, interactions, metamorphoses, all endowed with action, never still, always with mystery and fluidity.
80. To feel cleanly, through things.
81. I want to get into my poetry a kind of *hurling* quality, yet sensitive and rough.
82. Fill the poem full of the "clumsiest," strongest, realest, stump-and-smash you can, and make it imaginative and *close to* or *in* the action as much as you can, not generalizing.
83. Write deeply and passionately always, prose or poetry, and never knowingly.

{By August 1956, the date of the next entry, Dickey had left the University of Florida and moved to New York to begin work as an advertising copywriter.}

August 1956

"and memory
Closed in and set loose by sleep."

"the round(ed) sleep of a single memory."

"the patient scheming of art."
"the patient streaming of (its) form."

"and the earth
Vibrates ↑Vibrant↓ with solemn knowledge."

"emptiness behind //
So many perfect forms."

"he feels the change of color //
Of (the) arterial blood ↑the veinous↓ }

"and the change of color of blood
might well be magical, //
Giving up oxygen."

The sense of abandon: that is the essential quality of poetry. Unless poetry
conveys this, it is nothing.

The (Peasants) ↑Farmers↓
André Frénaud[61]

There are few meteors over the flat country of the old,
Few metaphors between the wagon and the ground,
No exploits for the mind, no leisure,
Not glory enough for the head to leap over the hills:
The modest face is not afraid

Of the memory of a long voyage
Through seed and straw,
Or, in spite of all,
Of the horror of working with beasts and muck,
Or, beyond <all> this,
(For) ↑Of↓ the truth of a man reconciled with his <parentage>
   <heritage> fathers.
When love gives him back (his) crimson ↑a red↓ face, he dares

To match the seasons of life with the seasons of the earth,
With the work of the underground river;
A language forms and barely ↑just↓ lives
By the deep pain learned since school days,
the indivisible common good shared (among) ↑by↓ the family.

61. Dickey's re-creation of Frénaud's poem appears in *The Eagle's Mile* as "Farmers."
The epigraph states, "a fragment with André Frénaud." The notebook entry, however,
creatively translates the entire poem.

He grows light, he reappears, he tries to speak,
he extends his figures with an exact clumsiness,
and the heraldry that changes every year,
               its green and yellow squares,
at each moment pronounces that one must dine;
teaches the etiquette that the power of man <instigates> ↑sets up↓
when he <sadly> couples sadly with the earth ↑(in a powerful yoke
    with the earth)↓.

Glory fooled always by the unforeseeable,
So kept ↑had↓ by his steps in the same ground,
So marked by his <knowledge> slowly won knowledge
And always uncertain despite (his)(valiance) courage,
so naked and poor all day long
in the immemorial,
the farmer never ends not knowing

the pasture's out of breath in <its> the furrow,
the <fields> inexhaustible fields, arid, avid,
the permanent slowness, the forewarnings according to (the) rules,
winter, and spring, the season which never ends,
And the apparition of misery, the separations.
A gravedigger on Sunday, he returns on Monday
to the ruling-out-in-squares of his laborious part ↑role↓.
The furs of snow do not come when they should;
<And> The moon has troubled the sown seed.

Notebook V

While Dickey's use of four bound and paginated ledgers facilitated his examination of literature and literary concerns, he also possessed a small blue spiral notebook that he kept with him throughout the day. His original intent for this smaller, more accessible journal was to record daily events or observations and to jot down thoughts or ideas as they occurred to him. Like the larger and heavier ledgers, however, the spiral notebook never realized such a specialized purpose. This fifth notebook consists of 105 handwritten, loose-leaf pages; the pages themselves are not numbered. Dickey likely began writing in this notebook in early 1953, after he had taught a semester following his return to Rice. On the front of the fourth sheet, he lists several books and more than half a dozen issues of literary journals he intends to order from the Gotham Book Mart in New York City. The issue numbers of these reviews indicate initial use of the notebook perhaps as early as January or February 1953. On the front of the seventh sheet, he cites lines from his poem "Utterance I," dedicated to his wife, Maxine; unfinished at this time, the poem was published later that year. Dickey used the fifth notebook for approximately twelve months. He noted the examination schedule for his classes on the back of sheet 87 in an entry dated Tuesday 2 February, thus confirming the year as 1954. Internal evidence therefore indicates that the fifth notebook simultaneously overlaps portions of the second and fourth bound ledgers.

The most notable feature of this notebook is the large number of poems that Dickey lists. Dozens of titles are identified, often in pairs that involve the deliberate selection of opposing perspectives. For example, "On Remaining In" is followed by "On Never Going Into," and "On Departing From" precedes "On Returning To." After citing "Man Considered from Above" as a possible title and then contrasting it with "Man Considered from Below," he extends the perspective once again by parenthetically replacing "man" with "child." This line of thought may have resulted in poems such as "The Father's Body," in which a young boy observes the physical differences between his body and his father's while he showers. Clearly, however, this pairing—and its use of opposing viewpoints—parallels or anticipates Dickey's later interest in imaginatively conceived points of view in which contrary perspectives are juxtaposed and then temporarily united, a poetic exploration apparent in such poems as "A Dog Sleeping on My Feet" and "The Sheep Child."

Other aspects of the notebook's poetic focus are Dickey's use of a series of poems and the cross-fertilization of poetry and fiction. Entries reveal at least eleven "Utterance" poems, the title suggesting the projection of a specific pronouncement or truth. Although the exact thematic concern of each poem remains unclear, their use in a series as well as another group on angels looks forward to Dickey's only published set of similarly related poems—his two "Reincarnation" poems, in which he intended, as he asserts in *Self-Interviews,* to show man being reincarnated up through the evolutionary ladder, beginning with the lowest forms of life. Doubleday having shown no interest in his novel *The Entrance to the Honeycomb,* Dickey began a poem of the same title that seems to center either on the military or on athletics. Both impose structure and discipline and both require belief and conformity. Dickey, in fact, considered the latter a trope for the former, and both metaphors for life itself. Other entries in the notebook identify poems that were eventually published, including "Between Two Prisoners," "Bread," "The Angel of the Maze," "Falling," and "Walter Armistead."

More than any other ledger except the first, the fifth notebook details the scenes and characters of *The Casting,* offering a fuller sense of the narrative and revealing Dickey's effort to avoid generality and provide presentational immediacy. Entries about this novel hint at particular aspects of *Alnilam*. Julian, for example, desperately desires to please his father and receive his love, believing himself "the end of a series." This emphasis on biological heredity looks forward to the intimate connectedness between Joel Cahill and his father, the shared set of abilities and sensitivities first seen by members of the Alnilam conspiracy and later confirmed by Frank Cahill's intuitive talents on the basketball court and in a Stearman plane. Like Joel too, Julian possesses an extreme imagination, and the actions and scenes he labors to set up or sustain are as deeply personal as they are strongly theatrical.

However, clear differences exist between Dickey's first attempted novel and his 1987 published work. In the latter, Joel Cahill has died under mysterious and compelling circumstances before the novel even opens, and his father begins a search for the son he has never really known. In the former, Julian not only is alive but becomes the character whose actions and attitudes are the center of the work. His father, moreover, seems only embarrassed by who his son is. Julian's relationships with Sara and Laverne are indicated if not explicitly detailed, while Joel's involvement with Hannah Pelham and Lucille Wick, who works in Supply and who many think is the Colonel's girl, primarily remains supposition. Then too, Julian's interest and participation in football and track contrast with Joel's acknowledged ability only as a good outside shooter in basketball. The large presence of Dr. Arrington, whom Julian is simultaneously at odds with and preoccupied by, as well as that of Julian's sister Ann, whose beating by their father the latter has photographed, has no counterpart at all in *Alnilam*. *The Casting,* therefore, establishes certain characters, scenes, and ideas that preoccupy Dickey and that eventually assume their final expression on *Alnilam*. The earlier work, in other words, is not a precursor to the later, a fact clearly indicated when one considers that the scene depicting Julian's nosebleed, which occurs as he masturbates following and perhaps as a result of Ann's beating, becomes transposed in *Alnilam* to one involving Hannah, whose own nosebleed results after sex with Joel's father and after he has paddled her at her insistence.

Three related features of the fifth notebook strongly underscore Dickey's commitment in the early fifties to writing. First, he creates a numbered list, though other entries occasionally interrupt it, of 169 books; they are overwhelmingly novels. He has read or is reading many of these books, and he notes them in other journals either by title or by commenting on them. For example, an entry in the first notebook identifies Henry Green's *Loving,* which along with others by Green is included in the listing. In the same notebook, Dickey refers to the "'eland' description of Robin Vote" in Djuna Barnes, a reference to her work *Nightwood,* which he also includes in his listing of titles. Included as well is Mann's *Dr. Faustus,* whose close reading Dickey reveals in the second notebook. However, other novels seem not yet to have been read. The last title in the list is Herbert Gold's 1954 novel *The Prospect before Us,* and several pages later Dickey notes the book and its publisher in a separate entry. Since the fifth journal concludes around February 1954, it is doubtful he has read the book, and the entry is most likely a reminder to obtain it. Dickey reviewed it for the *Houston Post* on February 21, 1954. Moreover, though he quotes from Joyce's *Finnegans Wake* in the first notebook, he does not include it among the 169 books. The catalog's purpose, therefore, remains unclear, but the number of works and the breadth of authors (including American, British, French, and German writers) testify to Dickey's intense reading and to its eclecticism.

Similar to this catalog of books is another feature of the fifth notebook that presents Dickey's dedication to studying language usage—a second list titled simply "What I want." It consists of sixteen statements that not so much codify what he hopes his poetry will be or do as attempt to define precisely the principles by which to govern his diction. The majority of these statements are single-word descriptions of the type of language for which he is striving—poetry, for example, that is "inevitable" or "athletic" or that possesses "empathy" and "unique perspective." Other statements, however, are declarations, self-directed injunctions that apply this new language specifically to aspects of the poem, including sentence pattern and dramatic situation. Dickey has used lists in other notebooks, to catalog, for example, new subjects he wishes to pursue in his writing or the steps involved in the composition of rational and immediate poems. The group of eighty-three statements in the fourth ledger even constitutes a kind of compendium of all aspects of language usage, including its experiential relationship to the physical world. In this much shorter listing, however, Dickey focuses exclusively on his poetic diction, attempting to differentiate the unique wording he believes requisite to achieve a vital poetry.

That Dickey has committed himself to the possibilities of language, though implied by the catalog of novels and his statements regarding poetry, is perhaps most clearly emphasized in the poetic lines and phrases he scatters throughout this loose-leaf notebook. They attempt to capture, in many instances, a unique perspective, as when he observes "The great smiling blond in the sun" or describes the effort "To stream his limbs / Into the hardening moon." These creative efforts also strive to achieve honest description, to be humanly true rather than merely literary, as when he sees "a wound dry as a nut" or notices "a delicate gold feeling." Dickey is struggling toward a language that surpasses fact when he characterizes a figure as one who "gazes so keenly he is blind" or when he describes "the slow / Forward" of snow. The diction reflects an understanding he learned in college. In *Self-Interviews*, he relates an experience at Vanderbilt that was like "the bursting of a dam for me,"[1] by which he meant his understanding that all art lies and, with luck, does so sublimely. In that lie exists possibility, its criterion of success being the effectiveness of the artist's manipulation of language. When Dickey writes in his notebook of "travelling like a mirror," he is attempting to convey a quality of experience beyond that normally perceived by the senses, one closely tied to reality but one that provides penetrating new insight into personal existence.

1. *Self-Interviews*, 33.

{Dickey began using Notebook V during the early months of 1953. He had returned to teaching at Rice Institute the previous fall following completion of his service duty.}

I like to use rime like Kid Gavilan punches[2]—in flurries, only when it's needed, and as a kind of surprise. It seems only a trick when it's used too consistently as an arduous convenience which the poet has taken on for no particular reason other than that it is a convention. There's always a "See! I did it!" air about the perfectly consistent use of rime in a poem when it's over.

Poem: "Merlin."
   ". . . (his) vocabulary
   Of springing and withering signs."

Poem: "Cold Water."
   ". . . shall go forth alone,
   Shaping a quiet paradox."

Poem: "Beginning on One of the Approaches to Madness."
   ". . . one side of the head bursts into flame.
   I am alone in the village of swans
   <With> Having now every way to speak ↑(cry)↓ ↑(say)↓."

Lee Barker 3:00 P.M. Wednesday Rice Hotel.[3]

Entrance to the Honeycomb:
   "passion or wind's heel."
   ["passion(,) or heel of wind"]

Book: Jacques Maritain — *The Limits of Reason.*

Ezra Pound — *The Spirit of Romance* — Selected Translations — New Directions.

From Gotham:
   Poetry January–February
   Kenyon Review Winter
   Hudson   "   "
   Sewanee   "   "

   2. Cuban boxer who became welterweight world champion on May 18, 1951, in a unanimous decision over John Bratton in Madison Square Garden.
   3. Barker was the editor for Doubleday who read and declined the manuscript of Dickey's novel *The Entrance to the Honeycomb.*

Partisan   "   January–February
Quarterly R. of Lit. (Vol VII, no. II)[4]
Accent Winter
Living in Time — Kathleen Raine.
Dylan Thomas — *Collected Poems 1934–1952* (Dent edition).
Denton Welch — *A Voice through a Cloud.*
The Denton Welch Journals — ed. Jocelyn Brooke.
Catalogue [Gotham].

"Utterance XI": "I tumbled with rosy dogs."

The Casting: epigram:
  "I," said the sparrow,
  "With my little bow and arrow (. . . .")
    The Death and Burial of Poor Cock Robin

Possible epigraph for "Utterance II":
  ". . . without ships the sea is not a sea."
    Hendrik Marsman[5]

"Utterance II": "change opened and calmed away by calm."

"Cyclops":
  "for shame the Cyclops
  Inherits any."

The Meditation on the Long Poem: possible subjects, themes:
  1. Culture, ↑religion↓ etc.: *Waste Land.*
  2. Hero in search of experience: Phelps Putnam.[6]
  3. National culture: *The Bridge.*[7]
  4. Man, city as microcosm: *Paterson.*[8]
  5. History, economics: *The Cantos.*[9]
  6. Inner life, metamorphosis of attitudes: Rilke.

4. Vol. 7 covers the years 1952–1954. The issue to which Dickey refers is the first of two published in 1953.

5. From Marsman's poem *Tempel en Kruis* (Temple and Cross), translated by A. J. Barnouw from the Dutch as "The Zodiac." The translation appeared in the spring 1947 issue of *Sewanee Review,* and Dickey re-created it for his poem of the same title published in 1976.

6. American poet (1894–1948) whose ill health contributed to his inability to complete an epic work centering on the wanderings of a hero called Bill Williams, an American Faust searching for experience. See Notebook IV, n. 10.

7. By Hart Crane.

8. By William Carlos Williams.

9. By Ezra Pound.

Speculation:

   1. Panoramic, splintered, with long whole sections.

   2. Fusion (and perhaps *confusion*) of inner and outer worlds.[10]

   3. 100 pages long, at least.

   4. Part multi-leveled, part purely concrete and local.

   5. In a sense Goethean [from low, local scenes to archetypal, high, symbolical (Blakean) scenes].

   6. Use of devices from the movies (cutting, panning, etc.).

   7. Some narration.

   8. Comic (Joyce: Bloom as Elijah).[11]

   9. Parts of it heavily sexual.

   10. No anthropology, little mythology.

   11. Subject: something (monstrous) to do with the individual's relation to and interaction with his culture.

   12. Diversity of styles.

   13. Religious, sexual, bored and local feelings.

   14. Theory of feeling for local articles and objects: theory of the pure, *archetypal moment,* symbolical.

Poem: "The Buffalo Dancers" ↑Lowie↓:[12]
   Song: "Summon me among those . . .
   (who go)
   One way among fire and theft."

"(As) ↑And↓ full of gleaming motions I die (down) ↑(still)↓."

"Utterance I":[13]
   One cry behind hunger
   Moves / like a harp
 Fled upon ↑into↓ arrows.

All Claudel, Supervielle in print.

Book: poems of O.V. Milosz.

Poem: "At the Moment of <Hoping> Believing."

---

   10. Compare Dickey's comments in *Babel to Byzantium,* esp. 287, regarding his poetic intent for *Into the Stone.*

   11. Leopold Bloom is the central figure in Joyce's *Ulysses.* Elijah was a Hebrew prophet of the 9th century B.C. whose mission was to stop the worship of foreign gods and to restore justice.

   12. Robert H. Lowie (1883–1957), American anthropologist who attained international fame through his studies of the American Indian, particularly the northern Plains tribes.

   13. See Notebook II, n. 90. The poem, published in 1953, opens: "One cry behind hunger / Roils like a harp / Drawn full to the head."

(Poem): "Before Opening."
(Poem): "Before an Opening."

Poems: "On Going Into."
   "On Coming Out of."

   "On Remaining In."
   "On Never Going Into."

   "On Departing From."
   "On Returning To."

   "On Staying Away From."
   "On Remaining With."
Perhaps combine titles.[14]

Poem: "The Theory of Assault."
   "The Theory of Repose."

"Her hair an element of redemption."

The young poets now: getting up a few names and chords into a poem.

"The mind's bone": (a structure of thought): "built into the mind like bones."

Books: *Anathémata* — David Jones — Faber and Faber. ⎫
    In Parenthesis — David Jones.   ⎬ from Gotham.
                                  ⎭

Campbell's *Baudelaire* — Pantheon.

Man Against Mass Society — Gabriel Marcel — Henry Regnery.

The Collected Plays of W. B. Yeats — Macmillan.

In the "Utterance" about giving up poetry, tell what he is "away from" —"the turgidity of insight" (trying to)(make)(smooth) the hoarse cough of meter into a scream, smooth as screaming, etc.

Poems: "Wells": use "Pursuit" from "Suite from Crime."

"Utterance II": end: "the (silent), living island" ↑mute and living island↓.

---

14. These titles suggest many of the stages or states involved in the mythic hero's rites of passage as described in Joseph Campbell's *The Hero with a Thousand Faces* (Princeton: Princeton University Press, 1949).

In most poetry now there is not enough of the living, breathing, unaccomplished world.

$$\left(\begin{array}{l}\text{Test: Feb. 12, 1952}\\ \text{English 200}\end{array}\right)^{15}$$

Books:

A History of the Borgias — Baron Corvo.
Desire and Pursuit of the Whole — Baron Corvo.
The Sign of Jonas — Thomas Merton — Harcourt Brace.
The Year One — Kathleen Raine — H. Hamilton.

Something like this: the poet ought to be someone who, when he bellows with rage, the bellow falls into a poem.

End line of poem: "And wreck this parable to joy."

Book list:
1. *Under the Volcano* — Malcolm Lowry.
2. *The Loved One* — Waugh.
3. *A Handful of Dust* — Waugh.
4. *Seven Pillars of Wisdom* — T. E. Lawrence — Besing.
5. *Journey to the End of the Night* — Céline.
6. *Death on the Installment Plan* — Céline — Barton.
7. *The Asiatics* — Frederic Prokosch.
8. *Victory* — Conrad.
9. *Swann's Way* — Proust.
10. *Studs Lonigan* — Farrell.
11. *Absolam, Absolam* — Faulkner.
12. *Light in August* — Faulkner.
13. *The Great Gatsby* — Fitzgerald.
14. *Tender Is the Night* — Fitzgerald — Palacios.
15. *The Image of a Drawn Sword* — Jocelyn Brooke.
16. *The Scapegoat* — Jocelyn Brooke.
17. *Antic Hay* — Aldous Huxley.
18. *A Long Day's Dying* — Frederick Buechner.
19. *The Delicate Prey* — Paul Bowles.
20. *Let It Come Down* — Paul Bowles.
21. *Ushunt* — Aiken.
22. *The Cannibal* — John Hawkes.
23. *The Trial* — Franz Kafka.
24. *The Castle* — Kafka.

15. The year is 1953. Dickey was still in the service the preceding year.

25. *The Morning Watch* — James Agee.
26. *Let Us Now Praise Famous Men* — Agee.
27. *Prancing Nigger* — Ronald Firbank.
28. *Valmouth* — Firbank.
29. *A Farewell to Arms* — Hemingway.
30. *The Sun Also Rises* — Hemingway.
31. *Look Homeward, Angel* — Thomas Wolfe.
32. *Of Time and the River* — Wolfe.
33. *Man's Fate* — Malraux.
34. *Man's Hope* — Malraux.
35. *The Naked and the Dead* — Mailer.
36. *Guard of Honor* — Cozzens.
37. *The Red Badge of Courage* — Crane.
38. *Pale Horse, Pale Rider* — Porter.
39. *Flowering Judas* — Porter.
40. *Portrait of the Artist as a Young Man* — Joyce.
41. *Dubliners* — Joyce.
42. *Sons and Lovers* — Lawrence.
43. *The Man Who Died* — Lawrence.
44. *The Education of Henry Adams* — Adams.
45. *The American* — Henry James.
46. *The Green Child* — Herbert Read.
47. *A Passage to India* — Forster.
48. *The Longest Journey* — Forster.
49. *To the Lighthouse* — Virginia Woolf.
50. *Mrs. Dalloway* — Woolf.
51. *World Enough and Time* — Warren.
52. *All the King's Men* — Warren.
53. *Invisible Man* — Ralph Ellison.
54. *The End of the Affair* — Graham Greene.
55. *Brighton Rock* — Greene.
56. *Moby-Dick* — Melville.
57. *Billy Budd* — Melville.
58. *Alice in Wonderland* — Carroll.
59. *Through the Looking-Glass* — Carroll.
60. *Young Man with a Horn* — Baker.
61. *The Tartar Steppe* — Dino Buzzatti.
62. *World Within World* — Stephen Spender.
63. *The Dead Seagull* — George Barker.
64. *The Bitter Box* — Eleanor Clark.
65. *Maiden Voyage* — Denton Welch.
66. *Fireman Flower* — William Sansom.
67. *Colonial Julian* — H. E. Bates.
68. *Falling Through Space* — Richard Hillary — Bennet.

69. *Prince of Darkness* — J. F. Powers.
70. *The Horse's Mouth* — Joyce Cary.
71. *Mister Johnson* — Cary.
72. *Of Human Bondage* — Maugham.
73. *The Man Who Was Loved* — James Stern.
74. *The Man Who Invented Sin* — Séan O'Faolain.
75. *Collected Tales of A. E. Coppard* — Coppard.
76. *The Young Lions* — Irwin Shaw.
77. *Miss Lonelyhearts* — Nathanael West.
78. *The Day of the Locust* — West.
79. *1984* — George Orwell.
80. *The Track of the Cat* — Walter van Tilburg Clark.
81. *The Oxbow Incident* — Clark.
82. *Conjugal Love* — Alberto Moravia.
83. *The Stranger* — Albert Camus.
84. *Sister Carrie* — Theodore Dreiser.
85. *Dr. Faustus* — Thomas Mann.
86. *A Handful of Dust* — Evelyn Waugh.
87. *The Seven Storey Mountain* — Thomas Merton.
88. *The Catcher in the Rye* — J. D. Salinger.
89. *The Way of All Flesh* — Samuel Butler.
90. *Native Son* — Richard Wright.
91. *Sanctuary* — Faulkner.
92. *Dorian Gray* — Wilde.
93. *The Christmas Tree* — Isabel Bolton.

End of story: "In the Loft":
   Roy pauses half-way down the stair: He stood there for a moment, gripping the rail, then formed a cruel, confident smile ↑, across his face↓, a broad one that was still on his face when he passed out onto the street. It was the only one he had ever had consciously to formulate.

Revise second chapter dealing with inheritance: I was only the end of a series, beginning with my uncle's entry into old age. Father's letters, etc., had now paid off: "I almost lost you for your father," etc. Leaves most of money as compensation, also some directly to Julian.

Poem about no one being able to create (the image of) his own brother: "an essential unlike to be understood": "to wreck the parable." No man can create his brother (if he try).

94. *The Heat of the Day* — Elizabeth Bowen.
95. *The Inheritance* — Allan Seager.
96. *Equinox* — Seager.

97. *Signed With Their Honor* — James Aldridge.
98. *Look Down in Mercy* — Walter Baxter.
99. *Howards End* — E. M. Forster.
100. *The Retreat* — P. H. Newby.
101. *The Power House* — Alex Comfort.
102. *Do I Wake or Sleep?* — Isabel Bolton.
103. *Brother to Dragons* — Robert Penn Warren.
104. *The Innocent Eye* — Herbert Read.
105. *Poor White* — Sherwood Anderson.
106. *Children Are Bored on Sunday* — Jean Stafford.
107. *Bamboo* — Robert O. Bowen.
108. *The End of My Life* — Vance Bourjaily.
109. *Head Against the Wall* — Herve Bazin.
110. *The Age of Reason**
111. *The Reprieve*
112. *Troubled Sleep*
    Jean-Paul Sartre.
113. *Nausea* — Jean-Paul Sartre.
114. *The Wall* — Sartre.
115. *The Conformist*
116. *Two Adolescents*
117. *The Time of Indifference*
118. *The Fancy-Dress Party*
119. *Woman of Rome*
    Alberto Moravia.
120. *Conjugal Love* — Moravia.
121. *The Transient Hour*
122. *The Barkeep of Blémont*
123. *The Second Face*
124. *The Miraculous Barber*
    Marcel Aymé.
125. *The Shining Scabbard*
126. *Journey With Strangers*
127. *Interim*
128. *The Fire and the Wood*
129. *Testament*
130. *Elephant and Castle*
    R. C. Hutchinson.
131. *Parade's End*
132. *The Good Soldier*
    Ford Madox Ford.
133. *Loving**
134. *Nothing**
135. *Caught**

136. *Concluding**
137. *Party Going**
138. *Dating**
139. *Living*
140. *Back**
141. *Blindness*
      Henry Green.
142. *Lions and Shadows* — Christopher Isherwood.
143. *Prater Violet* — Isherwood.
144. *The Aerodrome* — Rex Warner.
145. *The Adventures of Augie March* — Saul Bellow.
146. *Dangling Man* — Bellow.
147. *The Victim*
148. *Who Walk in Darkness*
      Chandler Brossard.
149. *The Weight of the Cross* — Robert O. Bowen.
150. *On This Side Nothing* — Alex Comfort.
151. *Titus Groan* — Mervyn Peake.
152. *Hadrian the Seventh* — Frederic Rolfe (Baron Corvo).
153. *The Desire and Pursuit of the Whole* — Rolfe (Corvo).
154. *For Whom the Bell Tolls* — Ernest Hemingway.
155. *The Last Husband and Other Stories* — William Humphrey.
156. *The Portable Faulkner* — ed. Malcolm Cowley.
157. *Children Are Bored on Sunday* — Jean Stafford.
158. *Boston Adventure* — Stafford.
159. *The Mountain Lion* — Stafford.
160. *A Long Forth* — Peter Taylor.

Art: aims at representing emotional truth through the imagination exercised in <the> a specific medium. The intellect aids the concept, or can, but the work of art does not depend upon it exclusively.

161. *A Woman of Means* — Peter Taylor.
162. *The Disguises of Love* — Robie Macauley.

Novel?: "There are two ways of hopping yourself up to face things," he said. "One is <to> drink and the other is exercise. Odd, though; <they> you can't mix them."

Poem: "Intrusion."
  (What is time?)
  "No more time than the royal deer
  Biting into our long-dead footfalls."
or "biting / Into our long-dead footfalls."

My whole area of responsibility in poetry is that of human relations at their deepest, most fragmentary, and most lasting.

163. *Delilah* — Marcus Goodrich.
164. *The Man Without Qualities* — Robert Musil.
165. *End as a Man* — Calder Willingham.

Bring out in the novel that Julian has always tried desperately to please his father, "believing it my only warrant for existence," but has never before brought himself, or been brought, to any kind of trial until the night of the game. His father *is* there, more than anything else for the purpose of being seen supporting his (the rich) neighborhood's team. His only remark: "I'm sure glad you're not going to play in any more football games."
"I had not remembered he was coming," etc.
The rest of the time he is alive, they stay apart.

166. *Nightwood* — Djuna Barnes.
167. *Friends and Vague Lovers* — Jack Dunphy.
168. *The Desire and Pursuit of the Whole* — Baron Corvo (Frederick Rolfe).
169. *The Prospect Before Us* — Herbert Gold.

Poem: "Beneath the Shell of Venus": a rotten (abandoned) pasture, the side of a hill: three sheep cross a bridge, unattended, etc.

Poem: "(The) Belief in the Enemy": importance, solidarity opposite to love, etc.

Novel: locker room as honeycomb. Use a figure to represent this.

Julian: "although I read a good deal of history, especially books dealing with the Assyrian conquests ↑and depredations↓, the Aztecs, and certain <fanatic> Mexican fanatic (religious) cults."

Poem: "The Entrance to the Honeycomb": 1st line:
    The entrance to the honeycomb is belief:
    Authority untouched by wrath.
    Doctrine is what relives
    Its laborers, is their dumb structured speech.

Poem: Wordsworthian poem on loss of the "insight" of innocence.
    "alive,
    Closing the instrument."

Theory of Prose Fiction:
  1. Concerned primarily with *act*.
  2. Motivation itself should be adumbrated by (symbolic) act.
  3. Attempt to convey by symbol and image what needs to be said. Let the psychological considerations come out through the act, scene, rather than through explanation.
  4. A minimum of introspection, "analysis."

Charles Ives — *Symphony No. #3.*
Walter Piston — *Symphony No. #2* — American Recording Company.

The Casting: brief account of Jack's throwing javelin (only the necessary adjunct, in the spring, to his football passing).

The Casting: tell or hint why things are coming to a head at this time: "maturing of a long process, possibility, which had appeared in images, symbols, and hints for years." (This in scene at lake, in box, with Laverne). [Give a few of these].

  Also, earlier, hint that with Sara: I must do something—soon. *The peculiarly humiliating defeat of never being able to bring anything about.* (First chapter, somewhere).

Book: *Selections from John Skelton* — Grove Press.

"Those That Die Late to Live":
  "thunder touches
  An old scar (it made) to make (us) smile,
  Across the aqueduct."

"Under the Venus' Shell"
  Under the Venus' shell, under a head
  Let everybody die. I went there once
  Without a feast I could not dream,
  Without a girl I could not shake
  To quite another. Resting a hand
  That changingly sought my other, on
  The back of my sleek not accurate
  Head, I closed my eyes
  Of growing stone, <and came> content,
  And came to this uncertain grief.

Sheep crossing a path, aqueduct, etc. Phelps Putnam-like dialogue. End line: "And let the knowledgeable also pray."

"Between Two ↑the↓ Prisoners." [16]

"The Captors."

"Landscape With Sounds": end line: "The battling of two legions armed with nails."

Novel: bring out Ann's age. Bring out fact that this beating is the only one he ever gave either of them.

Novel: his (J's) feeling that he is "a circle enclosing hysteria"—that he is never very far from hysteria.

What I want is an exuberance and freshness of feeling within control but not refined out of existence.

Cast "Venus Shell" in rough iambic quatrains. Write four or five a day. When the mind loses that alertness to relation characterized by an extreme looseness and flexibility, then what I want is gone. There is a feeling of recklessness here, also.

Eulogy for Willard Thorp: [17]

Since September there has been on the Rice Campus a new kind of hero: a Yankee one. He has flung graduate students around like dummies to see that they don't remain dummies, has caused ↑hordes of↓ undergraduates to flee through the dark stacks of Fondren Library like ghosts, <a little> pale, but from facts, live ones, rather than footnotes. He has unsettled <everyone's> all the minds he has come in contact with, only to settle them toward more permanent and valuable forms.

He has <taken in> directed plays, given programs, read papers and told jokes (intellectual ones); in short, has taken a part in campus activities which anyone associated with the school for twenty years would be proud to have done.

It is perhaps superfluous to remark that these references <might be> are pertinent to only *two* members of the English Department, and I regret to say that *I* am *not* the one they refer to. <I believe you know who I mean—Professor Willard Thorp.>

If I said so, I'm sure no one would let me get away with it, <especi> at least not while we have with us

Professor Willard Thorp.

16. "Between Two Prisoners" was published in the September 1960 issue of *Yale Review.*

17. English professor and historian at Princeton. He was a visiting professor at Rice while Dickey was teaching there.

Jack's pass: his arm shaping on the cold gauze of the air the merciless sudden curve of a hawk's beak.

Novel: in Julian's meeting with his father, his father is with five or six other men. One turns away embarrassed, another laughs, a <loud> low carrying laugh.

"You looked like a clown out there. I wish I'd kept my mouth shut about our number."

I tried to smile strongly, and (went on toward) the locker room.

Novel: in beating scene: father beats "I love you" out of Ann. He insists on it. "I love you, too," I screamed <crying> hysterically. "I love you too, I love you too."

"The First Poem": end line: ". . . settled out of vision, made with words."
"If you can find them, they will do what you say."

Story about the rich boy, idler, come home after the war to his old childhood. <His> The girl (Mary Ann White) and he in the half-built house.[18]

Books: Grove Press:
 The Marquis de Sade: A Study — Simone de Beauvoir.
 Count D'Orgel — Raymond Radiguet.
 Edwin Muir: Collected Poems 1921–1951.
 Rimbaud's Illuminations — Wallace Fowlie.
 Feeling and Form — Susanne K. Langer — Scribner's.
 Creative Intuition in Art and Poetry — Jacques Maritain — Pantheon.
 Ten Burnt Offerings — Louis MacNeice — Oxford.

"The Dawn Raid":
 ". . . lean
 Into clean (dissolving) ↑(and pulsing)↓ ↑and trembling↓ glass."

Poems: "The Cynic": "found / The flesh of crows his only to scorn."
 "The Old Knight."
 "The Burned House": long poem: my old childhood: enter the house whenever guilt is heavy between sleep and the night. Turning on a daylight bed, etc.

"A voyage never toward any childhood, but made /
By children."

---

18. A student at North Fulton High School who was a year behind Dickey and whom he dated.

"The Burned House":
  "walls /
  Erected into (conceivable) air
  Out of need," etc.

"Walls not of fire,
But fiery and uniform," etc.

"Night Briefing II" ↑The Benediction↓
  Sheltered, they stand beneath
  The shadow of another implement.
  Manipulation, not belief
  Shall move within the plant
  Of night, closing its veins upon
  One walking like a child alone,
  The land drenched from his single leaf.

  The chaplain's passion is their use.
  Falling ↑bluely↓ down their eyes
  Where cities lie imagined
  And unclean, they may
  Now laugh there, pray,
  Or deal in stones,
  But ↑(not)↓ never <ask to> (walk) among.
    ↑go blind to (walk love wed)↓

Wm. Humphrey: "obsessed with the virtues of his limitations." *Family stories.*[19]

Novel: pictures of Ann's whipping: "I could not bring myself to look at them often."

What a tremendously fecundating principle it is to have the rhythmic notation of the poem in advance! How much the imagination is helped by having an *order* in which to occur! A rhythm to fill out!

Dr. A. quietly: "That would justify anything, Julian."

Dr. A: "If you (can't) ↑don't↓ agree with what most people think is the way to live, they can't let you in." (But) "Sometimes you don't even know."

---

19. American novelist whose works are largely set in the east Texas area of Red River.

Beating scene: Julian has orgasm, leaning against a post or tree or tele-graph pole, his nose streaming (pouring) blood—"that quick, light, compulsive, dreaming series of outward strokes from the loin hitherto felt only in sleep."

Discourse with Doctor: "You've got to get in and battle with them, in free and open concourse, so to speak. How do you think I got this? Competition gave it to me. I won out. I dominated most of the others at med-school and, with luck, a few of those I shouldn't have been able to. Starting practice, the same thing. Now, I'm the best genito-urinary surgeon around here. Nobody gave me anything but the chance. The rest I worked for, and took."

J.—
Dr. A: "Now, hell, I can slack off a little, clip a few boxwoods, <enjoy myself> do stuff that don't mean anything, and enjoy myself," etc.

Pictures: any time Ann got "out of line," which was seldom, Father sim-ply dropped one of the pictures wordlessly before her as she sat at table, or she found it on her dresser, etc.
    She had run off with Hubert across the state line and got married.

Pictures: taking them. He has set up both cameras and photographer's lights, which he had had the wiring of the house changed especially to accommodate.

Succession of his father's friends: how he never seemed "in with them," as though "anything could set him back months, perhaps even destroy his entire achievement."

A little more about the routine of football practice—how he always warmed-up, did exercises, with such abandon and passion and ran signals so. "It was only when faced with someone else's will, who would fight, drive, that I lost heart," etc.

Novel: "Recover, possess, reject, ↑(transcend)↓: perhaps in some cases they were the same thing."

What I want in my poetry now:
    1. Verve, drive (Skelton): athleticism: through rhythm, "the free spirit hurled headlong" ↑athletic, muscular quality↓: *brio* ("The Anniversary").
    2. Insight, empathy: projection: Rilke—identification.
    3. Imagination: "soaring brother."
    4. Music (new metrics): *used* music.
    5. About real human situation ("The Burned House").

6. A hard, stony bounce—"riflestock": brilliant, swift, fast, imaginative.

7. "Used" syntax: Graham.

8. Speaking, writing, *out of the center of the experience*. The poet (or his protagonist) as engaged in the experience he writes of: *spontaneity, immediacy*.

Write a furious, driving lyric tomorrow—very fast:

   . . . / / ˘ ; / / ˘.

A poem savage and gleaming: <"all in my> "and full of gleaming motions I lie down."

In the final scene with Taz: Taz hesitates (fills J's throat with "lyric joy"), then comes on. J. swings (I was astonished at the force of the blow) but it must have been clumsy, for it missed, and a blinding, painless light bloomed <before> behind my eyes. I recovered immediately, though a little shaken, still on my feet, and he closed and missed. We grappled. For an instant[20] we swayed undeterminedly; then he began to give. Utilizing my strength less nervously, I was astonished ↑to find↓ how much stronger I was than he. I caught him by the throat of his shirt and his belt, heaved the lower hand up with all my strength, and upended him. (As if inspired,) I stepped away, releasing him to the air; he crashed to the floor on the side of his head and one shoulder, the room jumping. A lamp beside the bed reeled on its table, toppled, then righted. Taz gracefully extended one leg, then lay still. "If that's what they want," I said, turning to go. Laverne stood straight beside the open door. I walked to it, then looked back at Taz. I closed the door.

"Take off that robe, honey," I said.

She stood there.

"Take it off," I said, putting one hand on my belt-buckle.

She did as I said, and I led her like a child to the bed. I took off my own clothes and opened the blind and window to the sun.

I see the way to do the Assyrian scene now. Have the *whole* narrative told by an "imaginative historian," interspersed with single-line comments by Julian.

"The king stood up," etc. Then he jumps up into the mirror as the men gather round, J. despairing. J. is the young man hunting with the king. He is the prince, or the *young* Ashur-bani-apal.[21]

20. Here Dickey parenthetically wrote "over 2," and the passage continues later in the notebook. I have continued the entry to reflect Dickey's sense of continuity.

21. Son of Esarhaddon and king of Assyria (669–616 B.C.) under whose reign the country reached the climax of its wealth and fame. The Greeks called him Sardanapalus. In the notebook this entry originally preceded the passage beginning "we swayed undeterminedly" and divided the previous entry into two parts as indicated in n. 20.

The landlady is hammering on the door all the time: chaos: Julian laughs. As he passes her, he gives her a 20 dollar bill, "then went down the stair."

The scene with Corbett: Corbett's pass. They close in on him. He leaps and throws the ball "with his whole being"—"as though he were tearing himself apart." They batter him under, but the ball rides; it ends quivering tautly (this is only a desperation pass at the end of the game, but "the <teams> score did not matter, etc.). I rose, etc. The end catches the ball, then is hit and fumbles, or "interference was ruled" (all this is irrelevant). Dr. Arrington looks at him. After the game he and Sara (and the Dr.) walk out, "I looking at Corbett, but he did not see me." Describe a good deal here.

A passage somewhere about "all of them characters on a stage, and would do my bidding," etc.

Scene where Julian goes to Jack's room (or vice versa): gives him money (for something) as I had been doing for some time, but it was no good. *Then,* the part about the theatre, etc.

   Jack is drinking heavily. He looks very boyish and unchanged. They talk inarticulately, etc. Jacks get drunk: "Why (for such and such a college) with you and me in the backfield," etc. Then he gets drunker. "You've got plenty of money. I don't see why. What difference does it make if you could never've—."

   Julian goes out: stage metaphor.

   Jack's room: trophies and the *pictures* of him!

End of book: "many urgent voices, among which I walked quietly, untouched, and as happy as a stone."

"It would take him a long time to fail (completely), probably all his life."

Julian: "To break down artificial barriers is (almost) ↑(sometimes)↓ as important as to break down real ones. Who can say which is which?"

Novel:
   "Dance, Sir."
   "Ah, <DARL/ing,> let me be really disgraceful and say it." Then, primly, "Only horizontally, sir." [22]

---

22. Dickey indicated in a marginal arrow that the entry continues. I have maintained his intent.

After a while Sara lies down beside him. "I feel beautiful," etc. After a while she takes off her stockings and girdle. He seems to be almost asleep, yet his eyes are open.

She does a can-can fillip: bare behind.

Jean Stafford: "as though it were evidence of artistic 'detachment' to regard everything as faintly amusing."[23]

Novel: "Nothing real had happened ↑(had seemed real)↓ to me since I had left high school."[24]

Poem on sleeping with family, feeling youth go: "passed a long touch in the night."

"Between Two Prisoners": Rewrite very carefully; revise much. Send to Ransom; make clear.

Another short-line poem like "The Anniversary": rime: "devil" and "weevil."

Images of leaping, soaring, intense physical action.

". . . and the light comes out of the dancing."

Poems grafting Lorca onto Skelton, of which "The Anniversary" is the first. Strong rhythmic drive, rimes (Skelton), joie de vivre, strong visual and sensuous images (Lorca).

Poem: a kind of ballad about a girl searching for a ghostly "kingly" lover in the wood. He has appeared and then counseled her to meet him at a special place, etc. Question and answer: six-line, short-line stanzas: Skelton-Lorca. Describe his accoutrements.[25]

Ballad: perhaps ("After de la Mare") or "For Walter de la Mare."

Poem: "The Hanged Child."

Poem: "The Altar Flowers."

---

23. This entry in the notebook originally followed the paragraph ending "Only horizontally, sir."

24. This entry in the notebook originally preceded the second part of the passage referred to in n. 22, beginning "After a while Sara."

25. Compare with the similar poem "The Kingly Lover," which Dickey discusses in Notebook I.

Last name for a character: Leaf.

Poem: "The Virgin and (of) the Shades": dialogue.
  "The Virgin and the Sun."
  "   "   "   "   " Sea."

"Man Considered from Above."
" "   "   " Below."
(Child)

"(A) man spread(s) like a tree."

"A tree (stands) like a man."

"The immense confidence of one
Who at all times sees himself
Poised in a ↑(flowered)↓ dream to strike."

The theme music from *Limelight*.[26]

Poem modelled on B.V.'s "As I came through the desert": Sennacherib:
River of Dogs.[27]

A fairly long poem, more or less in the form of "Gerontion,"[28] "really
obscure," full of symbols, very carefully worked, and tight in rhythm.

"And the fish /
Circled alive in a spell."

The live practices of fishing ceremonies.

"I took their nets
And cast them down on a stone."

Some symbol to stand for aloneness now as opposed to community then.

---

26. The 1952 black-and-white movie directed by Charlie Chaplin concerns the artist's deliberate look back to assess his aims and art. The music was also by Chaplin.

27. See Notebook IV, n. 45. Each stanza in section 4 of Thomson's *The City of Dreadful Night* opens with the refrain "As I came through the desert thus it was, / As I came through the desert . . . ." A short-line refrain closes the first six of the eleven stanzas: ". . . I strode on austere; / No hope could have no fear." Both refrains are used by Joel Cahill in *Alnilam*, 430–31. On Sennacherib, see Notebook I, n. 142. "River of Dogs" is from Frederico Lorca. See *Poet in New York,* trans. Rolphe Humphries (New York: W. W. Norton, 1940), esp. "Unsleeping City" and "New York."

28. By T. S. Eliot.

Recast "The Mission" or write it as another poem. Take it up several notches.

"That cast their eye
(Anew) To custom and remorse,
<And> The steady, intolerable heat
Of sight, the narrow foundry's glow."

End with the figure of the forge as opposed to the waste.

Allen Tate's introduction of *specific* symbols, unrelated to the *logical* or *local* development of the poem, but commenting on it (the crab and the jaguar in "Ode to the Confederate Dead," the stag in "The Cross," and so on).

"The gaze of a beheaded man."

"The strength of ghosts."

End novel: "as strong, <and> (as) happy as a stone."

Poem: "A Spell for the Summer of Lester Mansfield": "nor drift of shadow of antlers."

"The mantis summer, the mask of stone."

Poem: "Who Shall Surpass Himself."

"The brutal arm distending its veins."

"The great smiling blonde in the sun," etc.

Lecture: "On Entering the Artist's Weather" or "The Artist's Weather."

Poem: "The Night Runner" or "The Deepening Runner": empathy, athletic poise, impulse.

Book: *The Achievement of D. H. Lawrence* — ed. Hoffman and ___ — Univ. of Oklahoma Press.[29]

"Annus Mirabilis:[30] The (Midnight) <Burner> Sprinter":
   comet above statues
   springs from blocks

---

29. Edited and with an introduction by Frederick J. Hoffman and Harry T. Moore. The book was published in 1953.
30. Literally, "the extraordinary year."

dead town
postured stone
thin limbs
olives
"heart bursting /
As with passion, remembers
(The wind) through," etc.

"The runner hunts
From his dead blocks."

"To stream his limbs
Into the hardening moon."

The blood created by his speed.

Writing: enter into the subject in an attitude of total enthusiasm, reckless and alert, and a little hurrying.

3rd novel: (boy with a gifted, dead father): concentrate on the mother: Jean Genêt and Virginia Woolf for style: 250 pages.

Book: *Poetry and the Age* — Randall Jarrell.
    Brother to Dragons — Robert Penn Warren.

Poem: "Spell for Piercing Stones."

"Leaves a stone in the air."

"The ear of a stone."

Before writing poem: let your instincts build up/on it.

Book: Yeats' letters to Sturge Moore.[31]

Immediacy, *immediacy* is what I want in writing.

Poems: (1) "The Idol": worshippers give it a kind of life: "mask," "mounted (ing) in the idol's view."
    (2) "The Feather": (new meter): floating: (soft) hedged (combed) teeth, white flame. White flame combed, etc. White flame combed and floating.

---

31. *W. B. Yeats and T. Sturge Moore: Their Correspondence, 1901–1937*, ed. Ursula Bridge (London: Routledge and Kegan Paul, 1953).

Poems: "Before Light."
   "After Light."
   "Before Dark."

Novel: to be called *The Scythians:* (wreckers, barbarians): a kind of genteel parallel of a barbarian invasion, overrunning.

"The Sprinter: Annus Mirabilis":
   "his speed
   Uncovers, (deep), a helmet and a bolt."

Shapiro: against any kind of officialdom in poetry. Poet: lifts up language
like Arthur's sword: the purely useless: like any vision useless, able to
work its changes only from within. *Ordinary man* who can do this.[32]

Poem: "Minos": uncreative man must be cruel and in an ingenious way:
his relation to the labyrinth and to the Minotaur. Look up the myth.

Shapiro article: dictum of "New Criticism": "make everything more
complicated than it is." Burke, Blackmur, and Tate. Shapiro does not
do this.

"The accessive grammatical accuracy."

The figure of the island: isolation—history: local—universal. Long
poem.

"The Dead Tree": man sitting, half-awake, at night thinks of this.

Book: *The Waking* — Roethke.

The Philosophy of Symbolic Forms — Ernst Cassirer — Yale University
Press.

Story: "Marry Me, Marry Me" (Pony Boy).

Poems: "Open Joy."
   "Closed Joy."

"A stone colored by washing."

"A delicate gold feeling."

---

32. Compare Dickey's statements on the poet in "The Poet Turns on Himself."

Poem: "The Brother."
    At the palsied fountain he is in luck.
    The leaves tremble, all heavy,
    Until one falls to the chill basin.
    Another being stills
    From his shadow as it crosses the ↑(fallen)↓ leaf.

Long poem: "Suite from Crime": in new meter, symbolic as hell, but not literarily allusive: two lines a day. Work on all year: fast, knotted, tangential, bold, oracular in part: part in 3- or 4-stress couplets. Plan as it develops. (Rape? Love?)(Robbery? Pride?).

"A wound dry as a nut."

Novel II: Matilda Weller: leukemia: boils, nosebleed.[33]

Joel's notebook: "Masston: blind, attacked with knife—Salt—Harris." F.

"The Deliverer":
    "where it is dark enough/ } Vary
    For light."

Instress: when you see, say, a heron, think: "There is something light and sharp and blind about <it> him." Let your mind dilate and catch quickly.

"Gazes so keenly he is blind."

Device: not simply adjectives, but *qualified* adjectives. Not "the *warm* shadow," but "the *still*-warm shadow."

Two-part poem: "(The Brothers)."
    One: The Living <Brother>: war: attempt to rediscover relation to dead brother, dead in childhood.
    The Dead: Dead trying to come at living: remembers his brother.
    ". . . saw
    My brother's face through water thin as steam."

Aiken review: ". . . line not like unknotting wadded twine."

New novel: don't stick exclusively to Mitchell: switch off to Elsdorf, to Brazek, to Marion. Have the scene where Brazek washes out Harbelis.

33. See Notebook IV, n. 45.

Harbelis gets a notion that there are other, more important things than this; he becomes, more or less, a man. "Civilian Contract School." Elsdorf and Miss Lawler: she rejects him in the end: he tries to make love to her.

Story about a fever case on Okinawa after hurricane. Onset of fever while watching a film: *The House on 92nd Street,* or one like it.

More and more I am coming to see that the *unique perspective* is what makes the poem, the perspective as it is realized by linguistic and rhythmical forms.

A poem has to be, or have,
  1. Unique perspective
  2. "Real"
  3. Imaginative.

Look constantly for, and encourage, the poem to go in a *new direction.* Give it its head and help it along as much as possible.

Of a poet: "There's too much clatter in the lines; they don't sing down!"

Novel: Mitchell's pool: built up membership by making it a "Gentile Club." The "Club" snobbery.

Novel: swimming pool: Mitchell: "the lights seemed to enter his head."

Two types of prose fiction:
  1. The Immediate (Lawrence).
  2. The Reflective, or Analytical (Proust).

In poetry the essential and relevant and hitherto undiscovered *angle* is of the utmost importance. The perspective—the way the subject is viewed, the *slant,* the peculiar vantage.

Story: "The Flower in It."

Poems: "Sea Bird and Brier."
  "The Sand Mirror."
  "Freehold."
  "A Drift of Antlers": (shadow) over sleeping boy.
  "Gladiator."

The *painterly* approach to poems.

Poetry: "Catching at the scene or object or feeling with words." But in a sense the words come out of a scene. *Then* you use them to catch *back at* the scene, object, or feeling.

"wave /
Raised from the open shadow
Of depth."

"(Dropped) ↑sunk↓ to the parable of flesh."

"Or silence(,) the dark of song."

Poetry: stay close to *things, real situations,* and bring them up to increased and unique life.

Poem: "The Center of a Kingdom."

"Love will not forgive the flesh."

Novel: first meeting with Selma: something (she does?) reminds him, or the way he is getting to feel does, of a similar feeling (that of the episode of the twins) which had opened into the most open emptiness, horror. He had (thought about?) swimming afterward.

Poem: "The Temperate Vision": "his face poured into light."

Poem: "The Thief of Light."
  "Water as Virtue."
  "Water as Sign."
  "Hunting."

"Hounds leaping (up) like fire."

Poem: "Among the Exhausted": "unable to search out the dead (for grief)."

"(Starving) light" in the "Father" poem: *starved* light.

Poem: "The Lost Stair(s)."

Poem: a system of new, *implied* relations. Implied by subject or implicit in the subject.

"Or, in the father,
That (silence) of the dazzled animal."

Novel: scene where one of the boys runs a long splinter under his fingernail. Describe this. Mitchell is quietly standing <beside> aside as this happens.

(Whiteside) for Mitchell? Whitehall? (Nowell)?

"The cry of drowning machinery."

Story: "The Flesh": about small boy and wrestling match. The sweaty bodies of the wrestlers. Uncle (Bill):[34] revelation of some affair with a woman: either his father or uncle.

Poem: "The Leaves of the Blind."
   "The Winter of the Blind."
   "Rehearsal of the Blind to See."

Poem: "The Enchantment."

("Among the Exhausted"):
   "I
   Fulfill their gesture(,) (by) imagining fire."

Novel: excerpt: "Snow's Battle."

The strangely glowing, lacquered faces of the cadets, he thought with amazement. *That* is life.

Mitchell's dream of the taxiing aircraft following him, turning unhurriedly, even pursuing him out of sleep, so that he had to turn on the light, feeling panicky and dead beneath the thin rinse of sweat.

Poem: "The Mantis":
   ". . . the butterfly
   Bewildered by a mask of stone."

Poetry: device: to offer something, take it away (refuse to disclose it), and give something better.

"The Mantis": "death is helpless and knowing."

"That there should be fire from a water's source."

---

34. Dickey's first cousin, the son of his uncle James Dickey. The family called the cousin "uncle" because he was the age of Dickey's father.

Story or part of novel: burning the camp on Mindoro.[35]

Novel: Mitchell's vision of the Air Base: apotheosis: the winter air base: boys going on dying good-naturedly, etc., smote him like a creative stone, and held his life motionless and trembling like a struck muscle—full of pain, and its own power and life, also.

"The Dead Tree": "wrestled shape."

"As a falling hand
Gathers by altering light."

"The corner angled nerveless, lost
In the steady maze of noon."

Poem: "The Angel of the Maze."[36]

One of the most valuable things you can know about poetry: to be able to look at a poem, or a section or line or word of a poem, or a rhythm or rime, and say, No, this does *not* do here what I wish, what the poem needs, and therefore I will change it. A stringent ruthlessness is the best revisionary quality a poet can have.

Poems: "Bread."[37]
    "Falling."[38]
    "The World of the Feather."
    "Traverse."

Rewrite: "The Day Sleeper," "The Night Sleeper" for *Harper's Bazaar.*

"The Childing Autumn":
    "Let the live image,
    stripped of words stand," etc.
    "Growing more desperate
    And kind, of my son
    Standing among the fallen
    Leaves."

---

35. In June 1945, the 418th NFS received orders to ready itself for embarkation to Okinawa. Because wood was rumored to be in short supply there, the executive officer, 1st Lieutenant Robert Walters, ordered all usable lumber symmetrically stacked. After the camp had been torn down and the wood assembled in a large pile, he decided to burn the lumber.
36. The poem was published in the June 1955 issue of *Poetry.*
37. The poem was published in *Poems 1957–1967* (Middletown, Conn.: Wesleyan University Press, 1967).
38. The poem was published in the February 11, 1967, issue of *New Yorker.*

Some variation on this. Work out *translation* of this image into the other: that of the circle.

Next two poems: long:
  "(The) Angel of the Maze."
  "A Vision of the Sprinter."

"Young Whore I."
"   "   "   II."

"Inoculation I."
"   "   II."

"Abortion I."
"   "   II."

My poetic genre: The Extreme: open, free, athletic, Baudelarian—The Extreme Decadent.

Poetry: take a subject and work at it thousands of ways, developing it in different directions until you find the best. Then work at it until it achieves its best expression.

Poem: "Survival (of 'beauty,' etc.)."

"Sprinter": "dead / Heat."

The fact that the poet knows what is going to happen is a powerful hand on his side against the reader. The poet has to make it (the poem) inevitable and unforeseen.

The three long poems: work on until spring.
  1. "A Vision of the Sprinter."
  2. "The Angel of the Maze."
  3. "The Sleeping Knights."

As a river, face-down and thinking to sing.

"the slow /
Forward(,) of snow."

Poem: "The (Mercy) Diver."
  "The Day Crossing."
  "The Night Crossing."

"Dead Tree": "of *acquired* light."

Novel: the bald boy (Pillon): the "washout": dreams: "Their hair's on fire. Comb it! Comb it!"

Joel's "escape": his own slavery to the dying girl: instructor's car: Joel's perversity gradually unravelled. Elsdorf thinks he has gone to Lawler. She is waiting for him, but he goes to Selma.

Mitchell and Lawlor:
   She: "I'll . . .
   He: "Do that," he said. "And —

"Looked at (him) with the unconcerned intensity ↑(accusation)↓ of animals ↑an animal↓."

Work on a poem a long time, building up and exploring. Example: "The Childing Autumn." If the improvisatory phase is no good, the poem doesn't have a chance.

Keep the *improvisational* element of the poem *open* always. It is what *discovers.*

Story or episode in a novel where someone is editing someone else's papers and comes upon a good deal of carefully written pornography: about sadism (the novel about the talented father and the wife trying to raise the boy as he wished).[39]

"The Angel of the Maze": Uncle Jim's garden: stone or marble angel: imagined: imagine his whole family: ivy halfway over the lawn, etc. His daughter: "an old man dancing": Valéry.

Poem about baby at the breast (see H. S. Sullivan).[40]

"The Angel of the Maze": old man: big house: wife dead (Uncle Jim): "angel" is what he might imagine in the summerhouse in the middle of his gardens. Passes the caretaker as a landmark and goes deeper, beginning to wish to be lost. Lies all night awake, his light hand on his breast: "shadow opens into. . . ": his tweed cap, etc.: the folded wheelchair. Imagines daughter, perhaps. The maze is the garden.

---

39. See entry in Notebook III, p. 135.

40. Harry Stack Sullivan (1892–1949), American psychiatrist who believed that psychoanalysis needed to be supplemented by a thorough study of the effect of cultural forces on the personality.

You let your good ideas get away from you too easily into slipshod, obvious, and thin work. Any idea for a poem is capable of almost infinite expansion in almost any direction, and so of greater concentration.

What I want: the human, imaginative music.

"Angel": "one ray of light crossing the summerhouse."

Poem: "Andromeda (at Night)":
"... he
searches above her
Bearing a thistle, a potential face."

End "Mantis":
"I enter
You like thirst, and *speak* my name."

Don't leave a poem until it is better than you'd have thought it could be. Keep after it, trial by trial.

When you improvise, be much freer. Push out and try *all kinds* of new combinations. The heart of a poem is improvisation. A poem is improvisation sorted through, ordered, and used, but improvisation is the element that goes out into and discovers life. The whole problem then is to discover the *most significant direction* of the improvisation: to order it, then to select, to implement, and to discover the most impelling and meaningful rhythmic structure for the whole load, given and discovered, organic and synthetic. In the ideal case, the rhythm enables the words to say more actually than they do. The final product to be integral, organic, unchangeable.

Use the dictionary more. You are too niggling with words.

Get away from the definite article.

Something immediate and profound.

There should be something in the novel about Joel's life with his mother, indicating that it has not been entirely satisfactory. Recount someplace what Mitchell knows of Joel's life.

Poem: "The First Energy" (love?).

Poem: "If I Were Buried Like Him <Her>."

Harper's poem: "shedding his (scarlet) ↑crimson↓ armor sleep by sleep."

Make the poem perfect both in overall creation and contributing detail. Keep probing for the outbreak into the unexpectedly relevant complex of images, relations, and rhythms. Cast grammatical constructions into a sharper, odder, more natural and varied and flexible form.

Rewrite "The Mission": long:
1. The Blessing
2. (The Weather of) the Chart
3. The Mission.

Poem: "Drummer Boy":
Civil War, *Red Badge*
Brady's photographs[41]   } think over.

"Whose foot
Grows down bloodily (into) ↑through↓ the stone."

Let no line or poem go that is not uniquely *your own,* if it takes ten years to write one poem or line. Cull, refine, solidify, penetrate, resolve, deepen, integrate.

You don't *ask enough* of words.

Civil War poem: "my brother at the spring": breastworks around the farm: "now they are like that."

Long poems:
1. "The Angel of the Maze."
2. "The Mission."[42]
3. Civil War poem: "The Burned House."
4. "A Vision of the Sprinter."
5. "The Sleeping Knights."
6. "The Ground of Elegy."

Develop a theory of the Amateurs: should have some affinity with Bergsonianism.[43]

---

41. Mathew B. Brady (1823–1896), American pioneer photographer whose work provided a vast visual record of the Civil War.

42. In the entry an arrow connects this title with "The Ground of Elegy."

43. Henri Bergson (1859–1941), French philosopher who advocated a dualistic world containing two opposing tendencies—the life force, or *élan vital,* and the resistance of the material world against that force.

What I want:
1. Inevitable
2. Unforeseen
3. Spontaneous
4. Unchangeable
5. Athletic
6. "Real"
7. Imaginative
8. Rhythmically compelling, inevitable, varied
9. Empathy
10. Immediacy
11. Unique perspective
12. *Used* syntax
13. Original and "solid" and imaginative imagery
14. All these adequate in an *unforeseen* way to the subject. Unforeseen and *contributing* way: enhancing, *organic*. The whole poem can be *held* in it.
15. Don't be so *bound* in the scene itself. Find what *relates,* comments, fits oddly and perfectly.
16. Don't be so predictable as to sentence pattern, either. Separate (elements of sentence), qualify. Let the whole thing delicately and surely and unpredictably and profitably, spontaneously dance. *Wholly* (in two senses) dance.

Any poem is going to be better for a real, articulated, *detailed* plan, a plan of intentions, transitions, and progressions worked over, worked out.

Example: Thomas: "Lie Still, Sleep Becalmed."
1. Sleeper with wound.
2. The Sea-dead.
3. How to get to them.
4. Us.

How valuable is the <conception> study of *conception* and *mechanics* (in full sense) of other poets, in particular poems!!!

"The sound of the violin before it leaves the tree."

Poem: "The Legion": "in a mountain pass bright thousands."

(He had) "the reposeful magnificence (//) of moving water."

Harper's poem: end:
". . . or a god for this moment believing entire
The perfect water of his blood."

Poem: "The Ground of Elegy."
    "On the Death of Walter Armistead."[44]

"Mouth exploding
Cotton and crossed sun-rays."

Armistead poem: "I listen(ed) for the island."

The Armistead poem should be a whole evocation of middle-class, rebellious boyhood, love, loss, and the rising out of this to the smashing of the war enemies, to be itself destroyed.

Work for a long time on the *structure*.

The accumulative process is most valuable to my poems. That is why these one-shot efforts almost always fail.

"Elegy": "... or (mount) the dull *speed of the sea*."

"(all those who were)
Dragged through the (gentle) fountain to survive."

No one knows what it costs an angel to hold his (particular) ↑(original)↓ space.

"The Angel of the Maze":
    (1). The Maze
    (2). Angel Becoming } suggested revision.

"Elegy": the living are "the sleepers who do not fall" or "the sleepers not yet fallen."[45]

Lecture: selecting poets' work: "a choice of exclusive weathers."

Immediacy (device):
    1. Commands: "Do such and such. Come toward me," etc.
    2. Now such and such happens.
    3. I do such and such.

Book: *The Prospect Before Us* — Herbert Gold — World.

---

44. The poem was published as "Walter Armistead" in *The Whole Motion*.
45. Compare Dickey's idea of the living as "sleepers who do not fall" with "Sleepers" and "Tomb Stone."

"As he walked (unfeeling)
the bones of animals underground
Remerged and fell apart."

"He is filled with the cold
That settles between door frames."

End of "Childing Autumn":
   "falling ↑fallen↓ down changing dark(ness), under inexorable control,
   Massive as food."

"Travelling like a mirror."

"Angel":
   "to pay
   Him through (the) Venetian blinds ↑the shuttle↓.
   Glance, glancing, a hind steps,
   Locked on a smiling coin
   Now running ↑runs↓, pattering lightly through the leaves
   Of ivy. Then stands.
   He lets a smile
   Peel from the dredge of leaves.
   Might a stag not stand
   (He may not see), making
   All the terror real," etc.
He does not raise the blind, etc.

Harper's poem: rime:
   "a god felt wholly
   By his perfect blood."[46]

"I am blinding into a mirror
As between trees filled with ↑(full of)↓ combed light."

Good poetry is written by endless improvisation, selection, and by inventing "what goes with" passages, "what would implement" passages.

Endless improvisation in or along or around a developing pattern.

Rewrite "The Burned House," and include the Civil War poem in it, somehow involving the dead brother.

---

46. The notebook entry has an arrow connecting "god" and "blood" to indicate their slant rhyme.

Perspective by imagining someone somewhere else, or by putting him in a situation likely to crystallize and exhibit the characteristics (and the imaginer's attitude toward him) that he wishes. Tartars.

"His grave opened ↑broken↓ by the Minotaur(,) (out of) ↑(for)↓ love."

Novel: on flight, Mitchell "vomits <painfully> painlessly (forward) into the (dark) cockpit" as they let down to enter the traffic pattern.

One must go deep enough into life so that it opens beyond.

Poem: "The Creation of Ceres' ↑Proserpine's↓ Field."

"Angel": her memory of
    1. Her youth: (marriage) banquet.
    2. Her old age, infirmity.

Improvise at least a week before attempting to give a poem any shape.

Poem: "The Flight to the Armory."
    "(A Place of Animals)."
    "The Gathering of Animals into Shelter."

Poetry: to keep a proper balance between improvisation and construction.

The relation of animals to the(ir) horizon.

Stephen Spender:
    The Destructive Element
    The Creative Element.

Sunlight on waves:
    "what a ground of holy depth
    To hold, light, such light."

"Angel II": "the green deadfall of light."

To achieve in poetry (especially toward and at the end of a poem) a kind of hesitancy and indirection that, cumulatively only, falls into full flight and overwhelming drive.

Long poem: "Crime": magazine-stand motif. Someone (the protagonist) reads. This leads into an account of a crime: *particularized,* participated in: decapitation, etc., which in turn heads into speech (by the head?).

The death of a girl hitchhiker found beside high school, etc. (the dance with the idiot boy in the murder house, etc.).

Sport: the basketball games:
(1) At Miami, behind the hotel, near the mess hall, leaves, etc.
(2) At Hollandia, wandering among the wrecked Japanese aircraft.
Leads into the game-like aspect of war, etc.[47]

Commerce: the efforts of a family to preserve its property from being destroyed by a freeway. Money: from Negroes. Keeps the family genteel, etc. Building: detailed account of this: get from Jim Sims or someone.[48] Traffic: automobiles, etc.

Maxine's poem: "The Creation of the Sleeper":
"his sleep /
Involving the whole landscape in different ways."

"Angel II": columns fallen into roses, brambled over, *opening, opening out.* End on this: she sees the maze open slowly // Clean ruins, the breathing of blood, strength, etc. She indicates this is a cycle, etc.

"As if the sculptor drowned
One hand in the clear spring
Of his childhood, with the other
Flowered stone <by> to dream
His mother's face."

The wife's *vision* is the garden. She *wants* him closed here, etc. Her vision, enclosing him and so on.

Re-improvise the parts that don't satisfy you: *let go the spring.*

{The following entry confirms the year as 1954. Anderson Hall is an academic building on the Rice campus. Dickey is teaching "Argumentation and Public Speaking," "Outlines of the History of English Literature," and

---

47. Dickey was stationed at Miami Beach, Fla., in late February 1943 as part of the 584th Technical Squadron. Less than a week later, he was assigned to the 412th Training Group to begin the process of determining whether he could qualify as a pilot, navigator, or bombardier. In January 1945 Dickey arrived in Hollandia, Dutch New Guinea, on a transport ship as part of a replacement squadron for the 418th NFS. Shortly afterward, he surveyed areas of recent fighting.

48. James Redding Sims was an associate professor of civil engineering at Rice when Dickey taught there.

two sections of "English Composition: Study of Fundamental Literary Forms."}

Tues. 2 Feb.
Exams

220	Anderson Hall	106	2:00
200	"	108 + 110	9:00
100 AI	"	108	2:00
100 H2	"	108	2:00

A poem must *change directions* with every word, line, with every stanza, so that the changes add up to the whole vector, which is the poem.

"Poem from the Midst of Wings."
"The Animals of the Medusa."

"Angel II": "the ruins of heaven."

"Changing, perpetually
Renewed in decisive, unattainable
Ceremony, which is the dead."

Poem: ("The Gentlest Creature")
    —for David Dowler—[49]

". . . and (cruelty) can rest
Only a while in that unshakable amber."

A poem grows slowly out of a great many spontaneities.

Maxine's poem: "He is singing into my shadow."

The Poetry of Dylan Thomas — Elder Olson.
The Structure of Literature — Paul Goodman.
    Univ. of Chicago Press.

1. Improvise
2. Consolidate
3. Improvise   ]
4. Consolidate
The notion is to improvise within increasingly, strenuously enclosing

49. An exchange student at Rice from Peterhouse College, Cambridge.

and directing bounds, determined by what has gone before (also perhaps by what is to come, if that has been determined), and yet not lose the free spontaneousness of improvisation, not close the poem off from new openings, new directions which may, if they are good enough, cause the present version of the poem to be junked in favor of a new beginning on their basis.

Novel: the country girl: "as though her being were composed of candle flame, fluttering with a sound like that of tearing cloth, or that of rage, before it goes out—as if her life were composed of a continuous series of these instants."

Joel: "entered her like a thread": "I don't suppose I'll ever tell anybody if I don't tell you," etc.

In poetry: don't make your move so early. Improvise until a real opening-toward-continuity appears.

Poem: "Any Landscape as Eden."
    "Poem Without Speaking" or
    "   "   for Closed Mouth."

"I wrestled with silence like a vine."

Novel: next day: the boys from basic: their aircraft: in snack-bar: leather jackets: very informed. "God, this fucked-up place." One of them remembers Joel as a new recruit at the base.

Someone remembers Joel at classification center screwing off; on this high grassy hill, lying in the grass watching the Colonel walk around in the hot summer; and then the parade. Joel: "I understand it all, now," etc. All the men in formation. His walking tours: very militarily and rapidly. Riddle: "Now you look like a soldier." Joel: "That's no trouble."

Poetry:
    1. Improvise
    2. Synthesize] Define
    3. Refine ⎤
    4. Invent. ⎦

A Summoning of Stones — Anthony Hecht — Macmillan

Poem about an old couple: "I am kind of their guardian. It is I who make their age."

"Two Poems for Sleeping during Crossing the Ocean":
  1. (The) Day (Sleeper)
  2. (The) Night (Sleeper).

"The space between throat and voice."

"The seasonal (depth) ↑death and birth↓ of my hands."

"The muscles of his back like trapped, disturbed water, and with that depth, and the sense of being moved always from uplifted *weight* and depth."

"The sanctity of openness."

Armistead: a vision: try to have a vision, but see only "light break from all his harness and his gear."

"Held a little, gently, the idea of dead ships surfacing."

Novel: *The Cost of the Earth*.

Armistead:
    "in an inconsequential corner of a warehouse
    Light break from out his harness and his gear."[50]

"What can we contribute to the dead?"

"The dead-locked sea."

"The (terrible) depth of confused power."

Armistead: intro.:

motorcycle	→	aircraft
↓	↓	↓
injury	dream	death
	of	
↓	children	↓
hospital	and	funeral
	invention	
	↓	
	resolution	

---

50. Compare Dickey's poem "Patience: In the Mill," which honors 1st Lieutenant Millard Hall, the engineering officer for the 418th NFS.

"Day Sleeper": "has the least elaborate hold on sunlight."

"Like a geometry full of flames."

"In the light of parallel lines."

"As a house alters about its door."

Novel: idiot: playing music-box backward: low, clear tones, plucked under silence: gray, high overcast.

"Day Sleeper": "Everything in his body is saying 'Give,' requiring a new principle of control."

In poetry I want a sense of headlongness in which there is something selective, and yet of excess.

"Where truth and fire dance at each other."

"Few have a death they believe in."

"Where the lightest things manage to fall."

Notebook VI

The sixth journal, like the fifth, is a ringed, loose-leaf notebook. This notebook has a red outer cover and contains sixty-five unnumbered handwritten sheets. None of the entries is specifically dated, but internal evidence suggests that Dickey began using the notebook in late 1954 or early 1955. On the back of sheet 23, he notes the death of James Agee, which occurred on May 16, 1955, while Dickey was still in Europe on the *Sewanee Review* fellowship. A notation on the front of sheet 52 reveals that he had begun teaching at the University of Florida. The entry is a schematic explanation of how students are to complete certain information for a diagnostic reading and language examination; within this schema is the date September 1955. Dickey states in *Self-Interviews* that, although Andrew Lytle had asked him to become his assistant, he primarily taught freshman English as he had done at Rice. According to the 1955 University of Florida catalog, freshman English, which was titled "Reading, Speaking, and Writing," was an eight-credit class that met throughout the year for four or more hours each week. It was designed "to enlarge the student's store of ideas and meanings and to increase his efficiency in the communication arts—reading, writing, speaking, and listening." Regular practice was provided in developing oral and written expression, extending vocabulary, and using body and voice in speaking. Students, moreover, were encouraged to read widely in order to expand their ideas and increase their ability to communicate effectively. It is likely this course to which Dickey's notebook entry refers.

The red notebook, as with the blue, was supposed to record daily ideas and observations, yet it became much more of a catchall than any other early notebook. Its sporadic use is indicated not only by its brevity (of all six journals, it contains the fewest number of written pages) but also by the fact that the fronts or backs of many sheets are blank. If the entries reveal a consistency, it is either in Dickey's continued experimentation with lines and phrases he hopes offer some vital perspective or in the lists of books that pervade the journal. Not surprisingly, these books are often French, since Dickey lived in France for much of his year in Europe, staying in Paris with Lester Mansfield, his friend and colleague from Rice. In a 1965 interview, moreover, he admits, "The poets that have influenced me in my fashion from the time I really started publishing books were foreign-language poets, mainly the French."[1] Indeed, although the notebook's initial list contains works of fiction, poetry, drama, and philosophy as well as collected letters and essays all primarily by British and American writers, later lists are more focused. One grouping is titled "French books," and Dickey numbers six additional lists. These consist overwhelmingly of works by past or modern French artists, including writers such as Jules Supervielle and René Guy Cadou, both of whom he specifically identifies in the 1965 interview, but also Michel Leiris, Pierre Emmanuel, Lucien Becker, Arthur Rimbaud, and others whom Dickey mentions in later critical essays or books.

Entries in the sixth notebook exhibit many of the ideas contained in the fourth and fifth journals, since this journal partly overlaps the former chronologically and sequentially follows the latter. For example, a notation concerning *The Romantic* highlights Mitchell's interest in the "mystery of consanguinity" and continues development of the work whose genesis lies in the fourth ledger and whose principal character remains preoccupied with his father. Two descriptive lines centering on a thorn tree suggest the novel *Done in the Thorn Tree,* which Dickey also identifies in that notebook. Moreover, brief entries on what he calls the "Phelps Putman poem" reflect his interest, evident in both the fourth and fifth journals, in an American hero searching for experience. Concern in the sixth journal with what he terms the two "skeins" of poetry as well as with the essential nature of poetic language also appears in the fourth and fifth notebooks. Indeed, in the latter journal, "inevitable" and "unforeseen" are the first qualities identified in his list titled "What I want." These traits reappear in the sixth notebook when Dickey declares that a poem or image "must have the quality of unforeseen inevitability." Such examples underscore the fact that the early notebooks are interconnected and, though not written in chronological sequence, must be viewed together.

Dickey's increasing involvement in poetry is reflected not only by the relative absence of entries focusing on his fiction but also by the correspondingly large attention given poems such as "The Entrance into Jerusalem," "The Swimmer," "Neva Flournoy," and an untitled effort he labels "angelic form poem." Both "The Entrance into Jerusalem" and "The Swimmer" concern the inability of an individual to attain that which in memory has now become an idealized image. The former poem is clearly autobiographical. Dedicated to Angelique de Golian, a childhood sweetheart whom Dickey worshiped from afar, the poem seems to compare the persona's entrance into a cultured and aristocratic

---

1. "An Interview with James Dickey," *Eclipse* [San Fernando Valley State College / California State University at Northridge] 5 (1965–1966): 5–20.

home with Christ's entrance into Jerusalem. "Neva Flournoy" reveals Dickey's early interest in sharks. Though the poem's dramatic situation remains unclear, a portion of the poem involves a dream sequence, a method Dickey frequently considered before later attempting to create situations in which the imagination blurs reality as reason and the senses perceive it.

The notebook's final entry, "Old Broadway adage: 'Don't tell 'em; show 'em,'" repeats a similar pronouncement from the first ledger where Dickey criticizes what he terms "the literature of 'analysis.'" Great literature, he asserts, not so much explains as renders implicitly, and he then declares, "'Don't tell 'em, show 'em'; or at any rate, show 'em more than you tell 'em." In a sense, the declaration provides the thread that unites all the early notebooks because the exploration of literature and literary matters, his "striking in," results in Dickey's knowledge that poetry must involve the reader, must commit him to the situation as it is created by the poet through the manipulation of language.

For Dickey, art is a war, a struggle to confront and achieve language that enhances the meaning of individual life by providing it with a sense of vital consequence. In his 1964 essay "Towards a Solitary Joy," he describes the conflict, declaring, "The battles of art are silent, bloodless, and usually result in defeats more total than any others."[2] *Helmets,* his third volume of poetry, also published in 1964, reiterates the military image in its title. The early notebooks, written in the decade before Dickey achieved published success, reconnoiter the literary horizon and record the initial skirmishes of an airman returned from Pacific combat, a veteran who had now entered another form of warfare. They are briefings that detail not so much the writer as a man but the man as he was becoming a writer, having dreamed, as he writes in "The Coral Flight," that he was "in flight, as never / Before, all the way out of earth, / Somehow still at war, / But a war that meant something / To the soul, at every / Floored mile we had flown in the dark."

---

2. *The Suspect in Poetry* (Madison, Minn.: Sixties Press, 1964), 118–20.

{Dickey began using Notebook VI in late 1954 or early 1955 as he was traveling in Europe on the *Sewanee Review* fellowship.}

"A blind bull gazing at his tracks."

"The (glitter) of (despondent) ↑(disrupted)↓ alchemies."

"Whose horizon is continuously uncut ↑undercut↓ and misshapen."

"Like one who sleeps in the works of a round ↑bright↓ lock."

"With the nakedness of (a) balance."

Construct the *rapidest* and most sensitive lines you can.

"The sun beat(ing) unobstructed on their appetites."

Novel: Selma's nightmare version of the hospital; she is afraid of the sun. She sees her death accomplished by blazing instruments.

"The earth stopped with light."

"A jarring in the midst of flame."

"Weathered intelligence."

"The sense of blood."

"Unanswered miracle."

Armistead:
    "but (at such and such times) a press of knocking passes me, following // A figure face-out, down, // Hands out, with an attitude of breasting // And I feel ↑And in a↓ (from) in a deserted corner of a warehouse // Light break from out his harness and his gear."

"The barriers at which hawks begin to sing."

"A thorn tree full of light."
"A thorn tree cleansed with honey."

"The body hair of a god."

Metaphor as a kind of short-circuit, passing across or through the usual pattern of connection between two poles, and connecting them nakedly.

Novel: Mitchell feels (touches) the vein in his foot: mystery of consanguinity.

The place where reality and imagination *cross*, intersect. Neither must be neglected. The place where they cross in characteristic and individual *rhythm*. Perhaps it is better at times to lean a little toward imagination, but this must be corrected at all times by reference to reality.

"Her body curved like paths of entry."

"The purity of stretched things."

"A cry like the drowning ↑dawning↓ of machines."

Write T. Weiss, expressing thanks.

A poetry not *reflective*, not *witnessing* but *participating in, involved in*.

"Time measured by water."

Novel: swimmers in the moment with film of water all over.

"As though the blood which composed (her) face had missed a beat."

Spring: "a (the) season taken ↑(from)↓ under a girl's blouse."

Two skeins of poetry:
1. Narrative ⎱
2. Elaboration ⎰ explore between.
The balance between reflection (generalization) and action (immediacy).

"Warm(ed) with the energy of secrets."

Novel: the dream is a waking image, more powerful than a dream image.

Aftermath of sex: the sun escaped from a sure trap.

I wait for (and try to induce, if I can) a certain fever of excitement to enter the poem and carry it on a little way. The task of writing the poem then becomes one of implementing and integrating this excitement.

"Like a salmon blinded by waterfalls."

Novel: at the end, Mitchell takes the girl partly because of his own terrible sexual hunger for her. She goes because of <her> the satisfaction of her own masochistic impulses.

"I burn you with my imagination."

The poem is a construction made to strip away.

To live with the maximum of self-discipline is the secret of spontaneity.

"The great drive and wandering" (of his verse).

Poem: "(The Entry into Jerusalem)": the small boy on Palm Sunday: the Catholic family: the older sister, the dancer: then the play in the spring woods (the miraculous flowering) and the entry: the grave children: house: the bleeding hearts, etc.: the leaded windows, etc. Ded. to Angelique de Golian, as a child.[3]

"Swimmer": "bind the flickering roots of their images / Into the swimmer's form."

Recast the beginning of "The Swimmer," telling how the image arose in some way and came to stand for the unattainable memory.[4]

There is too much stiffness in my verse; we want a harder, more reckless, quicker movement.

"Neva Flournoy": the (battle) with the shark (near the end). The Negro children burning up the salamander(s) in the clothes kettle.
    "The water, a sweaty earth of steam,
    Rose in a slow rush,
    And the tiny beast danced
    On four feet"—describe, etc.

This perhaps in Putnam poem: still Negro children.

"Neva Flournoy": dream sequence of the crab at the splintered window, picking out the cracked pieces: the putty, etc.

---

3. A childhood sweetheart from grammar school who was from a wealthy and cultured Atlanta family.
    4. "The Swimmer" was published in the spring 1957 issue of *Partisan Review.*

<Rolfe Humphreys — *Poems, Collected and New*>.
<Randall Jarrell — *Selected Poems* — Knopf>.
<E. E. Cummings — *Poems 1922–1954*>.
<Wallace Stevens — *Collected Poems*>.
<Ben Belitt — *Wilderness Stair* — Grove Press>.
Edith Sitwell — *Collected Poems*.
Mark Van Doren — *Collected Poems*.
<Stephen Spender — *Collected Poems*>.
<Brian MacMahon — *The Red Petticoat*>.
<William Gaddis — *The Recognitions*>.
W. H. Auden — *The Shield of Achilles*.
Howard Nemerov — *Federigo* — Poems: *The Salt Garden*.
Robert Horan — *The Riddle of the Sphinx*.
Goncharov — *Oblomov*.
Ronald Firbank — *Santal*.
Wright Morris — *The Huge Season*.
<Lorca-Belitt — *The Poet in New York* — Grove>.
<Edwin Muir — *An Autobiography* — Wm. Sloane>.
James Stephens — *Collected Poems*.
<W. B. Yeats — *Letters*>.
<*The Poems of Gene Derwood*>.
The Center Is Everywhere — E. L. Mayo — Twayne.
(Grove Catalogue).
Robert Richman — *Poems*.
<Harry Duncan — *Poems*>.
<May Swenson — *Poems*>.
<*The Lion and the Honeycomb* — R. P. Blackmur>.
<*The Letters of Sherwood Anderson* — Gotham (de bon marché)>.
<*The Selected Essays* — Wm. Carlos Williams>.
<*Poems: 1947–1954* — Weldon Kees — San Francisco: Adrian Wilson>.
<*An End to Innocence* — Leslie Fiedler>.
<Robert Graves — *Collected Poems* — 1955 — Macmillan>.
Robert Henri — *The Art Spirit* — Lippincott.
Herbert Read — *Anarchy and Order* — Faber.
<Kenneth Rexroth — *100 Japanese Poems* — New Directions>.
E. Pound — *Chinese Classic Anthology* — Harvard Univ. Press.
New American Poets — Untermeyer, Wilbur, *et al.*
<*Mid-Century French Poets* — ed. Gowhi — Twayne>.
<*Octavius Shooting Targets* — Arthur Gregor>.
Gotham list, magazines.
<Lionel Trilling's book>.
<*Predilections* — Marianne Moore — Viking>.
O'Casey — Plays.

Santayana — *The Life of Reason*.
Elder Olson's *Poems*.
Eliz. Bowen: novel.
Goyen: novel.
George: *European Men of Letters*.
More Stories — Frank O'Connor.
Ferril's *Poems*.
Croce — *Aesthetics* — Noonday.
<Checkhov — *Letters*>.
<Fry — *The Light is Dark Enough*>.
<*The Walker* — Patrick O'Brian — Harcourt Brace>.
<*New American Poets 1 and 2* — esp. #2: Louis Simpson>.
Lawrence's *Letters* — edit. and intro. by Aldous Huxley.

Poem: kicking, jolting movement of the verse as he kicks at the tapestry.

"Swimmer":
  "... and moved / my dry heart to the left."
  "The priceless drowned."
  "The sound is that when one person stops, in a moving ↑(marching)↓ crowd."

The Sewanee Review
Poetry
The Quarterly Review of Literature
Shenandoah
The Beloit Poetry Journal
The Hudson Review
The Yale Review
Accent
(*Botteghe Oscure*)
(*Encounter*)
(*New World Writing*)
(*Discovery*).

To get a little more *incantation* into my verse.

The sea: water burning away a game of which the rules are lost ↑water burning away the rules of a lost game↓.

See *Paris Review* and *Merlin* people in Paris.

"Neva Flournoy": the shark is a hammerhead.

"Fell to the depth of the wood."

"The hook softens through my bones."

Poem: "The Lost Game."

James Agee is dead. God keep him, in the depth and trembling of His open shadow.[5]

Phelps Putnam poem: "the skaters move over the green field."

"Changing helmets."

"Face screaming with heat ↑(cold)↓."

Warm rain: "a wall burned from around its nails."

Poem: "The Entry into Jerusalem": Palm Sunday: children: palm that crosses entry into Jerusalem: children playing in woods: non-Catholic boy at home of Catholic family: pictures of bleeding hearts: ballet: leaves: silver shoes, etc.: the de Golian family.

Title of Putnam poem: "The Cave Master."

"The Cave Master" or "Cave and Scaffold": images of climbing: the framework is by turns shaky and firm: scaffold and flight of stairs equated.

"The bones break lengthwise, farther than their length."

"A song passes through ↑(from)↓ his closed mouth."

"(You live under the sky)
As you live under your hair."

"The labyrinths which create Time."

Wood: "a green and black helmet."

A poem or an image must have the quality of unforeseen inevitability.

Boxing and running: power, savagery, concreteness.

5. Agee died on May 16, 1955.

Angelic form poem: it must have a kind of real grandeur about it, else it will fail. To include:

1. A description of one of the angels: red, Cyclopean eye.

2. A race between this angel and a superhuman version of the boy, between the trees, at night, about the stations where the boy's father had his chicken pens.

He ends in the coop flooded with feathers and enchains himself there, and looks savagely and panting through the boards at the dawn coming up.

The world should uphold the work of art, its unnatural ways, with its profound naturalness.

End novel: he felt the sun strike, fully open ↑opened fully↓, ↑through his hair↓ upon the spaced ↑shaped↓ silence of his nerves. She stepped sideways, a little forward, and he saw that where she had been, <stood> Truth, or its likely shadow stood, <but> and that it was trembling.

French books:
1. *Oeuvres Complètes 1 and 2* — Germain Nouveau — N.R.F.
2. All the rest of Éluard.
3. Luc Berimont.
4. *Défense et Illustration* — Jouve.
5. The rest of Maurice Blanchard.
6. *Ouvre Boite Colloque Abhumaniste* — Audiberti — N.R.F.
7. *Le Cornet à Des* (II) — Max Jacob — N.R.F.
8. Fargue — *Dejeuners de Soleil*
         Déjeuners de Lune — N.R.F.
9. Milosz — *Ars Magna*
         Les Arcanes — Béalu.
The books of *Malcolm de Chazal* — N.R.F.

Jarrell: confusion between "real" and "ordinary."

"Neva Flournoy": the creation of a new self by taking thought: the slow, direct process, halfway into which the process itself takes over, and she is left marvelling, as having passed into a dream that she foresaw.

"The Cave Master": the man in the poem (something like Putnam, Davenport, Russell Cheney, *et al.*) works in an office and tries to write. This poem is a kind of vindication of all those that try to do <so> this.[6]

---

6. See Dickey's comments in *Self-Interviews,* 43–46, on the difficulty of his own creative efforts while working in advertising.

<Elizabeth Bishop — *Poems* — Houghton Mifflin>.
<Brewster Ghiselin — *The Nets* — E. P. Dutton>.
Contemporary German Poetry — Babette Deutsch and Avrahm Yarmolinsky — Harcourt Brace.
<Louise Bogan — *Essays on Verse and Prose* — Noonday>.
<John C. Ransom — *Poems and Essays* — Vintage>.

"The Cave Master":
The enemy have to seek him out in the town: I gild myself in gold. The sun(light) leaps back into itself from the <point of> flat of my forehead. I go in supple gold leaf, etc. The battle, or at the encounter, the scene changes to something ordinary, domestic.
Part of the poem should be about the sublimation of "ordinary" heroic instincts that never get a chance to be tested.

"Light is the shadow of the sun."

Poem: "The Father's Body."[7]
("The Son's Body.")
("The Daughter's Body.")

Poem: "The Lightning-Game."
Book title also.
The Thunder-Game and Other Poems?
↑*The Rain-Game*↓.

You want the quick, hot, inward, Lawrentian flame—the plasm: the life warm, trembling, and unforeseeable.

Poetry: structures: geometric figures drawn with one line.[8]

#1
1. Michel Leiris — *Nuits sans Nuit* — Fontaine.
2. Jean Gênet — *Les Bonnes* — J.P.P.
3. Emmanuel Looten — *La Maison d'Herbe* — Seghers.
4. Pierre Emmanuel — *Tristess O Ma Patrie* — Fontaine.
5. Georges Schéhadé — *Monsieur Bob'le* — N.R.F.
6. Ernst Jünger — *Jeux Africains* — N.R.F.

---

7. The poem was published in the December 1956 issue of *Poetry*. Its reading at the University of Florida offended some women, and Dickey left his teaching position rather than apologize.
8. Following this entry in the notebook, Dickey drew a five-pointed star surrounded by a circle, using a single, continuous line.

7. Louis Émié — *État de Grâce.*
8. Jorges Luis Borges — *Labyrinthes* — N.R.F.
9. Norge — *Le Gros Gibier* — Seghers.
10. Paul Chaulot — *Comme un Vivant* — Seghers.
11. Yvan Goll — *Les Georgique Parisiennes* — Seghers.
12. Michell Marioll — *Therese* — Seghers.
13. Émié — *Romancero du Profil* Perdu — Seghers.
14. Béalu — *Ocarina* — Seghers.
15. Dodat — *Pour un Théâtre Olympique* — Seghers.
16. Norge — *Les Râpes* — Seghers.
17. Paul Gilson — *Poèmes* — Seghers.
18. Bosquet — *La Vie Est Clandestine* — Corrier.
19. Dodat — *Règnes* — Confluences.

#2

1. Jean Cayrol — *Pour Tous les Temps* — Editions du Seuil.
2. Alain Borne — *Poèmes à Leslie* — Seghers.
3. Michel Leiris — *Haut Mal* — Gallimard.
4. Emmanuel — *Orphiques* — N.R.F.
5. Emmanuel — *Tombeau Orphée* — Seghers.
6. R. G. Cadou — *Visage Interne* — Amès de Rochefort.
7. Chaulot — *Jours de Béton* — Rochefort.
8. Gênet — *Haute Surveillance* — N.R.F.
9. Supervielle — *Naispauces* — N.R.F.
10. Viereck — *Conservatism Revisited* — Lehmann.
11. *Anthologie de la Poésie Française depuis le Surrealisme* — Marcel Béalu — Bearne.
12. *Contre Terre* — René de Solier — N.R.F.
13. *Le Jeu et la Chandelle* — Georges Garampon — N.R.F.

#3

1. Jean Lescure — *La Place Ne Se Ferme Pas* — Charlot.
2. René Menard — *Coriandres* — Fasquielle.
3. *Poèsie Vivante*
    Livres 1
            2
            3
    Librarie Les Lettres.
4. *Shenandoah* (4 copies).
5. Jules Supervielle — *Oublieuse Mémoire* — N.R.F.
6. Philippe Jones — *Grande League* — La Maison Du Poète.
7. Paul Chaulot — *Contre-terre* — Le Cheval d'Ecume.
8. Picasso 1955.

#4

1. Jouve
   Oeuvres Poétiques
   Les Noces
   Sueur de Sang   } Gallimard
   Metière Céleste
   Kyrie.

2. \<Jouve> Michel Leiris — *L'Age d'Homme* — Gallimard.
3. Claude Vigée — *La Corne du Grand Pardon* — Seghers.
4. Jean Gênet — *Journal du Voleur* — Gallimard.
5. *Panorama Critique de Poésie Française* — Clancier — Seghers.
6. *Panorama Critique des Nouveaux Poetes Français* — Rousselot — Seghers.

#5

1. Léon-Paul Fargue — *Sous la Lampe* — Gallimard.
2. Henri Pichette — *Nuchea* — L'Arche.
3. Pierre Emmanuel — *Combats avec tes Défenseurs* — L.N.F.
4. Jean Dubuffet — *Prospectus aux Amateurs de Tous Genres* — Gallimard.
5. Rolland de Renéville — *L'Expérience Poètique à la Baconnière.*
6. de Renéville — *Univers de la Parole* — Gallimard.
7. Lucien Becker — *Le Monde sans Joie* — Gallimard.
8. Jean Lescure — *Le Voyage Immobile* — Les Presses de Hibon.
9. Rimbaud — *Bibliotheque de la Pléiade.*
10. René Menard — *La Terre Tourne* — Seghers.
11. Luc Decaunes — *Le Droit de Regard* — Seghers.
12. Edmond Humeau — *Epreuve au Soleil* — Seghers.
13. René Menard — *Granit des Eaux Vives* — Confluences.
14. Jouve — *Le Paradis Perdu* — *Les Cahiers Verts.*
15. Luc Estang — *Les Béatitudes* — Gallimard.
16. Alain Bosquet — *Quelle Rozanne Oublié* — Mercure de France.
17. Fargue — *Tancrède-Ludions* — Gallimard.
18. Luc Estang — *Le Mystère Apprivois*é — Laffont.

#6

1. *Oeuvres Complètes* — Raymond Radiguet — Grasset.
2. *Perce Neige* — Claude Vigée — Les Lettres.
3. *Barnabooth* — Valéry Larbaud — N.R.F.
4. *La Liste à Octobre* — Louis Émié — N.R.F.
5. *Le Dieu sans Tête* — Louis Émié — Laffont.
6. *Conseils à un Jeune Poète* — Max Jacob — Gallimard.

The *way* a thing is said is style—personal, and if good enough, indispensable.

Art: a deliberate construction.

The chief difference ↑and most obvious↓ between prose and poetry is that of metrical language. In poetry it is consciously employed *as such*— a kind of summoning of the *sonal* or *audible* resources of language in the service of meaning. In the best poems, we can say, sound and meaning are inextricable one from the other; are the same. In bad poems, the rhythm and meaning are at odds.

In prose there are rhythms, but they are much less consciously employed and are not so concentrated, stylized. Mnemonic quality.

{The following entry, which contains the date of September 1955, indicates that Dickey has returned from Europe and is now teaching at the University of Florida.}

Give out cards. Tell students to record grades on page 255 of syllabus. Explanation of meaning of grades on those and following pages and again on this week's lecture.

Code	next	percentile	per.	per.	per.	total
Test	words per	rate	for	role	rate	score
designation	min:	for	compre-	for	total	
Sept. '55	time	reading	hension	vocab.	compre.	

Clinic 3rd floor Anderson.[9] Anytime sign up for hours that suit him. Not a class schedule basis.

New Poets
<Series 1. May Swenson
    Harry Duncan
    Murray Noss
Series 2. Louis Simpson
    Robert Pack
    Norma Farber>.[10]

"The dark white of blindness."[11]

9. Anderson Hall is an academic building on the campus of the University of Florida.

10. Scribner's Poets of Today series. Dickey's first volume of poetry, *Into the Stone*, published in 1960, was the seventh in the series.

11. In the entry, "blindness" is circled and an arrow indicates Dickey's wish to have it replace "dark," so that the phrase reads "The blindness of white."

"Transparent magic(s)."

Alone and dancing in his mind.

Athletics: man becoming the *perfect* <beast> animal (Santayana).

The story is really about the fact that you can't possess the *past* of the other, the wife (here), as you wish to do on these occasions. Or finally, either, your *own* past.

"How do masked people age?"

The poet<s> says, "Trees and flowers, skies and winds, clouds and light, are in *my own way* alive with a special energy and character of *my* own."

"The colored hunger ↑lungs↓ of flowers."

"His ↑her↓ whole body holds my face."

A look breaks uselessly open on memory.

The staring-game of noon.

Honi soit qui mal y pense.[12]

Sentence in a C-3 paper the other day:[13] "Do you have any idea what is being worn on the male and female sexes, in broad daylight, on the campus of the University of Florida?" This is a marvellous dramatization of futility and inconsequence.

Someone said that the most flagrant abandonment of the fictional art is Balzac's "Thus passed fifty years."

Old Broadway adage: "Don't tell 'em; show 'em."

---

12. The motto of the Knights of the Garter in England as well as an old French proverb that is translated "Evil be to him who thinks evil."
13. The University of Florida designated particular comprehensive courses to make up its core, or general education, program. Part of this program was C-3, its freshman English course titled "Reading, Speaking, and Writing."

Poems

Dickey wrote the following poems during the fifties. While some were printed in reviews or journals during that decade, he never included any of these early works in subsequent books of poetry. Ten of these poems have never been published: "Canebrake," "The Wish to Be Buried Where One Has Made Love," "The Wheelchair Drunk," "The Mission," "The Coral Flight," "The Valley," "The Contest," "*Invitation au Voyage,*" "Hart Crane," and "The Archers." Taken together, the poems complement the notebooks by displaying how Dickey's search for subject matter and form, which the entries describe, manifested itself in the initial works of a major American poet.

A chronological presentation of these poems would provide a comprehensive view of Dickey's development and apprenticeship as an artist up to the publication of *Into the Stone* in 1960. Such an approach, in one sense, seems both necessary and consequential because it avoids egalitarian methods that distort or simplify. However, in an extended interview on July 24, 1995, Dickey asked that I group these twenty-four poems into three sections, each containing eight specific works. The present arrangement accedes to his request. These sections display neither a chronological order nor a single common subject, though the poems in each group generally concern family, war, death, and love, the principal subjects explicitly announced in *Into the Stone.* However, when examined together, the groupings propose another, more important perspective— Dickey's comprehension of himself and his mission from a vantage of some forty years following the poems' composition. The poems in each section, while exhibiting a stage or aspect of the psychological search for identity, also portray the emotional duality of the father-son relationship. The sections, in other words, do not so much present a linear pattern of development as they do a psychological complex in which the roles of the father and the son remain, at their deepest level, one and the same. The inherent need to move beyond one's present self is, in fact, the need to return to one's origins. Therefore, I have labeled the sections "Son," "In Search," and "Father," respectively, believing that they suggest Dickey's awareness of a pattern shared by the human tribe.

I. Son

The Father's Body

    His father steps into the shower;
In the rising lamp of steam
Turns his fatted shoulders on.
The boy is standing, dry and blue,
Outside the smoke-hole of water,
The ink-cut and thumb-ball whorl of planks
About him like the depth in a cloud
Of wire, dancing powerfully.

Back with him from the sea,
Light hovers-out the shadow of the sun.
The father's hair breaks down
Warmly under the shining.
He has come up from the river-bed, never seen,
Beneath the flowing of mirrors.
In the sterile, cross-lit grass

Of water, something descends into the man
Of ruined, unarrestable statuary
Not made by men: stone, blind
With the mule's gaze, sleeps itself awake,
And, before anything, is on the man's face
And through the boy's loins, and past,
Burning hairs up out of the earth.

The child watches the clean, shameful sight.
There in the moth-killing, trembling pine,
He thinks the frail moon of day is snowing
With silver readiness, the man
Up from the floor. His father's head
Is dark white, his mouth bell-shaped and drinking.
The boy steps into the water,

Re-shimmering its loaded height.
A movement comes down on his hair

Like the stiff bright headdress of fever.
In one immortal, preliminary posture
After another, he is cast
Down a ray of water. And knowing,
As a rain surrounds itself, how prayer
Kills out its breath, and beats, he bears

All of him in to his father.
They ride there, in beginning.
He takes a long drink of velocity
Shucking his face.
It keeps wearing out there,
Its pointedness running down,
So that his closed eyes pelt back at it, and see,
Uncontrollably, a wood

Where nothing pours. Grass comes gently
Down into being, in a ring.
He steps forward, deeper,
In the descended brow-light of a shell
Spreading the nerves of sound into itself.
Echo shouts slowly with the miracle.

In there, it is all intense
And mild, with flowers growing solid as a ball
And floated warm. As he looks into trees
Sheering the sun, his father asks

For his hands, and binds on the glittering chains.
Each ritual has the heartbeat of the first:
He lies then with his heart
Eating the center of the ring, his feet together.
His father at the edge of the fair field
Is uncertain, in his blue bathing-trunks.
Then the man is over him, as at night.

He is seen through gauze to be
Very faint; he reaches in where the boy's ribs
Are unformed, where they are wavering
Like the ribs of sand in water.
Sleep yells from ear to ear; his organs rise,
Lash clear, as from his mouth,
And he is overtaken from within
By weightlessness. His father draws his tongue out
With two fingers, and the syllabled dark from his throat.
("Soul," he cries after it with his last word.)

He is all beamed blood, with light between;
All matterly, but connected like a cloud.
The girl beside him, who is still wet
With him, screams: she kicks and squeals
As his father, his eyes closed,
Kneeling, molds her body.
He builds her freely
Strange, as the aging of a prophetic glass
Where all of historied time she is
Becoming the first and last of images,

And then, alone, the last.
In the silver-backed miles of blue depth
The weather blooms, tempered, as from warmth itself.
The boy begins to breath without his soul,
Lying there voiceless, pierced by a sprig of holly
Between the double freshness of his legs.
Her face moves from within. They are laid together.

The wedding blazes up all around.
She lies against him, glowing his mouth
To sweat like a glass of milk.
The bust of his father burns from his neck
Like a fountain waked in by a god;
His inner and unknown face,

Of a singing animal, breaks through.
Above them, his father's eyes, aging
With the sky, dancing about them
A pattern swum from wood, watched luminous from silk,
And he feels his father rise
Through his own slight, helpless loins
Into the frankness of space.
He falls through her from there, and her eyes change.

The shadow of the cross
Of a sword-hilt held awkwardly by his father
Imprints itself on his back, floating and burning.
He parts the girl's terrible legs; he shouts
Out silence; his waist points
And holds and points, empowered
Unbearably: withheld: withheld—

A loom is flooded with threads,
Showing him stretched on the nails
Of the inward stars of noon, released.

He has died, and his father flickers out
In the lengthening grass where he and the girl
Have been crowded down and crowned.
A little blood subsides into his heart,
And is his heart. Its word brings the girl's lips balanced
Through like water, and the multiple sleep
Of a shuddering herd calms over them.
She has leapt to the roots of his beard.
His father dies, and snaps the water off:

Snaps the descended and hypnotized leaves
Off in midair, and the warm ring of the wood.
They all three have been shining.
Yet the boy stands up in the stall of the cottage,
His face thought up
By speechlessness, bright with death,
And his father, withdrawing as he stands
Deeper in the grove, alone,
Breastward in the springing dream of seed,
In the bestial completion of sunlight
Hid up and down, branchingly sings.

The Swimmer

The river stands, a shadow balanced open.
I stand. My skull makes a motion of closing
Over stems, between upward and downward—
Closed, it is pressed white
Listening to thirst form singly from its vectors,
And lifted down, and the girl,
Each muscle of her body near a voice
Plucked and set beating harp-metal by the wedged sun
Between leaves and strings,
Falls from the opposite bank.

Toward the swinging paint of her shadow
Paired with a tongue that might be arched
And caught forever singing out
The dead intensity of the river
From the sleep of a blue mouth, brightening,
Yet is all sidling silence,

My head dips past its print, and the flesh goes,
And my eyes through the river's rain

(A wall burned gently from its nails) pass
From sun to moon: from sun to moon
Light of nausea, her hair dancing
Under the day-moth's dancing
Small step of suspension,
Ceases to shape back,

And under the water where I have loved
I touch it with the echo of my face,
And feel my legs, tuned to the river's magnet, follow,
Hum solid, changingly, like urns struck hard
Being filled, and light from the porch of a headless god
Binds down the trees of the abyss.

Behind my throat, a Presence
Is hooded out with bones, is trembling with whiteness
As white as the bones, between the bones:
In that dry, sparkling field under daylight,
Under the half-watered air

Of the strangling swimmer,
The current throws scars from the heart of lightning
Into the Hunt, and I leap
Up the branched channels of a vertical wind.
Death flickers light and broken: the thickets stream:
Above, her legs are shattering right, she pulls:
Form and Vigor
Tear out her saliva and rope it to the banks.
A hound passes its tongue through my shoulder—
My horns lift him, he staggers, his legs flail
The dancing sun of water, and I stand, at last,
In hiding, my antlers tuned to the dark of the wood,
And the sprinters with their lances pass,
Cleansed with young steam and honey,
As she beats back panic through the slow, clear wall:

Where my new flowing flesh stares up
She flogs toward the bush of the drinking deer
Whose stripped shadow under the stream, moveless,
Ceremonial, hung with dead leaves and dry
Sparkling, carbon and moonlight,
Draws with my patient gaze
Her lines of force from the spring
To the sea, through her nipples,
And through the kick of her arms
My stone ear runs and runs

Over the whole river, and a wheel
Meshes there with colorless flowers:

I feel at my brow the sleeping deaf
Press their violent foreheads up
To touch her, sowing greatly, in the lungs.
The crest of her geometry fires
And falls over the river, and vanishes into a bird
As she walks out. The lances of the sprinters,
The foam of the deer

Float unimaginably still. Tradition holds her safe,
Though we who made it,
The hunters and the hunted in her form,
Seethe in the current, cold, and things touch us:
My great eyes look at me from the air,
And I set my powerful, numb head

And hold through my stone ribs
The water carefully, but where she slept
Is past. I am stiller and not leaping
Back to my man-face and body rained to death
By the sun, where the spiritless eyes no longer
Are vacant, but know: her naked walking shakes them,
But onto me like no leaf
Falls, in the perfect gloom and body

Of the dark faultless field where shadows move
The forms of darkness dazzlingly,
And take no body back, that ever comes
To touch the bones of his bestial face
To the murmuring wall, late after love.
Turn back: stare in, through the multiple heart
Of proven water. Let the throat re-form.
God sheds the cloth of air.
Silence turns its following weight
Mindless, to rest Him freshly in the leaves.
Helen! Incorruptible extreme!
We have the blue eyes of prisoners.

Canebrake

Morning; it shows
Its suppleness, and the massed green bones of strength.
Beyond, the river rises

Like a serpent touched at the tip of the tail,
And sprung, thereby, in a flurry of feathers to the eyes.

The road is still, and does itself no good,
As you kick its ruts into the little field.
From your feet, far out above
Your head, is a silence made of sounds.
Is it the pencil leaves
Of the stalks, you hear, or the river sprouting, unseen?

Making not the shadow of a thing
Beyond the naked stems, the sun
Casts a game of jackstraws on ground.
It might be better if,
Feeling it hopelessly exposed, you put your hand
On one of the light, slim, jointed tubes.
Thus, in a dream some years from now, you may have entered

The sway of the sprinkled leaves on top,
And seen the serpent lift his blinding head
Out of the side of the river,
The hot green wind come forth,
Come in and thatch a staler roof
To the roof of your drying mouth.
Insect-like, among the grassy posts,
You still may learn which gradual sound

Is the river's, and which the fending of leaves.
Here is another place that moves within
If motionless. Stand, swaying a little, here,

Your hand a support of classic, columned
Yet untameable air, and feel for the needle's
Word to be split, in peace, on the tongue of the serpent
An army of angry children would stomp to death,
Afraid it would speak, as it will.

The Wish to Be Buried Where One Has Made Love

At dawn, in one move, a trout
Drew his body out the length of the river;

The sun smote the rocks into view.
We walked with the earthless footsteps

Of children about to be born.
We lay on the rocks, strangely flaming;

The trees from across the river
Came, in their next shadows, slowly;

A wind sprang out of their leaves
And broke, as I touched the guitar.

At dusk the boulders arose
Until they stood shafting in moonlight.

A curved muscle shook in the river,
As I stung the last note from the string,

And we lay, looking up through the stones
As through time, and saw there

A fish like a new current swimming,
A reflexing tree on the water.

We lie here, responding forever.

The Wheelchair Drunk

I never had arms before
Those five martinis swooped into my room,
And I can tell you now that the thing I am in will dance,

Dancing not against but with
The bricks of the building, and whatever
Holds the glazed floors still while the elevator drops through.

Those doors I double-burst
And jolt down the footless stairs
Looking anywhere for a bar. Who brought that chilled pitcher

To the foot of my throne now stares
Open-mouthed out the window as I reel
The spokes forward faster than they ever intended

And unwind myself,
A horseless sulky, an old-fashioned ashcan,
Top-heavily happy, spinning my wheels in the sun

With light chopped to bits around
My center of gravity. This is where I bump
Down off the sidewalk, crossing a street where drivers

Blanch at the thought
Of running me down, even though they have
The light and the law on their side—and now must find

A driveway somewhere
To come in off the street and join
Wire carts full of soap-flakes and babies. I have forgotten

Why I can't rise and walk,
Stand on the lawns, push my self-starting chair
Out under a truck and let them smash-stop each other,

Holding up delivery
Of the U.S. mail, Grandma Foster's Pies,
Clothing store dummies, toilet seats or rose-dozens,

But it's certain I can't,
And so must go as I am, in my dressing gown,
Toward the dark neon alive in the middle of morning,

Unrolling an endless rail
On either side of me out of my powerful palms.
But it will be hard, hard to get through those two blocks:

I desire to hear
At every crossroads all the unhandled other
Wheels scream helplessly dead, for suddenly I love nothing

So much as to whirl
In the middle of traffic, holding up like a thief
Of delight those bread-trucks, those frustrated bridge-players:

To sit here like money
Lost and found in the perilous streets, and spin
Myself on a magical dime, getting better and brighter and better.

The Anniversary

She is who
Aligned to joy,
A candle's blue
And quiet alloy,
Took me in wonder
Far into summer,
Allayed the ear
Come down through fear,
Broke clear as hazard
And perisht hard
Against the breast
The sun not help
Nor moon destroy,

Left whole the beast
And bled the boy.

By lights and signs
Beneath the arch
And breach of loins
We lay from other
And coined a stitch
To lace the river
An inch from sight,
And soaring brother
From that odd night.
Warm in such braces,
Mentioning grasses,
Grinning disgraces
And opulent faces,
We led each other
Two golds together,
That else would've been
No hue of the scene.

Now this is a stranger,
And letting the strings
Out over the river,
The slow grass ring
The hell of the ear,
I splay the guitar,
Bleeding my faces
Out of disaster
And into disgraces,
And kneel in time
Deep as a look
Where none may shine,
Shaping the book
The heart deceives,
Folding a tongue
In six dead leaves.

Genesis

When car-lights turn
The inside corner of the room
I wake to come singing up.
    I watch a woman burn

Who of myself is made
In the sun, and turned by her heart
Into the sea. Half-buried is she
   In water, on legs of shade,

   In the world's deep grave
Of dancing. Her look goes bluely out
Through the force of brow
   Of the new wave:

   Of a sudden, I know God
Himself, when the dewy man lay down,
Could not but flesh His hand
   In Adam's side.

   I, remembering,
Can catch the movement of woman
Back to the sea, who feel one rib,
   Bent in the ring

   Of others, touched
Like a thin tool, forkèdly singing.
She springs; the wave bites down on its window;
   Her body, new-hatched,

   Glides trembling over
The dead. In the heavy, draughting water
She lies alone, in divine, inessential life,
   And dreams of a wounded lover.

   Each time I think, she is born.
A man beats broken music from his ribs
Where she smiles, now, into the sea, and sleeps
   Face-down, upborne.

The Red Bow

   On side-showering wheels afloat, far off
I stopped from them, my bicycle leaning in-
side one tiring pleasant leg, as they came down
From the clear house, holding their bows.
Beneath us the fern forest weighed
The light on leaves as brightness moves
Somewhere along the pulling of a chain.
               The lawn dropped

As they crossed, the game and grace of the child
Gone somberly forth upon, through the first of the upper trees.

To hunt, I saw that one must see,
When approaching, the unmanned wood
As one stroke of life from the heart. I waited there,
Waiting for my heart, as the father moved,
The boy with his small vivid bow
Following. Each quick look from his head was out
Of the round gold smoke of the sun.

Small serpents, sparrows, insects, mice
Lay close, in their whole cloth
Of shovelled shade, but the child was making a thing
To be fallen upon in a sovereign blur from above:
Among the sensitivity of stars
Countersunk by the sun through leaves, not blood
But death, a run- or flown-down shape come green and full
Into trembling to stop and be struck there.
Slowly by their advances prey

Began to be hid among the trees. The leaves
Shook seriously, and the wood neared the whole sound
Of the secrecy of insects in the light,
A zone of fanatical grazing—
Yet on a sudden fining of the ear, the stand
In sound of a single fly was borne.

A hush caved in: went rising round
The balanced Game, whose heavy bush was blue
With the holding of years of breath.
There, going into the trees, one understands
The dancing of the world, mistaken for the leaves',
And the sense of dissolving
Forward, into the last great stone.

Deeply the dark bird sighed
Under watching, and a breeze fell short—
Then the ferns, nocked with drops, were still,
Again, with the only stillness.
At once more strongly: endless
Piling, the spring-loaded green

And ply of whole branches moved.
Near their feet, the leaves of a fern blew wrong-
side-out, and toiled, and knit once more

In the pattern of the muscles of a back.
A dead limb churned, breaking off something else in its fall.

There is no way first to place your foot
Inside the wood while the wind blows, and the trees,
Not equal to themselves, unearth from the very roots
The half-used, whelmèd postures of a god.
Uncertain, the father picked an arrow

As one he might as well lose, and crossed it with his bow.
A leaf turned brightness over in the wind.
He leaned back, pulling wide,
Until the quick of feathers touched his face, and powerfully let go.
Around them a mixture of little pines
In a shuddering brain-wave of needles went, and stood
The shade of the wood on end.
                                                A small
And yet a smaller and blacker stick, the arrow rose
And burned out a nerve of sunlight as it fell

Over into falling, off in height.
From there in a slow return
Of size, it came. Had one looked only then, it had appeared
Brought to bear by Heaven,
Not so much to fall, as fired with all intent
Straight down into the trees. A still cloud passed.
The wood of stars went out, and shadow profoundly
Opened all the way to the sun:

Out of the dimming piece-work of the ground,
Color, a butterfly, small, close, and unforeseen,
Flurred and stood up as it would
Just off the center of sight.

Light came up again
Around it, from the grass. The fern swept in and died;
The ribs of all of us
From the spine were beautifully swayed. Excited, released,
The father drew his bow. In the nervous, strong
Sharing of cord and wood, the hulk of air
Drew, huge upon itself, the tension of a bundle—
The green air leapt; the butterfly rose

Off-centered into light, resettled aimlessly,
Was followed. Where the wings
Moved among grass, exhorting the ground to breathe,
The father pulled the bowstring to his eye. Thin color blew

Away as the arrow shocked; the earth drove its quivering up
To balance in the shaft.

They went on, the man giving life after life
Waiting inside himself in line
In vigorous bronze, a chance to shoot,
While at his side, enseamèd air
In geometrical violence gave and danced
In the sound of a million marks of leaves being made
By shadow, restored, on light.

I saw them as lids
Asleep in the sun see
Blood shed alive upon the sight, and men in clouds
Come there, beyond Time, to act.
Seeing, I began to see
With something not in myself, the father drop his bow,
And kneel, and take up his son in his arms,
Sending me no reason at all for this

To be the time, and a shining breath across
My breast laid cruciform.
With the child, I stood looking
Into the wood, past the grounded arrow,
And knew, with him, at last,
The sun between trees can be ridden like a beast.

Suddenly the trembling Game, bright-black and red,
Was pinched upon the feather of the shaft.
Forgetting, forgetting, the man picked up his bow
And poised again, one knee set forward,
Like a centaur to pull the string,
And the son watched the hidden muscles rise
In themselves in ferns to take
His father from behind,
Drawing the shaken curve of the bow
By the strength of his right arm out of myth.

Behind his widened, humming hands
His face and chest split open like a bean: he fled
Into the wood, a vibrant field hung up in afternoon
Upon dilation and fatigue: half-dark,
Half-singing, half-burning with a sky.
Beside him the butterfly woke
On its wings, from a sleep in which something had pounded
Its shoulders into gold-leaf in a hole.

He stopped, and fully he was clothed
In all the shine and nourishment of sweat.
He knelt down there, and lay. Above, the butterfly rose
To the sun, above sound.

Warm dark, bright cold through the little sticks, he watched,
As the soul sees the bars of the rib-cage
Glow into Being, around
A long exhalation of moss
He made, bring dry from his honest form
The connected shape of weather of the years.
A moth crept beating in
And shifted down upon.

He heard a hill of grass go round the world
Day after day, year after year be made, and die:
Be made. And there some wind
Hulled among leaves and stalled,
As a step

Unseen, brought him the child with the red bow
Turning a singled way among the trees.
Every branch lived dead
Against conceptionless waiting,

As the boy placed one foot forward. He aimed
Directly at the wings, and
Pulling back the cord, drew the blaze of color
Out of the breath of his father.
The man sensed a sailing of arrows

Far off, in shimmering flight: a rain
Of eyelashes, or, as the grey leaves of the willow are
By river-water shown, a glitter of pencil-marks.
All those were lost, beyond. Each tree was filled
With a brave and fragile earnestness of speed.
The son took on in a rush what was always his: the power,
Where only his father was concerned, of striking
Out of an infinitude of light.

Yet he above some mortal in the bush,
A tomb, an unset boundary-mark
Of Man, a nest where bones of hares
Were trembling, trembled still,
Put forth his hand upon his father's brow,
His own as pale as a hanging of gnats is made, and makes
A transparent hole in air.

Below the spread of limbs, no leaf
Ever moved, the arrow was,
Come down. Out of the blur of floating
It opened its wild, stiff bud, and fell

Through the child through the heart, as he lay and wept
Above, trying his best to protect, and not to do
The living he must, of a thing to death:
Through the wings, which leapt alive, and in the mould of leaves
It held to a self-consuming shape. The father rose

To himself with the bow at the grasses' edge,
Whose man was the body of joy.
A crown of whispering came
All to be moved by trees. The boy got up to hear
The syllables of his name take place
Within that endless brink of sound.
They walked back over the lawn.

Holding the bones of motion in my legs,
A skinned-out form of metal and honed wires, I waited,
Waiting for my heart, until the room-lights leapt
And brought the windows of the House of Earth
Gold from the grass, laid flat to the dampening ground.
Under the moon's small broken loaf

In my seventeenth year, I kept watching
For the one step the fireflies took
On light, then to go on in darkness.
They were all about me in depth, and much dark,
And I loved my dead father like beauty,
And with sheer, bright, bodiless steps went down

To the wood, and the coming of all my sons.
"The trees show the shape of Nothing,
Moved. The moon stirs weakly, until the Day of age,
The place where one may make a bed of constant love
Of his own panting shadow. The dust in you has stood,
And next will sing, then watch again,
Having run. Who enters the trees
Has entered also the house, and been whole among those
Whose best-loved has not told his name."

II. In Search

The Mission
—1944—

 After the first long mission north
We flew, one hot night in the Philippines,
Before the sun came up
Mike Hall and I went down to San Jose,
And stood his jeep beside
A doorway of a pulsing thread of light,
And broke the thread, and went inside
A blacked-out house where a family sat

He knew. They flashed their steel-rimmed spectacles,
Their gold-capped teeth on Mike,
Called him MacArthur's little flying boy,
And brought the *tuba* out, a sweet-potato wine.
The oldest girl lit a candle;
I took a jelly-jar to drink,

And she and I went up the stairs, her gentle shape coming out
Of the eye of fire, and set
Upon my drying forehead as I climbed

Up under the roof, half-tin, half-leaves,
Where a blowing window opened forth
Its frame in stars, beyond the village.
A ghostly race-track far below
Into sight began to fade, in the valley's dawn.
I felt the roaring smile I'd held
Between the shimmering engine-disks, die out

And sink beneath my face, and sleep,
As my mind on the race-track wandered in the wind,
And into beautiful running, wake.
Hearing the little horses charge
For the far turn, I ran and ran

To catch them all before they surely died
Of outdone hearts.
Holding a fragile, calloused hand,
Hearing Mike and the still girl's family
Laugh, downstairs, and her sick brother,
Loved by me, unknown,
Sigh in the straw

Next room, I ran
With the marvellous horses,
Eyes and breath like theirs,
And a heart I could not trust for long:
Not leading, but in good position, there,
Home-stretched on the island-turned wheel.

The Coral Flight

In the hurricane wind
We crept into the aircraft, anchored
By their wings to the coral floor.
In the long roaring night we cramped
On the metal floor, along

The walls. I sat in the gunner's compartment
On an ammunition-box, leaning my head
On the bull-headed bulwark.
A flashlight burned in the craft.
In the wind, I was amazed

That we seemed to be airborne
In infinite flight, though anchored
To the sand-bagged stone of the island.
There was no pilot, though
One of us sat

In the pilot's seat, dishing up meat
From a tin can. At midnight,
The aircraft broke from its moorings,
And shuddered to the side, in a dance
of tons, actually flapping its wings,

And finally came to a halt
With its wing-tip ground down to pieces
By the side of a sea-creatures' cliff.
As we hung there,
The flashlight gone out without glory,

I believed we yet more securely
Flew, and winged
Through a gigantic dream of the war
Where we fought no certified enemy,
But the obstinate world itself.

On into the gray dawn we shuddered,
Gnashing against the stout coral,
Until, at the end, I sat up,
With sand dust deep in my eyes,
And saw where we were,

Not landed, but beached,
Absolutely wrecked,
The engines, the tail, the wing,
Everything, but come through
The shuddering of death,

Having, some of us, actually dozed,
But none of us not having dreamed
That we were in flight, as never
Before, all the way out of earth,
Somehow still at war,
But a war that meant something
To the soul, at every
Floored mile we had flown in the dark.

The Valley
—1945—

Steady, the simple pleasures
Of silence, of sea-blue sound
Coming up the valley from the beach.
They made us be things inside them,
Where slowly we sat on our porch,
Full of the large view of war.

The site they had given us to clean
And live upon, once laid of dust and every undug grave,
Had dazed us till we shone. When first we topped
And saw forth from the rise, Mike Hall had said,
"Good Jesus, what a place to live."
And what a place for many to have died.

The sun began to open. We tore apart some boxes and made floors.
The last two months of war

We lived in the long-legged huts we nailed
With their porches out over the valley.
Peace came, and the sound of terror died
In the wind the length of the leaves
We sewed in strips and laced above our heads.
All day and night the roof was whispering,
"It is all too good, too good."

Where is the thing that shoved coffins
Through the bright orange sun of the Philippines?
Where are the aircraft, tinning with rain on the strip?
And Appleby dead, torn apart and still
Kicking in dusty grass? And Lalley, his head cut loose?
And Ward, shot dead through the roof of a mill?

What was it all, thus come to, but our good?
In air we sat, and the stakes went down
Far under us, into earth.
Like the British, we drank tea. The box-tops of the porch
Hummed with a sand of termites, at our feet.
At night, rot leapt into the wind
And, humming still, began to pray for the hut

To fall, as once we prayed
For all us young replacements to go home.
I think of the valley, now, as Life:
Broad with great peace, such blueness everywhere
One looked or breathed or sang,
And death filled with relief,
And think of most

The insect treasures, mounting from what there is
Missing, in everything.

The Child in Armor

On such a day I see him at a window
Or a casement, urging shut
The sky in which the sun is caught
Above the stone enclosing that precise
Gray with which my fantasy is bought,
Not turning, but feeling with his mace,
That lifts itself, how
Free the outer air is, and of what pace.

On his light breast shine
Lion's paw, pine cone, in a crest
I cannot wholly take for mine.
His arms are weighted with a thought he has not furnished;
That which moves them is part me,
Part of my time and his, letting the burnished
Innocent falconry of arms
Ride the green fields, and burn or rest in them.

His face is shut from me,
A light and grated anvil. It is all lovely.
Somewhere a hound barks, and suddenly the window
Is green with moss, the sun is out,
The helm is opening. He lifts now
A sword with no will but his own,
And I sit here in the light, gazing not at his visor
But at my ancient son, with nothing but his armament
        renewed.

The Sprinter's Mother

She is, she must be lying
Under a wreath like holly.
It is sick
With lightning, here; the sparks grow;
There is her face, momentarily,
Against the hard leaves

Says the sun, alive in a diagram
Of fountains maintaining the dead
By overflowing hilltops
And choking: by dust-clayed leaves,
By chunks of rock laid endwise, flat,
Among each other, smoked and ghosted with weeds.

Whether interrupting or completing, the boy
Should take the roses from his hand
With his other hand, and put them forward
Onto the quick-limed cinders of the ground.
At the second hill, rain falls,
But the cut-out, preyless shadow
Of his mother's eagle rests between his arms
Struggling rawly with the light,
And the planed hill drifts to meet the cloud

Enough to hold him up
Beside her grave, which is blue
Slate. She would plead for the roses.
He holds them in his breath,
His mouth shucked. What music there
Of lightning thrown into sunlight,
Lightning like vines stripped
By a forgotten intensity of the moon,
Should be sounded, is looking for a way
To put his flowers down.
His legs are sleeping among the works
Of the great lock of daylight: it is terrible
For her to watch, to be rigid, to wait

For the staggered lanes, the boys crouching.
The shadow of the stone eagle
Explodes, the leaves at her forehead shimmer,
Dissolve: he stretches for the turn,
His legs and mind and backbone
All one jarring radiance
Forward: a light comes on in his mouth:
The nerve-strings of his teeth ache with her voice
Opening for him: the turn leans: she is rising
To touch the flowers: at his shoulder, a body,
Half, a tinge: he is alone: he is tying up:
The crowd surges together, in:
He must get his head down: No! the tape
Is there. He puts down the roses.
A bird streams thickly into song.
The dark roses are singing under the bird
To the rain, with speed and quiet;
Among the petals, half-hidden like rich drops,
Her cries are shyly balanced,
As though retaken by blood.

And, panting, blowing, he understands
How it is all proved, by childishness.
No small part of his body feels
The sun, light blue under the cloud;
Only the chest, back, and legs,
Warmed with excitement,
Glow over the graves in the changing light,

As she turns
Slowly into his face, not as a heelprint,

But as a held look he lets his breath
Gather to sustain, and the world
Flowed together in a new way, trembles,
Comes back at him, touches at his hair.

The Falls

Upon the light, bare, breathless water
To step, and thereby be given a skiff
That hangs by its nose to the bank
And trembles backward:

To stand on those boards like a prince
Whose kingdom is still as a cloud,
And through it, like a road through Heaven,
The river moves:

To sink to the floor of the boat
As into a deep, straining coffin,
And in one motion come from my mother,
Loose the long cord:

To lie here timelessly flowing
In a bed that lives like a serpent,
And thus to extend my four limbs
From the spring to the sea:

To look purely into the sky,
As the current possesses my body
Like a wind, and blows me through
Land I have walked on,

And all in a pattern laid down
By rain, and the forces of age,
Through banks of red clay, and cane-fields,
And the heart of a forest:

And at dusk to hear the far falls
Risingly roaring to meet me,
And, set in that sound, eternal
Excitement of falling:

And yet, strangely, still to be
Upheld on the road to Heaven
Through the changing, never-changed earth
Of this lived land:

And now in all ways to be drunken,
With a mind that can true up my body
In all the grounded music of the dead
Now nearer their rising,

I rest idly in the midmost of my smile,
With nothing to do but go downward
Simply when water shall fall
In the mineral glimmer

Of the lightning that lies at the end
Of the wandering path of escape
Through the fields and green clouds of my birth,
And bears me on,

Ecstatic, indifferent, and
My mother's son, to where unsupportable water
Shall dress me in blinding clothes
For my descent.

Two Versions of the Same Poem

I. THE CONTEST
Amputee Ward, Okinawa, 1945

What is it has mounted?
Hollowness whirled by the waist, it is.
In the blood cave, wind is falling,
Falling short.
Right and left are melted into one.
He doubles his hands.
He has closed them.

There on the page of the magazine
Where he knows
Her honest: where he knows her
As she is: as she is holding
The cold door of a Frigidaire
Burning with porcelain sweat,

Is a game of drawing.
You go between dotted, numbered points
Enclosing Shape;
These are stars. Around his leg
Riding in space as silently as the earth,

Led from star to star by the hand,
He feels their outline come to be.
The place of the island is bright
Upon the wind.
Head-down he follows, with his pencil.

As the last of marks would be made,
To Win (for *You*: *anyone*: a child!)
Joining one side of his thigh to the other,
Lining the island frailly out of water,
He thinks of her standing there coldly swinging
His body in through the door,
His face like a dancer's, deep in birth.

The pencil runs, runs on,
Runs down. His brain rustles: his lungs reverse
The vital haze of breath into a sound
Of asking. What would he win,
If he won? Where does it say that?
What does it say? *That his eye of a man
Is blinded.* His eye of an angel opens.
It is that, again, of sleep.

Beholding: it is all beholding.
At her hand, where the Winner's Money flutters,
And the island ripples
Its station in the sea up through the tent,
The frozen, mass-dazzling
Page of Heaven turns, and swings
Its eggs and fruit and crawling
Rain in streaks across his face,

And in his eye-lidded mask
He sleeps, somewhere between
His bed, and the broad, unloosable shot
Of distance. Then like a room he is waking
Behind the window clearness of his leg
Planted against the sun.
                         He and the girl go slow

With one another, round one another,
Flesh-tinted, in the bright ad,
And it is night. The moon, from its milk-teeth,
Sings into the dance they are making.
The shell-dusts of beaches quiver
Beneath his thigh, and there the air is pawing.

There is this he. Which? Now slowly alive
In the clearing of print with the money,
The girl, and the bright door crazed with cold.
But listen! It all has that greatness of hover!
The hover of muscle in sleep

That the bones cross, dropping,
Dropping: and there
The wool-spinning breath of a flock, but touched
To be broaded upon itself like fields, maintained
Of an inside dancing

Against no motion of otherness.
He scrawls on, writing in for the Rules of the Contest.
His lips not shucked with grief,
He floats like a shadow upon his mouth,
And now the running statue of his blood
Is tranquil in the missing of its stride.

From the earth's one side he has been cut,
And there she stands, in his last step.
He goes there, dreaming with the whites of his eyes.

Among the trees between, the surgeon stops,
Playing a country tune upon his saw,
Sun like a chicken's foot
About him tensed and timed.
Under him, a prone man is singing in unison
With the water-bending notes of the metal.
A mown plot of lancets lies
All-strewn and shivering with his face.

She moves from beside the ice-box, goes round
Their toothless song four times,
While they cut down his leg and throw it off
To the island dogs. *He weeps, she is gone.*
Then the branches bubble with lights;
The wind breathes hoarsely down his throat.
The veins of marble open

Beneath his back. A shadow opens out above his foot.
His voice spreads through the towels of his blood.
Will she not come

Again; will she not come?
With his hands down under him, he feels
Through the slab being lost among the leaves,

The floor of a church come up and stop.
He struggles to stand, the roof of his mouth
A shape of flame. Mosaic scatters his heels.
What step? She whispers.

"In Sleep, Death's Masque, God dances."
The heron-footed whirlpool at his waist
Gently: gently again
Corrodes into rain; his vanished pores, in a steep
Drowsing of motes, make a placeless water of light
Come still. There, in the swung sensation
Of a wound, she dazzles,
Dazzles the pool of urine in his loins.
In the faceted house of the tent, he lies,

Trying to hold on, yet moved
Inevitably from sleep.
Here, in the hoist of leather,

The swamp of gauze, the spittle-slick of rubber,
What can he do but close his eyes? What else,
In peace without shade?
Beside the sea—the farthest sound of brothers
Headlong loading lumber—
He shakes clean of his beard and starts to cry.

There on the page is drawn
A Polar Bear, in the place where the leg
Was starred and shining on itself, and now is gone.
Yet the paper keeps giving her off,
And the ice-box, and the Rules, and the money.
By God, by God
(And the night's moon, when it comes,
Stopped sheer at beauty, all around itself, by the sea),

He will cut her out. Just *her!*
A medic brings him scissors, and he grins.
The page turns, out in his breath; she slips and slips
The whiteness from her sides,
Trembling, becoming,
And her body is given unto him.
His heart stops all around him, in the sun.
He picks up everything and loves.

II. THE WORK OF ART
Amputee Ward, Okinawa, 1945

There, burned
By imagination slowly

Out of the hulk of leaning,
The walls of the tent began to glow.
His heartbeat continually fires
True, for his leg, and misses.
The wind blows the island on
Under a gentle shoulder of sun in the air.

An arm moves, filling temperately with land.
He says, with his head to the sand sheets,
"My courage is the inside of bright light,"
And a singled muscularity opens, in weight
Beginning to rain, a wildening space of God.
He steps back with his strange left foot
Into the blue-eyed floating of the soul.

On a skylight aging the smell of lawns,
The figures, in their stacked sparks
Of thread, are standing together.
Given the mica of their coats,
The hunters have gained, for years,
Their stiff, elected limbs;

The boar is stitched in fever from his life
Where the precious leaves have met to form his place.
The amassed geometer whispers
Into the sea, "The Lord of Tapestry is maimed."
His leg is mired to the thigh
In Creation, and lies on him breathing in threads.
"The Sword shall devour the Sun,
And there be no less light."

It hangs about him, all its rays
Constelled equal, killing its craftsmen with age.
He thinks the yeast of cloth is called
"Resurrection," death has everywhere so much
The shine of reliefless artistry.
In the place in him quivering dead in length
The shotted threads are moored.

And when the Limb, resplendent
In castle-green and black,

In the God-eaten white of cloud
And the canvas-gold of bone implied
Through the scarlet spool of the wound,
Hangs deathlessly, and the work is given to men,
What of the man himself, when the leg shocks out its gilt
How deadly still, into the still museum?
How to say that its unfigured man,
Forgotten by the cloth, has not yet died;
Has but devoured

In sleep the thread of the labyrinth?
He shouts between two screams.
The bubble of color
Rings mindlessly, in answer.
A hunting wall of sun
Comes down on the veil of the amateur.

Shines, like a marsh, the sun
On the crossed brow of listening.
He beats empty hands on his ears, and twists
All around his leg, white, edged gold, sewn flat
Beside a hooded falcon held by grass.
A procession of knights and hunters
Is watched around him into cloth.
He feels the move among the craftsmen's minds
Pull him up terribly to sit,

Facing, over his seed-pearled leg
The green and blinding thicket of the boar.
He braces his free foot on the sheets

And reaches through the weaving-bright of stillness,
Ablaze with mediation in his arm.
The silver sun
Catches one turn of thread alive
About his thumb, and begins to fall,
Unravelling, falling through the woven world
Into an upraised blade.
He feels its snowing vibrancy
Create his hand, its jewels hilt his palm, the blade

Shimmer in the bodiness stone of air:
The whole cloth burning and swinging, he yells,
"Pour la Reine," and brings it down,
Halving the green blaze, rippling
Across his thigh. The Work for an instant shines

For bright miles down the animal,
Fibrous moonlight of his nerves

As the leg begins its life.
His two hands cramping his thigh
Close from the rushing of the world,
He sees a Unicorn, a Serpent, and a Poison Tree
Flicker stilly from the void into the place
Which has been, until now,
Their absence by miracle. Before him,
The young hunter dies
Forever, asway in his silken cage.
The eye of Heaven grows, embroidered unsparingly

Into years of weaving,
Focussed where the sword fell
Historyless as cloud.
Not yet thought by the craftsmen, an angel's form
Is drugged by the green string of the hill.
It wavers on the tent-wall,

Seen gold through the bone of his brow.
He fades it helplessly back,
Increased, into the dance.
The tent feels his dampened flesh fall on
As the sun feels the backs of a herd through mist.
He smiles and licks his skull.
Memory and the Secret come apart
Upon the hovering fly.

III. Father

The Flight

Come to stand, the hawk
Now shows his share of the moth:
In summer already is
Another place, and snow become
The listening of a myth,
Having dispersed the body from the stone.

Here among this green your child
Has broken the famine of statues.
Through the immovable dream of the air
He feels with the bird the stone drawn
By high-pencilled rocks from his feet.
The summer starts to shine without its eyes.

There is only the hawk's way to plunge
Into the universe, a field at course
Drumming with flowers,
Past the wire-dipped cloud of the cage.
You drop the spread hammer of gravity
Toward him, as snow downfalls onto shape,

And at the center of the falling,
Where dark has kept the white wound,
The wings slant into the passing cliff.
You look to see him, turning those arms

In speculation, but he is not yet there.
He is floating in his last drink of water
As in the held breath of the sea.
He plucks the sex from the sleeping horse
Who drinks from the brilliant river.
There, the bill of the pitcher balances
At your throat, that of the clearest

Raging drinker. You see him as the rain
Must raise its limits to the inner crown,

To fall white, in summer, through the mind.
The cage, renewing and trembling,
Goes over the small, broomed grass,
Floating its bones where the mouse sleeps.
One by one we are all together

In the air-mass effect of the bars,
And the glade shimmers, intense, there,
Its stripes gliding inward as the wings grow
Over the heel-drafted, harlequin bed. Come:
Think your hand the tree

Where that bird might settle,
Having killed thus freely from his cage.
At every imagined touch, a branch may wander loose
Swaying inside the light. Your hand is like your face.
As the claws touch there, your roots release
The victim; dark strikes your heart in the child.

It is the way the animals lie there,
Bearing the earth, not able to ride it out.
The air-dead are on fire
With unknowable suspension, and from their wonderment,
Like that of targets, the summer begins again to snow

For the lost hawk. Beneath, your cry breaks
Into the tongue of a healing wilderness.
In clear summer there is light
Risen in thickets, smoked with thorns,
Wherefrom he rises like a ghost through the floors
Of an expanding home. Your heart looms

Impassibly and truly in your blood.
Distance changes the bright, flickering bruise
Under the eyelids of the dead,
And is nearing; the crystal cemeteries hang.
You look for your childhood buried in air,
But the small beasts dance in the open
Shadow of death, increasing in judgment.

Here the hawk in one of your pupils
Finds one of his wings, and stares across
At the other, branching your brows together
Head to head with the child beside you in fury
Over the light victim. But the mouse is lost in snow,
In imagination come standing fully round

In nothing at all but white:
But the cage enveloping snow.

He is flying there. Snow: white, conjectural solidity:
King-headed hydra, sifting
Brow and crown. Something loiters into its stride,
And you begin to sprint the paths of the park,
Your child beside you, padding swift,

Freezing with murder, a knife you have given him
In either hand: you are blazing green,
He is white and lost, you the season
Of killing, and he blind with chance
In the closed center of morning.
And as you go, the watching eye

Is suddenly nature's, from a bole,
From the slow ascent of a leaf
Falling upward unnoticed through Heaven,
The first trance of a shorn lamb.
Your face is the lines of a bush
Writing the wind in its head.
Your child whistles out into light
And scores with his eyes a brilliant right and left
Through snow into snow

Where you stop, the last cage panting around you,
And in the distance, diminishing,
Is the small shape with its mind lit
From the heart of nothing, its hands aflash,
Beautiful, low, and speeding. Turn your eyes

Like balanced coins, and on their outer side
The bird sits, the cage is falling like rain,
The dazed archer's mind of snow has brought
From itself the green of a beautiful prey
Immobilized and flowering everywhere,
Whose height the child marks in your side.
To be at all is to haunt the world.

The Ground of Killing

The heron's shade:
Black beak for orange.
Doubles God willed.
Wind riffles both,

Water, one. The scream
Of fish swells light
And blind and sharp
What neither cries.
The glow from opening
Sun takes white from
Feathers, spreads it upward,
Loses it weightward.
The water thinks down
A coral port, temper
Of bells, joining of cords,
Eyes drawn over font.
Who, deafening, kneels
Through lust to cold,
Lungs beating bright,
Comes at this weather
Under stone sail.

The diver enters
A weaving casement:
With level trident,
Warm mind for lamp,
Changes his skin
Passing the bill
Of the sentinel bird.
A pasture opens
Downward, under glass.
He hangs more ironly
To answer shade;
He tongues a dying mouth.
The striped fish in the last
Slant shuttle of light
Fans as muscle gathers
Its throat of arrows.
As the prongs drive slowly
From the thin hilt
Of blood, like metaphor
From soundless sleep,
The eye of the heron
Enters precisely the side
Of the fish and passes
Into the red village.

Invitation au Voyage

Rest on the bright decks
Among the others, all of them seeming your family.
When your eyes go out past the ship,
Often you can see
An immense ragged angel,
The sun, come on you from the water where you sit.

Your head is suddenly luminous,
And all there is
Trembles to you, through the circling
And weaving gulls, in and out
Of the great wild shape on the sea.

Night come, leave everyone,
And lean by yourself on the rail,
Where the god has turned
To silver, and thin
As a cross-cut saw on the little waves.
I shall be

Believing in the wide-spread, pale-blue dark,
And a man, there, close to himself,
Looking far over and hearing
Not gulls, but the sound of feathers.

Two Poems on Poets

I. HART CRANE

Sight, from the ocean dazzling,
Moved, within somewhere the rim
Of the actual wheel of glittering.
A gull before me shaped
Off, one wing down, then righted roundingly.

My looking out
Concealed it all.
I could not understand what he had meant,
Nor the surgical boil of the wake
Through which, a moment of the sea,

He piled and fell, a long slow presence of the pounding heart,
As the sea through a vastness of levels turned
Black, all over,

And breath, on a kind of saying, closed.
It could not matter, through the sunlight he was in;
No quiet of gull or froth could help,

But somewhere in the falling
Passion, his legs rebelled, and kicked
Most piteously; his arms fought off
Unstrikeable water, and the heart utterly gave out

In the man not yet all dead.
If one, along this unrelated beach,
Ran, as he could, and shouted with everything
He found inside himself, and did his best
To tear his body's life from him by every shred,

He would know that one must run
Or fall from a thing to be truly in it,
The hands in wind or water gone wildly for no hold,
The feet, there sprinting or terribly thrashing to say
Awarded, awarded, awarded.

II. To Be Edward Thomas

In under a flock of shade
Wired loosely into light, a generalized swaying of moss,
Those faceless beards with the breath of water
Stirring, I stopped with the old New England man

Between the leaves let down there,
The sun sitting patched and almost dead
In the white board chairs
We had left, to walk up and down a furlong of the sea's
Inviolable nakedness, in all its shining-level with the grave.

Just inside Florida we took our seats.
A bird's cry broke into four.
All around, mimosa, hibiscus,
Palms, the self-choking matted grass: slowly,
Where we were, we were inside

A shadow listening deeply to the light
Come out of a tree of yarn, the wild-wire gentle glowing.
I glanced at Frost, in him all loved old men
Composed, eroded, in the world's despairing search
For the time-born, original, singing and featureless face
That moved upon the making of its waters,

And thought, how vulnerable they are, the old,
Whose body in every motion is
Extending back through time: how valuable,
The good ones: how unafraid

As a wind blows out of the sun's dying
Increasing forge-red stroke
Down sea, down the great wild trembling shape
Cross-cut from water risen. Feeling the saw-edge in the wind
In the air going over us, a rocking from side to side,

The body warm from the sun shining into the brain,
I saw that a part of light would not
Be there, as it was, without three words:
"The team's head-brass." On the sea, from my mind,
Or another's, two horses, a horse,
His head with ornament alive,

Stood, on the quick soil of ripples, there. It was not Frost had said,
But Edward Thomas, whom he had loved.
The sun gave out. I could not tell if I
Could see the horse, or if he were, with

No light for bright head-gear, for hide,
And thinking instead of Thomas, poor, indeterminate, bare,
Writing acceptable prose, from cottage gone
To cottage with his family, and no live work near his heart,
And seeing the old man silent, in the gray dark straining with wind

Watching me, asked then like a body-blow from the soul
What it might be
To come to one's self, near the end of life in a war,
Under just this look:
To be brought forth by this.

From living in such friendship Thomas bent
Upon a tree, a horse,
A look that drew off Time, and put about the thing
Its end and its beginning, like a church. Its Being blazed
With reverence, upon head-brass and hide, or twigs,

Bark, wind in the interlaced boughs: these, beyond thought, at last,
What they must surely be: leaves, limbs, beasts in their holy reasons
Singled by him, but given by the world.
In his new poems the brooks and fields
Kept hearing the sound of their making: it was

As silence, and all restraint become
The classic restraint of tears, to let him speak:
Who brought also axes, hop-poles,
Hay-forks, shovels, in, and all
So still, put down just after work, or

Not used in years, whose men in the heat are drowsing
Deep in the brown ring of land, or dead
As drowsing. He drew close to cattle and plants,
And saw with unparalleled joy each thing his life required
Grow whole, in what he said.

Low mist lay in on water, where we were.
A tower no one had noticed
Made light, and none of it thrown,
But passed around, intact. We watched the double-handled hole
In dark, go by,

Brought off, brought on, brought off.
I looked up levelly. The beam came into my head
Through my nose and brow. In the momentary face,
Unblinkable, of light, I floated like powder
Assembling. Dark. Then light

Again, and a long-stemmed flash
Through the nose of the skull, of deep, precarious bright.
A battle-field framed in a key-hole.
Gone. Once more I waited, still. Shadow
Ignited, and behind it the whole
Light, full out of the blind of the brain,
In the gold-filled arch of bone.

Wire. White heat, not hot,
Spat, arced leaping among the harp-strung graven hills
About the fragment of an outline of a man
Struggling, in planetary blue. The dead,

Who inhabit the white of the eye,
Show forth, when shone upon.
This was Vimy Ridge, where Edward Thomas died.
Each time the moving light went past, I watched him, after it,

From his death, as grass behind wind,
Rise, never getting all the way to his feet, as the lamp-swung tunnel
Left him, seeming to sigh like a prow.
To be killed is suddenly to feel the self
Without the body, flash:

To fall wherever you can, upon the ground
Of shell-holes moved in a whorling drift, as from an oar,
And enter with the closeness of your eyes
The presence of many grains.

Killed many times, and risen off
Alive, alert, into dark, we got up at last
In our bodies, and stood on the long sea-wall
For one more look. The bright flag floated over.
There, in the wilderness glow
And moss of stones, a thicket of little fish.
Light shone them into being:

In the quick of it, from all one side of their weightless herd
Their collected vision swayed
Like dust among them: we could see the essential spark
Travel from eye to eye.

Closed in the dark, till the other arm
Rode out of the lamp, we stood: they had not turned:
A whiff out of bright: fire full of them
Swept, and their bush of inlaid burning
Quivered, once. They were gone with molecular swiftness.

You cannot choose whatever thing shall mean.
Out of the whole of chance it must occur,
The meaning felt, escaped into your head, requiring speech.
Fish, cold in the flight of fire
That speckled the sea with their eyes, may be recast,
And known, and memory rise like the dead,

Assembling the full of sense, as slowly the drowned recall
What profound, entire grip they had
With their hands, on the sea, when rowing.
The words may yet be said.

Around me, in the flower-lifted room
Of open dark, from the heavy, luminous man
Who had not said a word: from sight, from memory,
From air and fire and water,
A personal permanence, something to say

To myself from every side,
Grew, as having. I thought what friends of mine, known
Or unknown, as yet in the army of the brother
Lost, might serve me so.
As Frost, Edward Thomas, or whom so I might serve.
Back through the house of the wind

Walking, I would believe therefrom
In field, fish, dark, light, the flag-draped grave
To be seen in no outlying place, but in
A horse-headed flash from the sun,

A silence like Being, wherein you gently hold
What you have witnessed, and thence must love, as utter
Inviolable strangeness:
As it is, as you have found it,
Swung to you in all-human light.

A Beginning Poet, Aged Sixty-Five

This at my age this night
I do, and do by out-listening God.
All over the house is amazed.
The table shines, as if blindly
Thinking, on my hand, immersed in the ground
Of patience. *It falls, it falls.*

Yet the two or three images
Make all of that sound with their being.
These must become as a child
Who three years lived as my son,
And a horse my older brother owned,
Which stood, floated out of a field,

Cut off at the knees
From the earth, by a rolling ground-fog.
A cricket seizes slowly on my ear.
Part of that word I can use
For the silence won from the dead. It says
A river would move like a smoke.

It does, and then I think it.
Animals in it would stand, and this would change
Their eyes, as their thin lower legs
Dissolved. Their words on the page
Have no breath. Stand out, all things, to hear me
Call to the dead. Perpetually I see

The light of the sun strike stone
In space, and fall to the summer ground
Outside my house, stone dead
And bright. Amazedly down

Quietly under the wind, I speak, and under the moonlight and insect, as my hair falls out from the quick

    In a waterfall-shudder of silence.
Do not move from the cloud-top of earth
    Where you kneel without knowing it, horse.
    Child, do not believe to change
From death. Light, I am trembling fast
Asleep, in the ray where the moon holds on

    To throw the sun
To the ground, each second, around me.
    I write *the child and the animal,*
    And now my staring son
Has mounted the river's horse.
I see all their eyes as the same

    As in unbelievable flight.
Now they shall *move within death.* Almost it is said.
    Stay silent, son: one word, or two
    Together, more, and you ride
A pale, tall horse down the river
Of Heaven. I have come for the living and the dead.

The Archers

The boys are sighting with their muscles
Down the long crested shafts of the arrows.
Their forearms and somnolent eyelids
Are infinitely precious in the sun,
And the bold, cocked fingers of their right hands
Are tingling like springs,
As their beast's gaze, gone miraculously down
The feather-spinning roads of the arrows,
Refines the small treasure of the target
Beyond price, beyond aim, beyond the world,
Beyond the deep, surrounded gold of the center
Inflicted by this second only.

The First Morning of Cancer

    The first morning of cancer he awoke
And went with his eyes half all the way

From his grave room, as it wore in two.
All night in the dream of his mouth he had held
His life, by the tongue

To the sand brim, where the hourglass hears the whirlwind from its toe
Sing itself clear of the ground.
Upward of the bed, he passed, again,
The sense of floating brightly in a maze.

All two honest shapes
Of light, either one invisible, he lay there face-
to-face, in both the shadow's men: the Fallen,
And the Risen-from-the-Sun.
In the smell of bread-making flames he kept hearing,
"The thing that you are you have done."

Almost awake, he had the serpent's
Measure, of lying long, along
Each felled position of his life
In Light, prodigious casting of a center.
Halfway through the sun, he knew.
He closed his eyes, and suddenly he was one
Of an army of panting men.

His fear passed off, intact. Abandoned, sustained,
A loose chair came and rode
Partly down under his clothes. His shoes on the floor
In a kind of mooring swayed, by their weight signed slowly, again.
To where he was, he had come, his slight hair folded

Wrong, from the first, about his naked brain.
He laid the sheet aside, softly entered his hand, and with it fell
Upon his chest, spellbound with what it was doing.
As it drew air, he seemed to dip inside, at once,
All of the miles of breath upon the earth.

He thought what he would say.
All night he had heard the bed
About him, in the fluttering of a bush, be used
And flaked away, and on the saved-up word
To be said to his son out of sleep, had felt his lungs
The covering of his voices with a sack, and slept again
Headlong into a sound.

Now he looked. The child was gone
He had called, and a posture with jackstrawed hair
Fled outward, not gaining, through sleep.

Something, a pain, came out of him
And was shimmering by the inch and mile, at once.

Across his temperate skin, the child's flesh deeply blew.
An uncorrected gentleness of air.
Through this he stepped, and turned,
And in the clearing window was immersed.

Alone above the bed, he saw his son
Taken by leagues of sunlight from behind.
Much like his earlier fear, the pain passed off.
Slowly he filled with the singling blue of his eyes
To be gazing from love. It could not, then, be other.

He looked, out past himself and behind.
The wet crept up to the house, and the tended grass
Went on and under,
Beyond. Moment after moment out of air
His youth arrived. He began to believe in his blood.

The sun came over him, in a stroke of life.
His guts were burring with hunger.
His lawn on the very wings
Of Possession beat, and raised him, where he swayed
With the world's good pulse: the wings of a bird
In flight, which must shut
The bird each instant from falling.

His hair dumped over his forehead, he dumped it more,
And took off his shirt, and sat in the little of wind.
The chapped skin on his back stretched close
And bloomed like a hedge in the light.
The cancer rose in his brain, and yet therein
Made no dramatic stand upon an image.

A fathomless shawl on his back, he stooped
And took a double handful of the room
Out of the slept-in air. He dispersed the ball of his hands,
Having learned not a thing, but happiness,
Over again. Through the crawl of bloom on his neck
Slowly his soul from its watchful night came in,

Still lapping the bricks of the house. Anew, and doubly, he looked down
Where the lives of his wife and son streamed on,
Unlimited, into their crimson lids.
A stirring stopped. Nothing before

He moved had moved. A shell somewhere broke water:
An armored slug, a king-crab in a wig,
A turtle sparkling mossily from its back,
In its twilight of weight gone mad.
He was found in the window, and the universe struck, like flint,
Unreasonable eyes of prey.

About him in his yard, each paid-for rock
Shortened its shade, pulled on it like a scab.
Uneasily, he let his breath curve out around
The end of the sun, in his room,
The whole God, in a mask like a green-house, behind him.

A soundless cry went up and stood
In amazement between the beds, as if it felt the sun
Flattened on stone, of moonlight, then
Come back. He remembered he had shone himself all night
Into a helpless hanging-there of boughs.

He drowsed, and tried again. Along his arms
Some hidden branches came afloat. He kicked and pled.
They took him from the tree, and closed his sleeping body in the hill
Of light. He screamed in all his face
And it was singing from the rocks.
The air blew hard, and was a fire of dust

On all the roads. The bone of blindness turned
Among his brows, until it struck the light. The mountain moved.
It shrilled, and brought a man, his size, of sweat,
Superb, from the flight of the sun.
Beyond all light, his shadow shed
Through all of him to the wall. His son said,

"I will help." He heard. He set himself to call,
But broke. A thing, that instant, had grown
In the way a child, being lost in another's house,
Will fall to its knees and creep.

Astonished, the son rose up.
A two-shape the size of ironing-boards was pulled
To feathers on his back.
Vibrant as the haze of a propeller, from his miraculous head, one eye
Opened, and was followed by the moon's. In his light, inside the light
Of the first morning, he stood by the stone, and could hear,
Beyond, the death from the nearest of flesh,
In its basket of hands, nailing one

To another, and deadly, self,
Up and down and crossing from within.

Upon him, all his waking came to be
Where he strove with the starry stone,
His milled nails torn to mica by the weight,
And moving the rock not an inch.
Half dead from imagined screaming, he yelled out wide once more,
"And they found the stone rolled away."

Yet when the child arose
Beside the window's cave, the Being
Dropped from his breast, from sleep, into the sun
Wearing the soldier's dreaming mail.
The angel wept, as the child remembered
His father. For a moment the man saw brightly

Dilated through stone, the cross, an olive-tree,
Close with the Foe-within-Light, to ruin him into leaf.
From the boy he was
The distance where the soul appears, and all their eyes

Ablaze with intelligence, their face the face the horseman feels
Ascend to his, from the sprinting horse.
The boy came to him, and the cancer found

Life, in the motion of a woman unbinding
Her hair all the way to the bone.
It billowed about them like seaweed, and the man
Descended. God gave him up,
And smiled across his breastbone, in the light:
On his, like a crown, the candle-

dancing head of unconsciousness flickered. It was all in the fear
Of waking, returned in full, immense as the angel's
Alone in the sun, first watching the silent earth
From fire and shadow be made. There, he had come to be,
Unmystical, Love's pure bare Looking-On,
Not to notice, on pain of expulsion, who
In the world it was, the child gripped,
Trembling, by one hard healthy foot.

Appendix

Poems Published by James Dickey during the Fifties

"The Angel of the Maze." *Poetry* 86 (June 1955): 147–53. Collected in *The Whole Motion*.

"The Anniversary." *Poetry* 82 (June 1953): 138–39.

"Awaiting the Swimmer." *Kenyon Review* 21 (autumn 1959): 609–10. Collected in *Into the Stone, Poems 1957–1967*, and *The Whole Motion*.

"A Beginning Poet, Aged Sixty-Five." *Quarterly Review of Literature* 9 (winter 1958): 272–73.

"Below the Lighthouse." *Poetry* 94 (July 1959): 223–25. Collected in *Into the Stone, Poems 1957–1967*, and *The Whole Motion* as "On the Hill Below the Lighthouse."

"The Call." *Hudson Review* 12 (winter 1959–1960): 560. Collected in *Into the Stone* and as the first part of "The Owl King" in *Drowning with Others, Poems 1957–1967*, and *The Whole Motion*.

"The Child in Armor." *Poetry* 82 (June 1953): 137.

"The Confrontation of the Hero." *Sewanee Review* 63 (July–September 1955): 461–64. Collected in *The Whole Motion*.

"The Cypresses." *Quarterly Review of Literature* 9 (winter 1958): 268–70.

"Dover: Believing in Kings." *Poetry* 92 (August 1958): 283–90. Collected in *Drowning with Others, Poems 1957–1967*, and *The Whole Motion*.

"The Enclosure." *Poetry* 94 (July 1959): 218–20. Collected in *Into the Stone, Poems 1957–1967*, and *The Whole Motion*.

"The Falls." *Impetus*, no. 3 (winter 1959): 3–4.

"The Father's Body." *Poetry* 89 (December 1956): 145–49.

"The First Morning of Cancer." *Poetry* 90 (May 1957): 97–102.

"The Flight." *Beloit Poetry Journal* 6 (summer 1956): 16–19.

"The Game." *Poetry* 94 (July 1959): 211–12. Collected in *Into the Stone*.

"Genesis." *Commentary* 25 (May 1958): 427.

"The Ground of Killing." *Sewanee Review* 62 (October 1954): 623–24.

"Into the Stone." *Poetry* 94 (July 1959): 225–26. Collected in *Into the Stone, Poems 1957–1967*, and *The Whole Motion*.

"The Jewel." *Saturday Review* 42 (June 6, 1959): 38. Collected in *Into the Stone, Poems 1957–1967*, and *The Whole Motion*.

"Joel Cahill Dead." *Beloit Poetry Journal* 8 (summer 1958): 18–19.

"The Landfall." *Poetry* 94 (July 1959): 213–15. Collected in *Into the Stone*.

"Of Holy War." *Poetry* 79 (October 1951): 24.

"Orpheus Before Hades." *New Yorker* 35 (December 5, 1959): 52. Collected in *Into the Stone*.

"The Other." *Yale Review* 48 (March 1959): 398–400. Collected in *Into the Stone, Poems 1957–1967,* and *The Whole Motion.*

"The Performance." *Poetry* 94 (July 1959): 220–21. Collected in *Into the Stone, Poems 1957–1967,* and *The Whole Motion.*

"Poem." *Quarterly Review of Literature* 9 (winter 1958): 270–71. Collected in *Into the Stone.*

"The Red Bow." *Sewanee Review* 65 (October–December 1957): 627–34.

"The Shark at the Window." *Sewanee Review* 59 (April–June 1951): 290–91.

"The Signs." *Poetry* 94 (July 1959): 215–18. Collected in *Into the Stone, Poems 1957–1967,* and *The Whole Motion.*

"The Sprinter's Mother." *Shenandoah* 6 (spring 1955): 17–18.

"The Sprinter's Sleep." *Yale Review* 47 (September 1957): 72. Collected in *Into the Stone.*

"The String." *Poetry* 94 (July 1959): 222–23. Collected in *Into the Stone, Poems 1957–1967,* and *The Whole Motion.*

"The Swimmer." *Partisan Review* 24 (spring 1957): 244–46.

"To Be Edward Thomas." *Beloit Poetry Journal Chapbook,* no. 5 (summer 1957): 10–15.

"Utterance I." In *Soundings: Writings from the Rice Institute,* 114–15. Rice, Tex.: Owen Wister Literary Society, 1953.

"The Vegetable King." *Sewanee Review* 67 (April–June 1959): 278–80. Collected in *Into the Stone, Poems 1957–1967,* and *The Whole Motion.*

"The Vigils." *Beloit Poetry Journal* 6 (fall 1955): 21–23.

"The Work of Art." *Hudson Review* 10 (fall 1957): 400–402.

Index